HALFWAY TO HALFWAY AND BACK

MORE RIVER STORIES

WRITTEN AND COMPILED BY

DICK LINFORD
& BOB VOLPERT

Halfway Publishing
1328 NW Constellation Drive, Bend OR 97701

ISBN 13: 978-0-692-13625-6

Cover photo by:
Mark Unger, Sky Lakes Media

Cover design and interior layout by:
Tara Mayberry, TeaBerryCreative.com

"Just because I wasn't there doesn't mean I can't remember it."

From the short story Horseman by Richard Russo

Bill Center, circa 1975   *Bill Center*

DEDICATION: TO BILL

JOHN CASSIDY

BILL CENTER LIVED NEAR THE SMALL TOWN OF LOTUS CALIFORNIA, on top of a very steep hill above the American River. He built his house up there, perched on the very edge. It afforded a beautiful bird's eye view and he always liked to watch the weather coming up the canyon and listen to the afternoon wind up in the trees.

Bill paid a lot of attention to the weather. Just like he cared for and paid a lot of attention to everything natural and important. He and his wife Robin raised their family up on that hill, and from there he drove down to attend countless meetings where he spoke out for the trees and rivers and environmental protection of every kind. He was sturdy, articulate, creative and effective. Because of Bill Center, the land is a better place. Bill was our unspoken leader and the voice of the California foothills boating and environmental communities.

And it's because of that, and because he was a dear friend of ours, that we would like to dedicate this book to him.

PLAINSONG FOR A RIVER MAN

for Bill Center and all who knew and loved him

This cold morning the rain beetles tap
on the window—where did you go?
Man of rivers and mountains,
we wonder, where did you go?

Brash Fort Bragg boy rushing to the pier,
clambers upstream, following
the long salt tongue of the Noyo.
Where did you go?

Woodpecker, river, shambling bear,
bobcat, black oak, flea-fested lair, star-thistle,
poppies, switchback of wind—
all call you kin—where did you go?

Grey owl composed on the fountain rim,
quiet as winter, certain as snow,
held a robin in its gaze—
where did you go?

River warrior, green guardian,
keeper of souls, blue-eyed wild man
with the beamish grin,
oh where did you go?

When the stars were still pinned to the night,
you'd climb the high outcrops,
greet the first light. Wanderer,
saunterer, where did you go?

The boat's slipped its bowline, rolls on
to the sea, a dog's black-and-white bark
your company. You carry our love
wherever you go.

In the tide's breaking waves flowing
into the cove, droplets of light
scattering gold. Is that you?
Are you here? Where did you go?

Dear brother, dear husband, father,
grandpapa, friend, this sorrow's forever,
spills without end. We can't bear to,
we don't want to, we must let you go.

He's traveling now—no compass or chart.
Sweet Bill. Still we're blessed
with the thrum of his big kettledrum heart.
He knows where he goes.

—*Moira Magneson*

CONTENTS

FOREWORDS

DICK LINFORD

WHEN BOB AND I GOT SERIOUS ABOUT PUBLISHING a book of
river stories, we never considered contacting a commercial publisher. We knew that our stories were going to appeal to a smaller audience than a real publisher needed. In retrospect, self-publishing
gave us some leeway that we wouldn't get from anybody intending
to make money. What serious publisher would have indulged our
writing funny stories about each other?

Early on Bob, ever the optimist, told me, "You know we're
gonna lose at least five thousand dollars on this." That was a bit
sobering, and I was wondering how I was going to tell my wife
Suzie the bad news but it turned out not to be true. We actually
broke even after our first two months. Self-published books sell
an average of 150 copies. We have done many times that. We were
even approached by a real publisher for this book, but we have
come to enjoy being in total control of our product.

Still we haven't quit our day jobs. Not because we're cautious.
We no longer have day jobs.

On a lark, we entered *Halfway to Halfway* in the San Francisco
Book Festival. It won first prize for anthologies. Having no idea
how big a deal this was, we googled what other people said about

winning the award. One woman said it was the best thing to happen to her other than giving birth to her child. Another woman said that it was like being elected homecoming queen at a high school with a population of five. We figure we're somewhere between.

Creating *Halfway to Halfway* brought some unexpected pleasures. It stimulated memories of people and events that had faded, and brought us in touch with many old friends. Perhaps most important, we heard from new people with stories to tell. Of the twenty contributors to this book, nine are new. And, if we might brag, four of the new people, Callan Wink, Moira Magneson, Adam Tanous, and Tate Higgins, have MFAs in creative writing. Callan has had a story published in The New Yorker, Moira has had several poems published in both books and magazines, Adam makes his living as the editor of Sun Valley Magazine, and Tate has published stories in several literary journals.

We have already started collecting stories for a third book. But what do we do for a title?

BOB VOLPERT

I SURE HOPE THE PEOPLE BUILDING SELF-DRIVING CARS are paying more attention to the road than Dick and I did when we ventured down the self-publishing highway. We made plenty of mistakes. Our biggest shortcoming was a propensity to mishandle orders. One December, Dick and I both screwed up orders just before Christmas and my wife Mary summed up the situation perfectly. "I can't believe you two idiots are successful at anything."

Despite our incompetency, every month brought a payment from Amazon that was directly deposited to our Halfway bank account. Most payments weren't enough to buy a burger and a beer but having something come in for 51 straight months was fun. And then we hit the jackpot. We had a financial bonanza.

"You won't believe how much money we made last month!" shouted Dick when he called. "We got a payment for almost $8,000. We're rich!" Well, we weren't. Dick had made a withdrawal from his retirement fund and given his broker the wrong account information. His retirement money sat in the HW account for about a month. The correct amount that month was something like $9.40, but for a while we thought we had a bestseller on our hands.

This new collection was difficult to pull together. We had nearly 100 stories to choose from and even on the day we finalized the selections, another very good one showed up. Keep sending stories.

My contributions to this book have a glaring omission. I was unable to complete an essay about our son Matt. He is absent from this collection. Matt and I couldn't agree on the cause of his flip at Cramer the first time he rowed the Middle Fork. He claims the boat wouldn't have gone over if I hadn't high-sided on the wrong tube. I have a different opinion but this disagreement will have to wait resolution. He will be in the next book.

Thank you to all our friends who have contributed to the success of the Halfway to Halfway books.

CONTRIBUTORS

JOHN CASSIDY misspent his youth guiding river trips in California and Idaho through—out tthe 1970s. In the forty years since, he married, raised two boys, buried one dog, and paid off a mortgage. In 1977 he co-founded Klutz Press, a publisher of how-to and children's' books. He is now retired and divides his time between Palo Alto, California and Stanley, Idaho.

SUE CAWDREY, a published freelance writer and public relations consultant, has devoted a large part of her career to promoting and writing about the outdoors. She has represented a number of river rafting outfitters in California, Oregon and Idaho, and has served as publicist for the Lake Tahoe Concours d'Elegance (vintage wooden boat show), Marin Rowing Association, Parcourse Fitness Systems and the Northern California Olympic Committee.

STEVE CUTRIGHT started rafting in 1969 while in college and has run rivers throughout the West and overseas. After graduate school, he moved into outfitting and served as ARTA's CEO for five years before working with Bob Volpert at Outdoor Adventures. In the late 1980s, Steve became a municipal firefighter in the East Bay, eventually becoming a fire chief. Now retired, he and his wife, Rena reside in the Bay Area and travel extensively. Steve continues to boat on whitewater rivers, guiding occasionally with Idaho River Journeys.

JOE DALY was raised on the Susquehanna River in rural New York and moved to California to teach high school. He stated guiding in 1971 and he and Dick Linford started ECHO River Trips in 1972. He served as president of the Tuolumne River Trust for twelve years. He lives in Berkeley, California with his wife Sue.

JENNER FOX is a musician on the river and road, splitting his time between river guiding and touring the states performing original folk music. He has four studio albums, and spends his winters guiding and singing around the fire on the Futaleufu River in Chile.

PETER FOX guided in California, Idaho and Chile through the 1980s, and was on the first rafting descents of the Futaleufu in Chile and the Grand Canyon of the Stikine in Canada. He worked as a professional photographer for years and is now retired and living in Bend. His wife Susan and their daughter Kaela were river guides and his son Jenner divides his time between guiding and music. Peter teaches whitewater rowing and is working on a book on the subject.

TATE HIGGINS grew up in South Carolina, learned to river guide in Colorado, and found his true river home working on the Middle Fork of the Salmon in Idaho. Tate also works as an instructor of wilderness medicine, an expedition leader in East Africa and Nepal, and is completing medical school at Oregon Health & Science University. His wife Trina is a fellow river guide, and their daughter Penelope has inherited their love for wild rivers.

JERRY HUGHES grew up in tiny Hazelton, Idaho, eighteen miles from Twin Falls. He first floated the Middle Fork of the Salmon as a Boy Scout in 1963. He became a guide in 1967. He played football at University of Idaho and attended law school there after graduation. After passing the Idaho Bar Exam he decided he would rather be a river guide than a lawyer. Jerry and his wife Carole established Hughes River Expeditions, Inc. in 1967. They are gradually turning the company over to their son, Colin.

JOHN HUNT guided in the 1970s and 1980s. He stays wet by surfing, rowing an ocean dory and doing river trips with old guides and family. He has a Ph.D. in water pollution assessment and works in watersheds around California. John lives in La Selva Beach with his wife and fellow ex-guide Teresa Clayton, and plays stand-up bass with the Troubledoors.

DICK LINFORD grew up in Wyoming and New Mexico but migrated to California for college. He started guiding in 1970 and, with Joe Daly, started their own company, ECHO in 1972. He is now retired and lives with his wife Suzie in Bend, Oregon, where he bores people with river stories.

MOIRA MAGNESON guided in California, Oregon, and Idaho through much of the 1970s and 1980s, and earned an MFA in poetry from the Writers' Workshop at the University of Iowa. She teaches writing at Sacramento City College and lives in the Sierra foothills with her husband Eric.

MICHAEL O'MALLEY has served in marketing and business development positions in the Utah Governor's Office of Economic Development since 2011. Previously he filled a similar role with for the Utah Science Technology and Research (USTAR) Initiative. He was past president of the Utah Lacrosse Association and recently retired as a lacrosse official. In his spare time, he is a Deer Valley mountain host and hiking guide. He first became a whitewater raft guide in 1979 and remains a licensed Idaho guide. He lives in Park City, UT and is a graduate of Pomona College.

MARK PALMER started guiding in 1981, while an undergraduate at UC Berkeley. He faded out in 1987. He now lives in Los Angeles with a beautiful wife who is a lot smarter than he is. He has two small dogs, and writes television for children because it allows him to use shorter words than if he were writing for grown-ups.

MARY PAPALE claims she became a secret operative for the CIA after college and then became a river guide. Her view of the river was often from under her boat so she moved on to IRJ Headquarters where she became the Queen of Reservations and Menu. To keep her and husband Bob Volpert entertained they had three sons, Will, Matt and Skip. Mary counseled the boys to become accountants, attorneys or teachers but they all decided to become river outfitters. With four outfitters in the family, Mary will always find space on a river trip somewhere.

BOB RAFALOVICH has been a whitewater and fishing guide for 43 years on the Rogue River. He is the former outfitter owner of Rogue Wilderness Adventures. After selling the business, he continued to work as a river, fishing, and trail guide. Bob lives in Merlin, Oregon and guides for Briggs Rogue River Trips and Morrison's Rogue Wilderness Adventures.

DAN STEINER came west seeking adventure after graduating from Yale. He guided for Bob Volpert in the 1970s and 1980s, mainly on California rivers. He spent one summer trying to develop river trips in New Mexico, a state notorious for its lack of rivers. He now works at a desk in Washington DC but still harbors dream of becoming a river outfitter.

ADAM TANOUS put his chemical engineering degree from Stanford to good use by becoming a river guide on the American, Tuolumne, Rogue, and Salmon Rivers. He is currently the managing editor of *Territory Magazine*, *Sun Valley Magazine*, and *Taste*. He lives in Hailey, Idaho.

MARK AND MICHELLE UNGER own Sky Lakes Media based in Medford, Oregon. They produce promotion videos for websites and social media platforms. Their videos showcase the spectacular natural beauty of Southern Oregon and the Pacific Northwest. They graciously gave us permission to use one of their photos for the cover of this book. The person rowing is Covey Baack. And, yes, he is wearing a PFD. It is under his shirt.

BOB VOLPERT became an outfitter when his prospects for earning a living on Wall Street faded with the mid-seventies bear market. Now retired, he outfitted on rivers in California, Oregon and Idaho starting in 1978. Bob and his wife Mary Papale live in Point Reyes Station, California.

WILL VOLPERT lives in Southern Oregon with his wife, Julie, and their kids Emma, Carson, and Elijah. He owns Indigo Creek Outfitters, a whitewater rafting company operating on the Rogue and Klamath rivers. Off the river, he has served on the volunteer Board of Directors of the Siskiyou Mountain Club since 2011.

STEVE WELCH is President of ARTA. When he was twenty-five, Steve was given an existential choice. He had been accepted to a graduate program combining business administration and computer science at Claremont College, and he was given a chance to run a failing rafting company. He chose the rafting company, thus avoiding the possible moral hazard and complacency that often comes with wealth and security.

CALLAN WINK is a fishing guide on The Yellowstone River in Livingston, Montana. His stories and essays have appeared in *The New Yorker, Men's Journal, Playboy, The Best American Short Stories* and others.

Adam Tanous

LAST CALL

ADAM TANOUS

I SUPPOSE THE GOATS MIGHT HAVE BEEN AN OMEN.
But, really, who would expect an omen to come along on a Friday afternoon? Right there on the Dwight D. Eisenhower Highway, a bumpy stretch of asphalt choked with commuters and glacier-dooming exhaust?

I was with Buford and Rico—old friends—all of us part-time river guides with much more good humor at our disposal than river skills. Buford is a welder, Canadian Club drinker, and a man with a merciless wit. Rico I've known for the great majority of my life, and I can say that during most of that time together we were laughing about one thing or another. In a pinch, Rico could make a beheading fun.

We were on I-80, somewhere between San Francisco and Placerville. People with real jobs were jockeying around for the exits to an endless string of suburban gems—San Pablo, Pinole, Hercules, Living Hell. We, on the other hand, were on our way to kayak and otherwise fritter away another weekend of our precious lives on the South Fork of the American River.

Buford was driving, clipping along at 70. I can't say why, except to chalk it up to the screwy power of omens, but the three of us glanced over at the car next to us at the same time. Just spitting distance away was a Ford Country Squire station wagon. It was an old car, sun-bleached, and rusty in places. Just another beaten down, 60-year-old white guy was driving. But I was transfixed by him, and yet wholly unable to form the thought of what I was seeing. I was actually stammering, which doesn't normally come easily to me. Rico, even more voluble than I, seemed equally perplexed. Finally, Buford, ever the man to unveil an elephant in the room, proclaimed, "Goddamn, that car is chock full of goats."

Indeed, there were 20—maybe more—live goats stuffed in the back of the Country Squire station wagon, all standing stem to stern like so many sardines in a can. Equally unnerving, the fellow driving seemed absolutely nonplussed by it all. He was idly staring off into the middle distance, as if he were pondering whether he had left his stove on at home.

A carload of goats is not that easy to explain. Was this a relationship gone sour? Had this poor bastard finally mustered the courage to leave a soul-crushing marriage? Just packed up his goats and left? Or—admittedly, this was a stretch—perhaps he was involved in some sort of goat trafficking? These did not look like particularly rare goats—something, say, worthy of trafficking. But, then again, could I pick a black market tortoise from of a lineup of house turtles? Probably not.

And then the basic logistical questions came to mind. How did he get them in the car in the first place? What could the back of that station wagon possibly smell like? Was there food back there? Having suffered a summer at our company's Idaho guide house with a goat named Achmed, I know a thing or two about goats.

One is that they eat incessantly, and it doesn't seem to matter if it is of this earth or not. I suppose it was possible that this guy pulled over at rest stops and let them graze a bit. But, really, how did he manage that? And where in God's name was he going with a carload of goats? It was all so puzzling.

Puzzling and great fodder for the rest of the drive. That was all it took with us: one weird little moment and we could launch into hours of bantering back and forth, each of us trying to out-funny the other guy. And this, it has occurred to me over time, is really the heart of river guiding. In fact, it is the enduring memory of my working on rivers for much of my adult life—not the no-shit-there-I-was whitewater, not the still river canyons, nor the space-blue skies under which I have been sheltered for so many days. Rather, it is simply the relentless pursuit of laughter. It might start with someone finding a decrepit bone in camp, say, a raccoon or a marmot jawbone—nothing regal, certainly. And though they may be otherwise intelligent people, river guides will spend hours trying to make each other laugh with that stupid little bone. The effort is unremitting and exhausting, but as much fun as anything I've ever done.

By the time we got to our outfitter's guide house (the outfitter for whom we all worked), we had played out every imaginable goat scenario. The air had finally cooled, and we settled in for dinner with a couple of other guides. The house, which was as close to a commune as you might experience during the Reagan era, did, in fact, have a spectacular perch over the South Fork of the American River. It also had a scratchy green carpet, furniture a smart man would never sit in, and dust—all the dust of Ethiopia in one little house. By the time we had had our fill of cheese quesadillas and leftover beer, it was 11 p.m.

"How about a quick pop at the Round Tent?" Buford said in his usual peppy way. "Last call and all."

The Round Tent was a bar in Placerville and not one at which river guides were particularly welcome. Hard, tough men living with a bit of a bitter taste in their mouths drank there. We were the antithesis of all that: soft and weak, full of laughs, and bright futures. Still, we knew our way around a bar.

Chris, a young and strapping guide, eager to be a part of the fun, chimed in, "Is it all right if I come?"

We all considered the moment, though perhaps a little longer than we should have. Again, it was Buford who broke the silence.

"Chris, I like to drink," he said. This was the stern Buford speaking. "So does he, and so does he. And when we drink together, we *really* like to drink."

"Oh, I'm in," Chris said. "I AM IN."

Of course, last call wasn't technically last call. There were shots that went around—Canadian Club, tequila, ouzo, schnapps. There were beer chasers and a little Kahlua for dessert. And then suddenly, as if the hand of God itself had reached down and touched us all, there we were at midnight in the Round Tent Bar in Placerville, California, the three smartest and funniest guys in the whole wide world. It was a miracle. Certainly, we needed a bigger stage.

Along the winding road to South Lake Tahoe, Nevada, Chris discovered some ugly truths about the life of a guide. After he threw up the first time, we pulled over and cleverly put him in the back of the pickup. There was a camper shell and plenty of fresh air, but that was about it for amenities. And just in case he turned out to be a sleepwalking drunk, we locked the camper shell. That was that; our woes were literally behind us. We carried on, as if we were people with something vitally important to accomplish.

Caesars Tahoe at 2 a.m. was everything we had hoped for—loud, fun, full of pretty women, gambling, and free drinks. Even the pit bosses seemed cheerful. We were winning money but not enough to worry anyone. Nobody in the entire casino was having more fun than we were. Bernadette, a tall and lithe African-American woman, was quick to notice and sidled up to us.

She claimed to be the headline comedienne at the casino, though it occurred to me that she wasn't all that funny. Nonetheless, she was laughing at our jokes, so that was fun enough. Truly, my first thought was that she was a hooker and, somehow, this was how the fun would end. We'd wake up on some dirt road outside of town, toothless and broke.

Lovely Bernadette proved me wrong. She simply thought it might be fun to throw in with three village idiots for a bit. And who were we to refuse the company of a good looking black woman with access to all of the comps a casino had to offer?

It was not long before Bernadette invited us up to her suite for a little party. Granted it wasn't Las Vegas, but it was quite nice—spacious, big hot tub in the living room, views of the Tahoe strip. As the night wore on, all sorts of people rolled in and out of the suite. Presumably, they were friends of Bernadette, but who knows really who they were? There was plenty of champagne, dancing, swimming in the tub. Room service appeared more than once—we ate eggs and bacon, French toast, lox. Someone had a roast chicken.

When I woke up, I was heartened to discover that I was not face down in some meth head's crappy little yard. All 32 teeth were still in place, and, as far as I could tell, I hadn't been robbed. I was, in fact, still in the suite, folded into an overstuffed leather chair.

In the floor-to-ceiling windows, a giant orange sun was rising over the Sierras and the middling high-rises of South Lake

Tahoe. It was beautiful and not a bad way to wake up after an all-night party. At least, that was, until my eyes focused a bit and I saw before me Rico, sleeping butt-ass naked, cupped in a goofy little Roman couch. The image was nauseating, but I soldiered on. Buford was across the room in a bed snoring like only a welder can snore. Bernadette and friends were nowhere to be seen.

At that moment, I remembered Chris in the Caesars parking lot. Locking the camper shell seemed brilliant at the time. Now, I wasn't so sure.

"Shit, we've got to go," I announced to the room.

Happily, we had no bags to pack, no bills to pay. Four minutes later we were marching across the parking lot, the Caesars marquee towering above us with Bernadette's name spelled out in little round light bulbs.

All a little nervous, we unlocked the camper shell. Mercifully, and yet another reason river guides are infinitely cooler than rock stars, Chris had not choked to death on his own vomit. He was sleeping like a teenager on the corrugated metal truck bed. He didn't seem to know or care what he had missed. He did seem a little more concerned that he was due to lead a commercial river trip in a few hours and here he was with us in a Nevada casino parking lot, a river nowhere in sight.

As much as Rico, Buford, and I wanted to while away the day playing Keno in South Lake Tahoe, we really did believe in the show-must-go-on stuff. Chris had a trip to run, so we had to get him there. With a little ambivalence but more guilt, we filled the truck with gas and hustled back down Highway 50 to Placerville. We dropped Chris at put-in with a hearty handshake and a tall cup of coffee.

. . .

Three hours later, after our second breakfast, Rico and I were on the river. Kayaking was the perfect hangover recipe: refreshing and quiet. Things moved along swimmingly. At least, that was, until we approached Troublemaker—a class III, sometimes class IV rapid. I had an inkling things weren't quite right when I started to see people wandering around on both sides of the river. Closer still and the crowds thickened. We paddled into the eddy above Troublemaker, and I could hear country music playing out of boom boxes.

People were everywhere—maybe a hundred or so—gathered around the rapid. Some were in lawn chairs drinking beer, others scrambling over big rocks like ants on croutons. Toddlers were on the shoulders of their dads. It might have been a splendid summer barbeque except for one thing: the ropes. Ropes were stretched across the river from both sides, like a giant game of cat's cradle. And all of the ropes led to the Troublemaker rock in the center of the rapid. There, plastered to the rock with the full force of the river, was not one boat but two boats. It was the perfect double wrap.

My heart sank. Scrambling from one side of the rock to the other, sweat spilling off his pale brow, was Chris. He looked spindlier than before, and there was a desperate look in his eyes. It was the look of a man willing to do just about anything to change the trajectory of his life.

Over the noise of the rapid, men were shouting unintelligible and, no doubt, unhelpful instructions to him. Dusty little kids were chucking sticks into the river; dogs were fetching them. And the Placerville heat, dry and crushing, seemed only to magnify the confusion.

. . .

It was awful—the river guide equivalent of being stoned to death in the town square.

Rico and I were still bumping around in the eddy, as yet unnoticed by the crowd. Rico turned to me, "Oh, dear God. The poor bastard. We should do something."

"Oh, I think we've done enough," I said.

And with that, we slipped out of the eddy. Heads shamefully bowed, like two snakes in the water, we paddled out into the rapid, past Chris and the ugly snarl of gear, ropes, and humiliation.

I never saw him again. I went back to guiding in Idaho and Chris stayed in California. But I know Chris got off that rock and I'm sure he went on to become a fine man, to meet better people and have a better life. It wouldn't have taken much.

Rico and I paddled down river another mile or so and had lunch beside the river. There was a big oak there, so we lay down under it to nap for a bit. I fell into a half-sleep, and my mind drifted back to the goats. I wondered how they had fared. I suspected that they would reach their destination safely. It might take days, but the Squire—dependable, if weary—would deliver them. No doubt, it would be a bright morning when they arrived, the sun spilling over the hills. Someone young and hopeful would see the car roll to a stop, then sprint across a great field, fling open the tailgate. In a shining moment, a carload of goats would bolt for freedom, each and every one leaping for a life in some verdant land far away.

ELWOOD AND DONNA

DICK LINFORD

I CAN'T LOOK AT A CAN OF SPRITE WITHOUT THINKING OF ELWOOD and Donna Masoner and their nightly ritual on river trips.

Elwood was a pioneer river outfitter in Idaho, and an industry leader for many years. He was a well-respected member of the outfitting community. There was considerable mistrust between the hunting outfitters and the river outfitters in those days, and Elwood helped to bring the factions together. To use a double negative, nobody didn't like Elwood. He served on the board of directors of the Idaho Outfitter and Guides Association for over a decade, and was its president from 1984 to 1987. Those were critical years for outfitters on public lands, as the major Federal agencies were intent on taking our permits back and putting them out to the highest bidders. Outfitters everywhere united to stop the plan. Elwood's steady hand in this united endeavor was invaluable.

Like most of the early river outfitters, Elwood got into the business almost by accident. He and his wife Donna owned a music store in Twin Falls, Idaho. Elwood became a Boy Scout master, and his troop started running rafting trips on the Middle Fork of the Salmon in the late 1950s. The only rafts available in those days were military surplus seven-and ten-man assault rafts, made mainly to paddle ashore from ships. They were very hard to come by. River runners scoured army surplus stores looking for them. They were also very heavy—maybe 250 or so pounds compared to the 135 pound boats today. They came with special notched cones designed to be pounded into bullet holes to stop leaks. These would have been great if people had been shooting at us, but were pretty useless when it came to patching the long tears that came from hitting sharp rocks.

Jerry Hughes started his career by working on Elwood's Boy Scout trips before his senior year in high school. He remembers the Scout trips as a ragtag combination of boats and boatmen, none of whom really knew what he was doing. The western style of rafting was with oar rafts. That is, one person rowed the raft with large oars. Elwood, however, put the Scouts in boats that they had to paddle, and everyone knows that paddle rafts are much less exact than oar rafts. "We went places on the river that no man had been before, where no man wanted to go, and where no man has been since," Jerry recalls. Jerry also says that the experience changed his life. He has been a river guide and outfitter ever since.

Elwood's Boy Scout trips were hugely popular, and this was when Americans were rediscovering their great outdoors. Soon, non-Scouting adults were asking Elwood about river trips, and he realized that he just might be able to make money taking people on raft trips. It didn't take long before he had a viable business, and a business that was a lot more interesting than running a music store. He named his company Whitewater Adventures, and he gradually faded out of the music business. The company was the biggest on the Middle Fork in 1970, when the Forest Service put a cap on river use, including the number of outfitter permits. He gracefully conceded to cut back on the number of people he had been taking in order to reach an allocated use agreement that all the players could live with.

Elwood also picked up outfitting permits for the Main Salmon and the Selway River. The Selway was a major coup because only four permits were issued. The Selway is the most exclusive rafting river in America, having only four permitted outfitters and allowing one commercial trip and one private trip to start on a given day, and these trips are limited to sixteen people each. That's a total of 32 people a day. Compare that with up to 174 people per day on the Middle Fork of the Salmon. And the Middle Fork is considered a closely regulated river.

Elwood's Selway exploratory trip was an epic experience, worthy of a story in itself. It involved several flipped rafts and people missing in the canyon for two days. A lesser man would have taken the Selway off his list, or maybe even quit rafting. But Elwood was undeterred.

When people think of river outfitters, they generally envision macho outdoors types. This image is usually not right, but it was especially not right for Elwood. Elwood looked like someone who would run a music store, or maybe teach music. He was moderate in stature, he had a large nose and ears, and big brown eyes with lashes any model would envy. And he certainly did not swagger. His demeanor was that of a very thoughtful, kindly man. And yet he was catnip to women.

Elwood was a mentor and father figure to a generation of guides. Some of them, like Eldon Handy, Jerry Hughes and Bob Sevy, became outfitters themselves. When some of my guides started their own companies, I was furious. I felt somehow betrayed. But Elwood was welcoming and helpful to these guys, who were becoming his competitors. He was even helpful to Californians like my partner Joe Daly and me, and this at a time when California outfitters were personae non gratae in Idaho. Joe and I did several deals with Elwood, and we trusted him completely.

Elwood also made sure that his Boy Scout troop received an outfitter permit, allowing them to run six trips a year. As far as I know, the Scouts were the first nonprofit organization to hold an outfitter permit.

He was very generous in giving advice to newcomers. When he sold his Main Salmon business to Jerry Hughes and Carole Finley he sat them down and told them that the success of a river company depended on three very basic rules:

1. Never let your food costs exceed ten percent of your gross income.
2. Never let the Sierra Club reserve all the spots on a trip. They will hold the spots until you can't sell them and then not come through.
3. Don't let guides break eggs with one hand.

When Jerry and Carole laughed at this last rule Elwood told them it was no laughing matter. People don't like eggs shells in their eggs.

Elwood and Donna got married in 1939. She was eighteen, he was 21. Donna worked with Elwood at the music store, and then helped in running the river business by doing a lot of the off-river work. She was a pretty, slight, small-boned woman with little interest in being on the river. Plus, this was before women broke into river guiding. But when she heard that Elwood was confronting temptation from the fairer sex on trips, she decided to save him from temptation by going on every trip with him. And Elwood did go on all of his trips.

So for over 25 years Elwood and Donna were on every trip together. That's like camping sixty or more nights a season. Talk about inseparable. The one small glitch in this setup was that Donna was a good Mormon girl and disapproved of drinking, while Elwood, whatever his faith, really enjoyed a drink or two, or maybe four. So Elwood and his crew worked out a system. Early at camp he would pop a can of Sprite, drink some, and leave the can on the table. When Donna wasn't looking one of his guides would pour whiskey in the can. Elwood would drink that down a bit and a guide would again top it off with whiskey. This would go on through the evening until Elwood was feeling just fine. Donna must have known, but chose never to talk about it.

Elwood passed away in 1997. His death hit the river community hard. Scores of guides had worked for him over the years, and he had friends from all walks of life. His funeral was well attended. Many of his old guides came. They brought a case of Sprite and a few bottles of whisky, and drank several tributes to their old boss and mentor.

Donna and Elwood had been married for 57 years when he died, and it's hard to imagine a couple who were closer. Donna visited Elwood's grave every day until she died in 2015. She was ninety-three. That's eighteen years of devotion after his death. She also convinced Elwood to convert to Mormonism before he died, so they could spend eternity together in a Mormon heaven. The only problem I can see with that is, who in Mormon heaven will spike his Sprite?

Callan Wink, photographed near Livngston, MT

WHAT DID I DO WRONG?

CALLAN WINK

IT'S A FAIRLY TYPICAL FALL DAY on the Yellowstone River. We'd managed a few whitefish, a few trout. I'd told my one and only joke and it had gotten mixed reviews. We saw a bald eagle. We saw some mule deer. I got a text from a girl I'd been chasing all summer and now I was trying to respond surreptitiously while rowing. "A trout just rose," I say. "Right next to the bank. About 3 o'clock." My client casts frantically.

I text: *Murry bar. 6:00 tonite?*

Sounds good 😃 She texts right back. Things are looking up.

After lunch, clouds form and the blue wing olives hatch. Regattas of sailboat-shaped mayflies ride the current film, getting picked off left and right by trout. We catch a few decent rainbows, 14-inch crowd pleasers that jump and pull hard. All the while I'm keeping my eye out for the *one*. During a hatch like this it seems like the bigger fish, usually brown trout, post up in the more difficult lies—inches from a mid-river rock, just underneath an overhanging branch, right along the edge of a current break—where it's nearly impossible to get a natural presentation. These are the challenging fish, the really fun ones that can drive you crazy.

Eventually, I spot a good-sized snout poking up rhythmically in a pocket between two boulders. It's moving in the small area of calm water, not even bothering to fully submerge after eating, just swimming back and forth near the surface with its mouth agape.

"Goddamn," my client says. "That thing is huge. Over 20 for sure."

It's a nice fish. Probably more like 18. I check his leader for windknots. I put on some floatant and blow the fly dry. "There he goes again," he says. "Look at that thing."

I detect a faint tremor in his leg. The guy is from Texas. He does something with oil—sells it, or buys it, or finds it—I can't remember. This trout has his leg shaking and it makes me like him a whole lot more.

I tell him he's ready to go and he starts casting. All day he's been doing a decent job but now he loses it. Too hard, too fast. The wind has picked up and he's forcing it. The line slaps right on top of the trout's back. The fish bolts, leaving a wake. It cuts just in front of the boat and we get a better look. It might have been 20 inches after all.

The client sits. We don't say anything. He digs a beer from the cooler, drinks and belches. "Well," he says. "What did I do wrong right there?"

I get this question fairly regularly. *What did I do wrong?* As if there is just one thing, a single problem to be fixed by a simple, silver-bullet answer. The answer I like best is the one I never say:

What you did was, you didn't drop out of college at age 20 and move to Montana. You didn't work crappy construction jobs and go fishing every single evening. You didn't rent dingy basement apartments in an overpriced resort town, just so you could live a stone's throw from the river that stole your heart. If you had done that, I want to say, I guarantee you'd have caught that fish. Easy.

Instead, I say something like, "Well, I think maybe you were breaking your wrist a bit on that cast. You need to tighten that up. Don't worry about it, we'll get the next one."

Maybe we will, maybe we won't. We'll give it a shot and in the end I suppose it doesn't matter. Catching a trout is a rather inconsequential thing to be good at—something I try to remember to keep my own ego in check. There are jobs of great importance to humanity and guiding fishermen will never be one of them.

Just before the takeout I see another trout working, maybe not quite as big as the first one but still respectable. It's already been a good day and I'm tempted to just row on by. If I hustle we could still make happy hour. Instead, I drop anchor. When you've reached a point as a fisherman where the possibility of redemption on a big fish no longer excites you it's probably time to hang it up.

"All right," I say. "Lead him. Nice and easy, we got this one."

I slide my phone from my pocket. This is a bit painful. She has '50s pin-up girl stockings tattooed from ankle to mid-thigh. Very intriguing.

I text: *Fishing is good. Gonna b late*

Steve Welch and Family—Sam, Steve, Sandy and Mac

THE MOST AMAZING THING

STEVE WELCH

I'M NOT THE BEST RIVER GUIDE IN THE WORLD, but I've been at it awhile so I've gotten pretty good at easing through those situations in which seven people find themselves in a confined space with nothing to talk about. Admittedly, this is a skill with narrow utility and infrequent demand, but you must admit that when needed, it is a skill of the highest importance. You don't get stuck in an elevator all that often, but if you do, it's nice to be able to break the ice.

My go-to move for starting a conversation in these instances is to ask: What is the most amazing thing you have ever seen? Everyone has seen something amazing—or at least has something that is the most amazing thing they have ever seen. By the time you go around the raft or the elevator, you have a pretty good chance to come up with some sort of interesting follow-up question: "How long were you in China?" "What does a volcano smell like?" "Did the dog die?" etc.—and you are off and rolling. Ice broken. Awkwardness ended. Disaster averted.

I distinctly remember the third day of a Rogue River trip in the early 1980s where I had to use this tactic in order to get through the flatwater section of Huggins Canyon. Usually, by day three, the early-trip shyness that causes those awkward silences has been replaced by the casual comfortableness that comes from 72 hours of shared experiences and constant proximity, but on this trip, on this day, in this raft, silence fell and we drifted into the dreaded discomfort zone of dead air. And then, just before I got that feeling of failure that all guides get when the conversation dies and you think that people in your raft are getting bored, I popped my go-to question:

"What is the most amazing thing you have ever seen?"

I had asked the question often enough to know that I should I always have low expectations for answers. Few people have been to China and the dog always dies. But my expectations on this day, in this raft, were even lower. The group, although kind enough, didn't seem to have any dynamic personalities or charismatic jokesters. There was the standard assortment of teenagers, accountants, and lawyers and given their three-day audition leading up to this moment, I wasn't expecting any bombshell answers. Certainly not from Joe, a 40-something year-old something-or-other whose prior distinction on the trip was to have been the most quiet person anyone had ever met. As we went around the raft, hearing about sunsets and TV shows, I was a little surprised when Joe told a story about Bob Beamon, the guy who long-jumped 29 feet at the Mexico City Olympics—a jump that broke the existing world record by almost two feet and which would remain the world record for over 22 years. Anyhow, Joe and Bob Beamon had taken a public speaking class together at the University of Texas at El Paso and for the final, each student had to give a speech in front of the entire class. The speeches were given in the gymnasium, and when it came time for Bob Beamon to give his speech, he walked up to the podium and said: "My name is Bob Beamon."

Then he stepped off the stage, walked across the basketball court, stood directly below the backboard, pulled a quarter out of his sweat pants pocket and held it up for the crowd to see. And then, flatfooted, he jumped up, set the quarter on the top of the backboard, came down, re-coiled, jumped back up, snatched the quarter off the top of the backboard, landed and again held it up for the crowd to see. Then he walked back across the court to the podium, stepped up and said: "Any questions?"

Holy cow! I did not see that coming. To this day, that is still one of the most amazing things I have ever heard anyone say they saw. Sometimes I think that seeing Joe tell that story is one of the most amazing things I have ever seen.

Anyhow, we finished going around the raft and heard about some waterfalls and then the conversation went right back to zero. No common Marine World experiences or unchained travel memories; no curious follow-up questions or spin-offs. Just silence. Even Joe's story didn't leave room for much more than "Wow!" This was bad because we had a long way to go and I didn't have that many more questions. I was about to go to my next one: "Do you think there is intelligent life somewhere else in the universe?" when Joe said, "You know, there is one other thing I once saw that was pretty amazing" and commenced to tell the story that follows this paragraph. His version was much longer and more detailed than mine, and included nuances that I have long forgotten. He told it in a humble, almost shy manner, but with a bit of bravado—sort of a half-embarrassed, half-proud tone. I remember he got sort of emotional during the exciting part, but he never got overly animated; just stayed matter-of-fact the whole time. I can't do it justice, but I will attempt to tell it here as I heard it on that day, in that raft.

. . .

"I grew up in the Florida Keys and spent a lot of time in and on the ocean. My dad had grown up in the Keys as well, so boats and fishing and motoring about on the open seas were in me from my childhood. I can't remember a time when my family didn't have at least one motor boat and we often had two. Everyone did. At 10, I was pretty comfortable tinkering around in the Gulf and by 12 I could pretty much tune up an outboard by myself. That's not bragging. That's just how it was.

"Anyhow, we used to do all kinds of stuff in boats that we weren't supposed to do. One of our favorite things was to go out, catch some bait fish and then start chumming for sharks—you know, cutting up the fish and chucking them in the ocean so that the blood would attract them. There were a lot of sharks in the Keys back then, mostly little ones, three or four footers, lemon sharks and blacktips and bull sharks, so it was pretty easy to get a big crowd of them around the boat. Then we'd start rationing the bait fish so that the sharks would do that frenzy thing. I don't know if you've ever seen that—a frenzy—but it is really impressive. Sort of scary. In seconds the water would just be a mess. Sharks everywhere. Then we'd throw in another chunk of fish and it would go even crazier. And crap, we'd be in this little open 16-foot aluminum boat just laughing our heads off. One of us would wet his pants every time. One time, we thought it would be funny to stuff one of the pieces of fish with a cherry bomb. Cherry bombs were these big firecracker-like things that had a waterproof fuse that we would buy from the older kids at school. They were pretty expensive. Anyhow, we stuff this cherry bomb in the chunk of fish, light it and toss it out into the frenzy. And then we wait. One. Two. Three. Nothing. We thought the fuse had gone out and then, about 20 feet away from the boat there was this big explosion and this fountain of water gushes up from the ocean. And there were chunks of shark floating up and we were all frozen for a second and then we all started laughing our heads off. I think we all wet our pants that time. Then we looked around and noticed that the sharks were a lot bigger than before so we left.

"Another time, my best friend Peter and I took the boat out in a big storm just to see what it was like. It was like hell. To this day I've only been more scared than that one time—and we'll get to that—but at the time that was the most scared I'd ever been. I remember we were trying to keep this little boat headed into the waves to keep it from capsizing and the waves just kept getting bigger and we just kept getting further from shore and the waves just kept getting bigger. It was horrible. We were helpless. If the motor had died, we would have died. I learned a lot that day.

"But the most amazing thing that ever happened to me, the most amazing thing I have ever seen, was when I was 14 and Peter and another friend of ours and I took the boat out to go marlin fishing. Marlin are big, mighty fish that can get to be 14 or 15 feet long and weigh fifteen hundred pounds. And they're beautiful. They were our siren's call, our Moby Dick, our holy grail. We talked about them all the time. All we wanted to do was catch one of them, a big 15 footer, and then motor back into the harbor with this giant fish lying in the bottom of our boat. Like Santiago in *The Old Man and the Sea*. Except without a shark eating it. The harbor where we kept our boat had about a half dozen sport fishing boats that would take tourists out on deep-sea fishing trips and the captains of these boats didn't really like us kids. We were always monkeying around on the docks, trying to get seagulls to crap on things or putting Peter's sister's dolls in the bottom of their bait buckets. Stupid kid stuff. Anyhow, the dream was to catch one of these big fish and then come into the harbor right alongside the sport fishing boats and the captain would see it and then he'd see us and then one of the tourists would say we were better fishermen than the captain because we had caught this big marlin and all they had caught were some grouper. Then the captain would see that we weren't punks and he'd hire us and we'd be rich. That's all we wanted.

"So, the three of us got up early one morning and went way out on the Atlantic side where the marlin were. It was a beautiful day, no wind, no chop. Flat as a pancake. You could see forever. We had two rods out and we were trolling these big plugs that are meant to look like bait fish swimming really fast. I don't know if you've ever been marlin fishing, but marlin are really fast so you have to troll really fast. Trolling isn't really the right word for it. In our little boat it meant going almost flat out. So not only are you going fast, if you aren't catching anything, you are going far. And another thing about marlin fishing is that if you aren't catching anything, it is really boring. Just motoring across the open ocean staring at these little plugs skipping across the surface waiting for something to happen. We had our house painted once and while the painter was waiting to put on the second coat, I said: 'Isn't that boring, waiting for the paint to dry?' and he said: 'Yeah, it's like marlin fishing.' I'll never forget that. Anyhow, it's boring if you don't catch one.

"And on this day, we gave it a good long try, but we didn't catch one so we eventually got bored and wanted to do something else. We were a long way from home, so we decided to just keep going and check out some islands that are out there. We had plenty of gas and we had some food and we didn't have any cherry bombs, so we just kept going. Like I said, it was a beautiful day and we could see forever.

"Anyhow, after about another hour, we saw an island and we headed for it. There was no surf, so we were able to drive the boat right up on shore. We got out and pulled the boat way up on the beach. I don't know if you've ever been on a little island way out it the ocean, but the first thing you think is: 'Crap, don't lose the boat!' So we pulled it up the beach as far as we could and went to check out the island.

"These islands out there are pretty big. There are dunes and trees and bushes and stuff and lots of sandy flat areas. No one lives on them or anything, they're just out there. You can climb over the dunes and sort of get lost in the trees and sometimes you can find cool stuff. We were old enough to know that there weren't any pirate's chests or anything, but we had heard about ship wreck stuff that would float up on shore or shipping containers that fell off of the big ships. Mostly we found shells or dead birds. But there was always the chance and we were 14, so this was better than anything else we were allowed to do. And I should say, we weren't really allowed to do this. We had a strict radius that we were supposed to stay inside of and we were way outside of it. So even if we didn't find a shipping container, it was fun to just be breaking the rules.

"Anyhow, about two minutes after pulling the boat up, Peter sees this box down the beach and we start running towards it. I mean, already this was better than a dead bird, right? A box! As we got closer, we could see it was more of a chest than a box and then, when we got to it, we could see it was this wooden crate thing, about the size of a suitcase. Like the classic wooden crate you see in old movies. It said US NAVY on it and it was nailed shut and all sealed up. And it was heavy. We couldn't lift it, so Peter ran back to the boat, grabbed our big fishing knife and then came running back and we pried it open. There was some waxy cardboard laying on the top which we pulled off and then there was some brown paper wrapping and when Peter cut through the brown paper and ripped it open, we all froze and just stood there staring.

"I tell you right now, I'll never forget the moment we saw into that crate. Inside the box, neatly stacked into little individual cardboard sections were 48 hand grenades! Hand grenades! Hand grenades! Holy freaking hand grenades! Forty-eight of them. Three layers of sixteen each. Forty-eight. All just sitting there waiting for three 14-year old boys to come along and find them, right?

"And then we looked at each other and we just started laughing our heads off. Like really laughing and shouting and jumping and hugging. And peeing. If we had found a chest of gold we wouldn't have been as excited.

"And then we got scared. This was a big deal. These weren't cherry bombs. I remember thinking we were going to get in trouble. But then I thought about where we were and how there was no one around and no one would ever know so I relaxed a bit. And then Peter took one of the hand grenades out of the crate and held it out in front of us like it was some sort of sacred object. Like when Indiana Jones holds that idol at the beginning of *Temple of Doom*. You know what I mean? Like this. And we all just stared at it. It had the pin and the handle and looked just like the ones we had seen in the movies. And then he put it back in its little crate section and we all looked at each other and started laughing again. And then Peter took the same hand grenade out again and before we could say anything he ran about 50 feet up to the top of the beach, pulled the pin, and reached back and hurled it over the dunes into the trees. He even did that grenade throw move like in the movies. And then he threw himself down on the sand and put his hands over his head and before Terry and I could even figure out what was going on there was this big explosion and all this dirt and tree and shrub stuff flying up into the air and crap. And then Terry and I hit the deck too but it was too late, of course. We would have been dead if there had been any shrapnel or anything. But there wasn't. The leaves and bush and dirt didn't even hit us .they were blocked by the dunes. So we got back up and there was Peter standing at the top of the beach screaming. At first we thought he was hurt, but then we saw that he was jumping up and down and screaming from pure adrenaline. And then he came running back down to us and said, "Holy fucking Mother of Jesus did you see that?" I remember those were his exact words because Peter never said stuff like that. His parents were big into church and Peter was one of the nicest kids I knew. He never swore. But this was a little different. He'd probably been waiting his whole life to say that and man, it was the right thing to say. 'Holy fucking Mother of Jesus did you see that?'

"And then it was bedlam. We went crazy. At first we just kept throwing them over the same dune and then hitting the dirt and covering our heads but after about 12 or 13 of those, we started to look around and get more adventurous. We also got a bit more comfortable with them. This isn't something I thought I'd ever say, but after you throw about ten hand grenades the thrill starts to wear off. I mean it was exciting, but it was sort of the same. Run up the dune, pull the pin, chuck the grenade and hit the dirt. You could feel the earth shake when it blew up, but it wasn't like the movies, mainly because we couldn't see the explosion because we were on one side of the dune with our faces in the sand. Eventually we figured out that two of us could sit on the dunes way back from the other guy and we could watch him throw it and we could see the tree blow up, but even that got old because we weren't all together and the two that were watching were *waaaay* back because we didn't know how close we could be and none of us wanted to die—not with all those hand grenades left. So after a couple of rounds of watching, we got bored and decided we should play army and go on a mission. Terry went back to the boat and got the little back pack we had brought our lunch in and I got the tackle box and dumped all the fishing gear into the bottom of the boat and then we went back to the crate and loaded them both up with hand grenades. Well, we didn't actually 'load them up' because that seemed dangerous, so we took about eight in the backpack and another eight in the tackle box and we headed inland to blow up Nazis. Peter even took the big fishing knife and stuck it in his belt behind his back, just in case.

"We wandered around a bit and blew up some stuff and hid behind trees and dug some foxholes and had a great time. The highlight was when we found this little fisherman's shelter that someone had built out of driftwood and palm leaves and corrugated tin. These weren't all that uncommon because fisherman who got out in a storm would sometimes beach their boats to wait it out. They'd build little sheds and hunker down on an island, then go back to fishing when it cleared. Sometimes they'd come back to the same island and use the same shelter. Over time they were almost shacks. Anyhow, we found this one and we blew the crap out of it. We built a bunker out of logs and we covered our faces with mud and we stuck leaves and branches in our hats and we crept around on our bellies and we threw the rest of the grenades. Our arms got tired. It was really fun.

"But then we ran out of ammo, so we headed back towards the crate to get some more. As we were walking back, I remember worrying about two things: First, how were we ever going to get our friends to believe us and second, how we were ever going to keep our parents from finding out.

"The next thing I remember thinking was that I didn't have to worry about either of those things anymore. When we came back up over the last dune that was at the top of the beach where our boat was and we looked for the crate, we all stopped dead in our tracks. Peter had been concocting a wild premise for our next mission and I swear he stopped talking mid-word. And remember when I told you that I would never forget opening that crate and seeing those hand grenades? Well, I'll never forget what I saw next either.

"No, our boat was still there, no worries about that. But surrounding our boat and fanned out across the beach were about 20 guys in full military gear with their guns drawn. Actually not just drawn, but drawn and pointing at us. Right at us. 20 guns. Some pistols, some big military rifles. Some of the guys were down on a knee. The whole thing. I remember thinking this is bad. I remember thinking we were going to get busted big time. There was a Navy station on the mainland and everyone knew that you didn't mess with the Navy. We were only about 90 miles across the ocean from Cuba and this was 1959 and Cuba was Communist and you didn't mess with the Navy. Everybody knew that. I remember thinking that we should have thought of that before we went around throwing US Navy hand grenades all over this little island. I remember thinking I was going to go to jail.

"Then it got worse. One of the guys yells, 'Manos arribe! Manos arribe!' Yeah, in Spanish. None of us spoke a word of Spanish but each of us knew enough to put our hands up and not move. It turns out that 'Manos arribe!' means 'Hands up' so it's a good thing we did that. If we hadn't peed so much already that day, we all would have wet our pants right then too. With our hands up. Or worse. So we're standing there at the top of the dune with our hands up and then about half of the guys start coming at us with their guns still drawn. Yelling shit in Spanish that we don't understand. Remember, we had mud on our faces and we were all camo-ed up with branches. We didn't look like three stupid 14-year-olds who got bored while fishing for marlin. We looked like what we were trying to look like: army men out on a mission.

"So anyhow, these guys are advancing on us and we are fucking scared and about to start crying and they keep yelling louder and we keep raising our hands higher and they keep advancing and we keep trying to look as unthreatening as possible and Terry throws the backpack towards them which fucking scares them and almost gets us shot and then I drop the tackle box and we do everything we can to show them that we are harmless. Eventually we realize they want us to drop face down in the sand and lie there. So we do. We drop face down and lie there. And then one of the Cuban Navy guys sees the knife in the back of Peter's pants— remember?—and he fucking stomps his big-ass boot down on Peter's ear and stomps his head into the sand and he starts yelling and sticking his gun in Peter's face and Peter is crying and I am crying and Terry is whimpering and we all think we're about to die. Then another guy comes up to Peter from behind and grabs the knife and the first guy gives Peter's head one last good shove with his boot and then steps off of him.

"And then there's this bunch of yelling back and forth in Spanish and one of the guys still down the beach by our little boat starts yelling at the others and then they all start yelling but not in that threatening way any more. Sort of in a funny way. Shouting more than yelling—if you know what I mean—a little different. Better, that's for sure. And then they start laughing. 'Ha, ha, ha! Pescador! Pescador! Fisherman! Fisherman!' And we start shouting, 'Si! Si! Si! Pescador! Pescador!' I guess maybe we knew two words of Spanish. And then they are really laughing and putting their guns down and explaining to us, I guess, that they figured it out. They saw all the fishing stuff in the bottom of the boat. Just a bunch of stupid boys goofing off on an island. 'No invasión! No invasión"!"Si! Si! No invasión.'

"What a relief. I remember looking across the sand at Peter's face—remember we are still laying on our bellies in the sand—and Peter's face is still red and sandy from the guy's boot—and I remember seeing Peter almost laughing, like: "Yeah, man, this is the coolest thing ever."

"And it would have been if they had just let us take out little boat back home. It would have been really cool. But they didn't. They had to take us in. We were on a Cuban island or something—yeah, oops—and they had been dispatched from their big ship to figure out who was bombing the homeland and 'El Capitán' back on the big ship wasn't just going to let these guys come back without something. So they put us in their boat and two of them got in our little boat and off we went. They were nice about it and the guy who stomped on Peter's face gave us water and kept apologizing and every so often, the others would make fun of the stomper guy because he almost killed a little kid. I guess. I don't know what they were laughing about. But they were nice and I wasn't scared, just sort of wondering what the heck was going to happen next. Like, how is this going to end?

. . .

'Well, the next part of the story is kinda boring. We got to the big ship and got taken up to El Capitán and he spoke some English and told us that he was going to take us to Cuba and make sure we weren't American spies and make sure we weren't invading Cuba. "Standard procedure" he said. I remember that's exactly what he said because later on when Terry and Peter and I would tell the story, that was Terry's favorite part because he could do this really good Spanish-Cuban voice and he would always say "Standard procedure" just like the boat captain. But when the boat captain said it that first time, I remember thinking: "standard procedure?" I was only 14, but I had lived my whole life in the Keys and I had two older brothers and never once had I heard of three stupid boys getting hauled off to Cuba for throwing hand grenades. I think I would have heard of that if it had become "standard procedure."

'Anyhow, they take us to their outpost and haul us into the courtyard where the next Cuban military guy is waiting for us. It was a courtyard like the one in the end of *Butch Cassidy and the Sundance Kid*; you know, adobe, tile, dirt. And we were right out in the middle. I don't know how to say "lieutenant" in Spanish but this was clearly the next guy up the ladder. And this guy doesn't think this is funny. He hasn't really caught on to the subtleties of our particular situation. He's in charge and it's getting dark and he has three Americans in custody and he is looking at an international incident and there is still a chance that we're spies so he's not happy. So there's a bunch more Spanish and it starts going back towards the yelling kind, like the opposite direction of before, and this roller-coaster that we've been on for about six hours now takes a steep dive and starts heading for a tunnel. We're back to being *espias* or *merodeadors* or something bad and it starts to get scary again. We get handcuffed plus like I just said, it was getting dark and, shoot, we were only 14. And then the lieutenant guy does the thing that scares us the most. It wasn't until years later, after we'd told this story hundreds of times, that Terry and Peter and I realized that for each of us, the scariest part of the whole event was what happened next.

"The lieutenant split us up. He separated us so that he could interrogate us individually and make sure our stories matched. So that he could find out if we were lying. And right then, I got as scared as I have ever been in my life. More scared than when Peter and I were out in that storm. I don't know what it was, but until it happens to you—and God I hope it never happens to any of you—you don't know what it is like to be scared until you think you are really close to dying alone. That's a crappy feeling.

"Anyhow, they split us up and take us to different rooms around the courtyard. When Terry tells the story he calls them "cells" but they were just rooms. Desks. Chairs. Just rooms. And they start asking us questions and every so often I can hear a Cuban cackle from one of the other rooms and I slowly start to realize that even though I don't know what's going to happen, but I'm pretty sure I'm not going to die alone.

"And now it gets really boring. They call the US Coast Guard and report three Americans rescued from the open ocean and being held safely in a Cuban port. The Coast Guard notifies our parents and tells the Cubans that they'll send a boat for us in the morning. We will spend the night in Cuba and go home in the morning.

"So we have this Cuban dinner at a picnic table in the courtyard. Nothing big; beans, pork, water, and they let all three of us sleep together in the bunkhouse with the other soldiers.

In the morning, the Coast Guard came and got us and took us home. I remember my parents were relieved but had to pretend they were really mad at us for going outside our little radius. They didn't know about the hand grenades. Shoot, I don't think it was until I was forty that I told them that part. But you know that Terry and Peter and I told our friends that part. And they believed us because we had kept a couple of the pins from the hand grenades and we showed them. I remember telling that story at school a hundred times. Our friends could never get enough of it.

"I also remember I didn't get to borrow the boat again. Ever.

"Then when I turned 18, I went to El Paso and met Bob Beamon."

When Joe finished his story, our raft was floating in the eddy in front of our campsite. I don't know how long we had been there or even how long it took us to get there, but it had been a long time and no one in the raft had said a word. We were spellbound; speechless.

Then the raft drifted into shore and Joe hopped out, pulled the raft way up on the beach like he was over-reenacting his story, smiled at us and then walked away. After a few steps he stopped, turned back and said: "Anyway, that's probably the most amazing thing I have ever seen."

The only other thing I remember about that trip and about Joe—and this part has bothered me ever since—is that the next day, at take-out, after we had given out T-shirts and said good-bye and everyone was in the van, I remember waving goodbye as the van pulled away and I remember seeing Joe in the front passenger seat of the van staring right at me. And as I waved at him, he nodded and smiled at me. And then he winked.

MAKING KAELA

DICK LINFORD

KAELA FOX IS A RIVER GUIDE FOR MY COMPANY, and a very good one at that. She is strong, hard working and conscientious. She puts great social energy into trips, and she's as cute as a bug's ear. Guests love her. At least once a year I tell Kaela that she owes me for her very existence, and I explain why. She is too polite to tell me she has heard the story before.

How can I make this claim? Bear with me. It's a long story, but in the end you will see that, by closing one door I opened another one that made Kaela possible.

Peter Fox came to us in 1980, when life wasn't going exactly as he expected. He was the son of a Harvard professor, and had been an honor student and an All-New England running back in high school. From there he went to Stanford, where he had walked on—and then off—the football team. He graduated in 1975. He lived the hippie life for a while, with the obligatory Volkswagen bus. He shipped out on a freighter, worked in a photo lab, took creative writing classes, wrote poetry, cut firewood and pounded nails. But he wasn't getting traction anywhere. He was unfocused and unhappy. He found us in the spring of 1980. He was the star of that year's training class and an outstanding guide right away. Pete was the total package—strength, intelligence, stamina, and personality. He was about six feet tall, maybe 210 pounds, and handsome. He had the body of a fullback, and the most muscular legs I had ever seen. One woman told me "Peter's legs scare me." The three things I heard repeated about him were, "Pete Fox can row anything," "Pete's in charge even if he isn't the head guide," and "Never split a pizza with Pete. You will never get your share."

He truly loved rafting, and he had no plans! We were a perfect match. We have always relied on smart, strong, adventurous, people with no plans. People—especially parents—have accused me of ruining careers. I don't buy it. River guiding has delayed many careers, but that is often a good thing. It gives people time to find themselves, and to make more informed choices, both about mates and about careers. Once in a while people—almost always male-—will stay at guiding too long, and wake up in their 50s with worn out bodies and no job prospects, and more than once I have told men that it is time for them to develop a life beyond guiding. But most of our guides go on to exceptional careers, and they seldom experience mid-life crises and the accompanying divorces. They don't hit middle age wondering what they missed.

So here was Peter's chance to do something he loved, with people he loved, while sorting things out. And the longer it took for him to find his way, the better for us. I thought he would be around for years. I didn't expect him to fall in love —at least with a non-river guide.

But fall in love he did, and with a woman who didn't guide. He and Arden moved in together, and she didn't want him gone all summer. Not an unreasonable request, for sure. But I was shocked and hugely disappointed when Peter called me to say he was giving up guiding. He had been so happy as a guide, and he did it so very well. Of course I told him that I was disappointed but understood, and I wished him luck. Disappointed? What an understatement. And I didn't understand.

A few weeks later I had a brainstorm. What if he were making a mistake? Might he end up resenting not guiding? Had he forgotten just how much he loved it? After all, he had once said that rowing a raft was as addictive as heroin. Maybe his decision should be tested. Why not invite him to join us for the last few days of our 1981 guide—training program, just to make sure he knew what he was walking away from? I called him, and he leapt at the chance.

In those days we did our training in the California foothills in late March or early April. We would meet on a Friday night and end on a Sunday, nine days later. We would be on the river all day and have off-river instruction at night around a fire. The weather would be cold and likely to rain or even snow. It was a brutal pace and a way of testing the trainees. If they could remain upbeat and positive after enduring several days of rafting and camping in the cold and wet, they had the toughness, fortitude and love of rafting that we wanted. Also, the hardship and adventure they shared caused training groups to develop a bond, both with each other and with our company —a cohesiveness that would last through their guiding careers and beyond. My partner Joe Daly and I would join the group on the weekends and spend weekdays at the office. That way we could set the tone, wind things up, tend to business and—no small matter—sleep in warm, dry beds most of the week.

In 1981 the weather was about perfect. It was cold, wet, and miserable the first several days. One person told me later that, if he had had a car, he would have quit and gone home. Then it cleared up. The last few days were cool but clear. The hills were green, the poppies and lupine were in bloom, and the side streams were pumping. The rivers and the foothills were at their glorious best.

As an added plus, the training class of 1981 was an exceptional group. Many of them stayed with us for years. I am still in contact with sixteen of them. Their bond was so strong by the end that, when one trainee found out that his sister had died, he opted to finish training before going home. Two trainees later married each other.

And Peter was in hog heaven. The last night was a great party, fueled with beer, filled with stories from the week, and featuring silly awards. At one time people started racing rafts across the river and back. Peter beat all comers. He was in his element. He was the bull goose.

Peter called me the following Wednesday to tell me that he had broken up with Arden and wanted to guide. In as solemn a voice as I could muster I told him that I knew it had to have been a hard decision, and I asked him how Arden was taking it. "Not well," he said. I told him that in the long run they would both be better off, and better now than later. When I hung up I whooped to Joe, my partner, "We got him!! Pete's back!"

Peter went on to guide for another five years. He worked for us on the Tuolumne, our most challenging river, for most of those years. He spent several winters on the Bio Bio in Chile when it was the wildest rafting river in the world. He also guided in New Zealand and was on the first rafting descent of Chile's Futaleofu, now the world's wildest commercially run river, and Canada's Grand Canyon of the Stikine. He was our personnel director when I stopped doing the job, and managed our California operation. Over fifty guides reported to him.

In 1984 he met Susan, the real love of his life, at a touch football game in Boston. He lured her to California, and she too became a guide. They got married in 1988. They are still married and have two adult children: Kaela, whom you know, and a son, Jenner, who played varsity soccer for Yale, where he majored in cognitive science, with an emphasis on how music affects the brain. And what does one do with a degree in cognitive science from Yale? Become a river guide and musician of course. Peter is a professional photographer and Susan is a yoga instructor. The family of four owns seven rafts and several kayaks, and they spend at least twenty days a season running rivers. Last year the whole family ran rivers not only in the US but in Bhutan and Chile.

In my forty-three years of outfitting I have seen many relationships form and almost as many unravel. Guides tend to be young, attractive, adventurous, and stunned by hormones. They live intense, physical lives in close proximity, and pairing off is inevitable. I can name twenty-one marriages between people who met through my company, and these marriages have produced at least thirty-three children, all of them above average.

As the person in charge of hiring and scheduling, I often played a hand in these relationships. Guides often asked me to schedule them with whomever they were attracted to, and asked me not to schedule them together when they broke up. I obliged when possible. I gave advice on matters of the heart, whether asked for or not. I even played cupid a few times, putting people together that I thought would make good couples. But Peter's relationship with Arden is the only one I ever purposely torpedoed.

So what does this have to do with Kaela? Isn't it obvious? Without me, Peter's life would have taken a totally different path, and he would never have met Susan. And only he and Susan could have made the Kaela that we know.

So I meddled. I was underhanded. I was manipulative. Am I ashamed? Actually I am. A bit. Am I sorry? Not at all. Is Peter? No. Is Susan? No. Nor is Kaela, although she is tired of me telling the story.

Tate Higgins

Loon Creek Cowboys

TATE HIGGINS

FROM THE AIR, THE MIDDLE FORK COMES AS A SURPRISE. The Idaho mountains are deep here, stacked like salmon in a crowded eddy, and the river is tucked into the heart of this wild country. As the small plane banks into its descent, I want to say I noticed that the valley around Loon Creek spreads out from the banks of the Middle Fork like the spilling hair of a beautiful woman leaning back to catch the sun. But that's a lie. I'm on an emergency flight to replace a sick river guide, and I'm watching the pilot, wondering if it's true that this is one of the most dangerous landings in America. I'm too anxious about the upcoming landing to process metaphors.

The pilot drops altitude quickly, taking us into the shadows of the valley and banks into a hard left turn, inches from the tops of the tallest Ponderosas. I can't see a runway, not even a dirt one. The walls of the mountains loom around and above the plane, blocking any escape for another pass if the pilot's made an error. It's like trying to land at the bottom of a bucket without touching the sides.

"Don't spill your coffee in my plane," he says just before putting us down.

A couple summers before, I'd sweet talked my way onto a Middle Fork crew with a well written cover letter and phone interview with Dick Linford, a partner in a large rafting company. I'm sure that first season, they expected someone more qualified to show up. I'd been guiding rafts in Colorado and fallen in love with being wet, sunburned, and tired all the time. I'd gotten pretty good at running technical class IV paddle boats and living the guide life, but those were day trips. The Middle Fork was a whole different league. Until my first day of work, I'd only seen the Middle Fork in the way folk's faces changed when they told me about this best place. I'd heard the stories of the full-time gypsies and decided I wanted to guide on the best rivers in the world with the most talented guides, and the Middle Fork was at the top of a short list.

Then, one day ambition turned to responsibility, and there I was, a boy from South Carolina standing at Boundary Creek looking down at my boat bouncing in the eddy. It was the first trip of the year, snow pouring from the sky when we left the guide house in Salmon, high water and fast-beating hearts, and I had to ask veteran guides Hata Hill and Tracy Blashell how to rig my boat.

Within the first river-mile, I wasn't sure I had it in me to become a Middle Fork boatman. At Tepee Hole, minutes into a hundred-mile, six-day trip, Hata and Tracy were grinning like men possessed with glory, and I was scared. I had barely been able to control my boat through any of the first couple miles. My practiced finesse in a 14 foot paddle boat did not fully translate to a heavily loaded 18 ft. Avon Spirit and tree trunks for oars. My arms were already gone. I was a paddle boat guide getting his ass kicked on the sticks, thinking, "If I am unable to do this, if I am in so far over my head that I can't get this boat down the river, what the hell am I going to do?"

Well, you don't grow up to live in your truck full-time and get paid to travel the world by being a quitter, so like the times before when my ambition out-talked my experience, I plodded on withhard-headed ignorance, dumb luck, and a lot of help from my friends.

By day four of that first trip, I couldn't hold a beer in my left hand because I'd over strained my forearm with my rookie death grip. When I surfed my big boat in The Tappans and popped an oar, I had to grab my left index finger with my other hand and use my finger as a tool to release the buckle on my spare oar. It was one of the best trips of my life, and the Middle Fork became the center of my whole world, the place where I always wanted to be, the place I planned the rest of my life around. The place where I learned to row a boat, to grow a beard, to talk to cutthroat trout, and to realize there's always room to try harder, always room to get better at everything. I was in love. Still am.

Eventually, I turned my back on her and moved on to other places that I don't love nearly as much because there's something inside me that won't sit still. And now, in deep winter, far from any home I've ever known, she catches me by surprise as I'm walking, takes over my mind and heart like a first love gone away, and I remember her waters, the cobblestone bars, impassable sheer canyons, starry skies, a turquoise mountain creek joining the main flow, a bridge with a swinging gate to keep the horses at home, ancient logs holding a pool of hot water, and long days and nights with people I almost can't believe I'm lucky enough to know. It's a restless feeling that comes from so far inside me it literally hurts. Maybe I won't ever be able to sit still. I worry that I've been ruined by the power of moving water, and I'll never find a place to stay put because of this rat inside me that I have to feed. A part of me that always wants more, that always wants to feel that first mile, that first trip when everything is new and hard and so full of possibility and magic.

Loon Creek Camp is about halfway down the river, the middle of the trip and about the center of the whole world for me during those summers. I was halfway through my fifth summer with guides who had become family on and off the river. All of these beautiful men and women who are talented and hard working and imaginative, pure hearted despite their drinking and their story telling and their vagabond lifestyle. We'd found our river groove, and at Loon Creek we were about as happy as a band of gypsies can expect to get. We had a big party going on the cobblestone beach. Zach Byars' parents Rick and Monica, former river guides and musicians, were entertaining the guests, so we sneaked off to the sweep boat to drink moonshine, tell lies, and celebrate our good fortunes.

The sky was heavy with stars when guides from the other companies started appearing out of the darkness that hung over the river. Loon Creek is within reach of a handful of other camps, and if you're camped upriver, you can float down in a couple overloaded duckies after your guests go to sleep, have your guide time in the hot springs, then hike back and your dudes won't miss you. Some of these vagabonds were our good friends who shared a launch with us every summer, and some were new faces, another company on a shortened trip who had caught up to us. We were used to getting attention from other companies because for decades we had the most and the best looking female guides on the river. The kind of women that make you laugh and make all the girls you met up to that point seem not good enough. Before long our beach was a full-on party with the guide crews of at least three companies.

Even though guide time in the hot springs is one of my favorite Middle Fork traditions, there are nights when your body is tired from rowing all day or all summer and you just want to go to sleep. Tonight, I was tired. It'd been a big couple months, and I was trip leading my tenth trip in a row, but the stars were out, and night-hawks were piercing the night. It was one of those tired nights when you're lucky to have a Texas boy like Zach Byars around. He works harder than most, but never seems to get crusty, and he won't let anyone get away with going to sleep early and missing out on good adventures. So we headed up to the hot springs in the dark. Zach and I decided summers before not to use a headlamp at night when hiking because using a headlamp to walk at night was for the dudes. I'd only walked off one cliff all summer.

I bet there were ten people in the hot springs and more spread out on the rocks in Loon Creek. I've had some wild times in the Loon Creek tubs, a couple stories that I probably won't ever tell, but I'd never seen the tub so full of happy people. There was moonlight and stars and laughter everywhere, and the best part was that every naked body belonged to a Middle Fork guide. We love our guests and literally would not be here if not for them, but it's nice to not have to wear clothes, and not have to be dis-creet about passing around a bottle of whiskey, not have to watch how you talk.

Some of my favorite summer people. One of the special moments. Soak in the hot water till you're woozy, climb out and lie face down in the icy water of Loon Creek for a moment of rich clarity. Repeat. It took me a couple trips in and out of the hot and cold to notice a skinny bearded stranger with cutoff jeans sitting quietly in the corner, sipping from a bottle of whiskey, a large tattoo of a wolf in crosshairs on his shoulder. Turns out, he was the caretaker of Loon Ranch. I'm going to call him Cuss, but that's not his real name. I'd seen him a couple times before, but never without his hat or a gun on his hip.

After a couple hours, we ran out of whiskey and beer. This is usually where the party would end, and a lot of the guides had already sneaked off to bed, but Cuss invited those of us left to come down to the ranch for a night cap. I was beat, but it was on the way home, and I'd never been inside any of the ranch buildings. We sat around Cuss's table and told lies for hours. By the time we'd finished all the whiskey Cuss was willing to admit he had on hand, it was deep into late night, and a few of the guides from another company were getting real loose. We could hear them stumbling around in the front lawn and hanging on each other and singing songs. We'll call them the rookies. They were young guys, free from the eyes of their guests, living the dream, and they were acting like it.

We were in the kitchen when a cowboy came stomping inside, dressed for a day of work. He was one of Cuss's ranch hands, and he ignored us, put on the coffee, and began frying an egg.

"Are they being too loud out there?"

"Too loud to sleep," he said.

"Are you making breakfast?" It was the middle of the night. No sane person should be drinking coffee.

"Might as well get started digging those irrigation ditches before it gets too hot. I can get a full day of work in by lunch."

That's some real cowboy grit, I thought, and my cue to get to bed.

I was on early breakfast duty, and tomorrow was my day to drive the paddle boat. I imagined that at least part of my job as head guide was to be able to get out of bed on time. I was easing towards the door without saying goodnight, when I hear Zach say, "Hey Cuss, how about we ride some horses." We'd had this idea before, but not sitting inside the caretaker's house.

"Maybe next time," Cuss said. He'd changed into blue jeans, his gun and hat, but no shirt so he could show off the wolf tattoo. Zach explained to Cuss that the boys from the other company were too drunk to make the three mile walk home, and it was our guide duty as fellow guides to make sure they made it home safe. Best way to accomplish this was on horseback.

"Horses are all turned out. We'll have to catch them," Cuss said like this was going to deter Zach. It didn't.

Zach nodded, and Cuss must have recognized something in his Texas stare. They stood up together and bolted out the door and into the night.

Sometimes you have no choice but to support your friends, and before I knew it, I was holding open the gate, admiring the stars of the summer triangle, and kinda hoping they wouldn't be able to catch the horses, and we could all go to sleep when the herd came stampeding into the corral with Zach and Cuss hooting and hollering behind them. "Damn, here we go," I thought.

Zach and Cuss and I saddled the horses while the four rookies stumbled around in a sloppy mess. One of them was petting a horse on the face and whispering into its nose how much he loved it. Another one was laid out in the dirt and horse shit talking to himself and puking.

"These guys going to be okay on the horses?" I asked.

"These are pilgrim horses. They don't care about anything," Cuss said.

And just like that, off we went, sitting high on our horses along the trails I'd walked many times over the last five years as a Middle Fork boatman and hot spring soaker. I'd stumbled off these trails in the dark before, fallen down steep slopes when the earth surprised me by not being there, and here I was on a horse whose name I couldn't remember. Looking down into the canyon at the Middle Fork rumbling past, I smiled and felt totally at ease, filled up with a world bursting under a bright moon in a world where the horses knew the trails better than any of us.

We rode above a silent Shelf Camp, the guides we'd shared the hot springs with now laid out under the stars and on the decks of boats, getting a little rest before another early day. I wanted to call out to them, "Look at us! Look at what we've become! Look what we've done with our lives," but I didn't dare wake the guests sleeping in tents on a trip of a lifetime. We rode on in the night, and a couple miles later eased our horses down to the edge of White Creek Camp and right up to the rookies' tents. Zach, Cuss, and I were careful to be quiet so we didn't wake anybody up. The rookies were loud and sloppy, and I was happy to be done babysitting. They fell from their saddles and stumbled towards the quiet circle of tents like zombies, not even turning back to see what happened to their horses. Some of them may have even crawled into the wrong tents.

I was feeling pretty inspired. Sober enough, sitting proud on my horse, under the moonlight, passing quiet judgment on these guides who couldn't keep their shit together. I decided to adjust my stirrup. I'd worked on a ranch briefly one summer before. I knew what I was doing, sort of. What I didn't do was look down.

I was too happy, too confident, too everything, just like the time I thought I didn't need a headlamp and stepped right off into space.

I swung off my horse, my right leg coming down to find the ground, my left foot still in the stirrup. There was no ground beside my horse, only a deep depression, a pit house dug hundreds of years ago by the Shoshone Indians. My foot found only space, my upper body swung downward, and I hit the ground hard enough to knock the breath from my chest and see stars. My other foot was still caught up in the stirrup. I can understand why my horse got scared. To him, it must have looked like some invisible force of the spooky night had ripped me from the saddle and was now sucking me down into the earth. There were ghosts in these canyons, asleep under Ponderosa pines. I'd felt them leaning down to me and almost whispering in my ear, and with my foot tugging on the stirrup, it must have felt like this force was trying to pull him in as well.

So I don't blame him for spooking. I just tried to stay calm, turning on my butt and arms to take the violence of the drag, calling out his name steady and low so he knew I was okay, even if I wasn't sure yet if I really was.

"Easy, Horse. Horse. Easy," I whispered quietly so as not to embarrass myself in front of Zach and the cowboy.

Lucky for me, this was a pilgrim horse, used to the roughest country in America, used to wolves and gunfire, and used to fat rich guys from Kansas who could afford expensive outfitted hunting but couldn't bother to learn to ride a horse. This horse had way more days in these mountains than me, and once he realized I wasn't being slaughtered by the Indian spirits, he quit dragging me.

I stood up and dusted myself off, grinning, relieved that nothing seemed to be broken. I went right back to adjusting my saddle like nothing had happened in case Zach or Cuss had noticed any of the commotion.

The only acknowledgement of my mishap was from Cuss. He walked over, eyeballed me and asked, "Stirrup too short?" And we both just nodded at each other in the dark.

On the ride back, the three of us talked quietly, soaking in the wild country, and it felt like the most important things in the world were right there underneath us. Zach and Cuss and I chatted about the area, about how it takes a special person to be drawn to the rugged mountains, about how once you find your place here, you'll never be happy anywhere else in the world. I knew I was leaving. I've always left, but that's also how I got there in the first place, leaving somewhere else, and every word of love I professed, I meant.

Back at the ranch, Zach and I helped unsaddle the string of seven horses, brush them, and turn them out, then walked down the meadow to our sleeping camp. The sky was getting light by now, stars clocking out a little section of the sky at a time. I climbed on my boat, set my alarm and laid down across the hatch for twenty minutes of sleep. One of those blink-twice-and—call-it-a-nap kind of efforts, and next thing I knew I was starting the coffee and the other guides were slowly getting up, and I wanted to tell them what happened, but I was doing my best just to hold myself up, so I just said good morning and avoided eye contact.

Katrina Cornell lowered her cup and gave me a questioning look.

"What happened to your eye?" she asked, making a face and leaning in closer.

"What?" I asked, figuring they must have been bloodshot from lack of sleep, and reaching for my sunglasses hanging around my neck to cover them up from guests.

"You got a black eye."

I took a big sip of coffee, felt the Idaho morning sun on my face, and remembered my pilgrim horse and the pit house.

"Fell off my horse," I said like it was the most normal thing in the world for a river guide.

She took one look at my sly grin and decided not to indulge my story telling, just shook her head and went off to break down the fire pan and load boats.

That's the only time we ever rescheduled margarita night, the big dare-wear party we throw for guests and ourselves. I guided the paddleboat all day, running good lines. And telling corny jokes. Zach drove the sweep. We handled it like professionals, but we both went to bed early. Well, I went to bed early. Zach never gets tired, and when I fell asleep I imagined he was wearing a cape, entertaining the guests with songs on the mandolin, and trying to get the group motivated for a bacon bomb.

I've got this idea that life is about learning. This idea that people become the most dangerous and worthless right at the same time they convince themselves that they have everything figured out. The Middle Fork had a way of reminding me that I had a lot to learn. On my best days, I remembered how little I knew when I got here and reminded myself how much this place had taught me, how much all the other guides had taught me.

I heard later that the other company's guides got in a bit of trouble for waking up their sleeping guests at four in the morning. They may have even blamed our bad influence and were told to never visit our camp again. Too bad. We could have taught them that just because you're riding a horse doesn't mean you're a cowboy, and you've got to show up to work looking fresh even if you don't feel like it, and sometimes you've got to keep your sunglasses on all day to hide a black eye.

Bob Volpert

The Importance of Lists

BOB VOLPERT

WHAT'S SO DAMN HARD ABOUT PACKING FOR A MIDDLE FORK TRIP? It's no more than six days and five nights. What could that possibly amount to? Five clean shirts for camp, four or five T-shirts to wear on the boat, a couple pair of shorts, a baseball cap, a toothbrush, sunscreen, and maybe a cheap rain poncho. I'm only going for the first two days of our trip. I won't need anywhere close to all the crap that Idaho River Journeys suggests our guests bring, and besides, I've done this enough times to pack in my sleep. No list for me, and certainly no reason to pay attention to the admonitions of my wife, Mary. Although I pretend to listen, I give her words no merit.

Even after packing the essentials and adding a towel, a couple of packs of beef-jerky, two Snickers bars and an extra set of flashlight batteries, my stuff is impressively compact. Nothing speaks to experience and competence like packing for a river trip and filling less than half a dry-bag.

When Mary and I check in at the Mountain Village Lodge in Stanley the afternoon of our pre-trip meeting, one of the lodge

managers off-handedly mentions that colder temps are in the forecast. Big deal, I think to myself. How cold can it get?

The next morning we shuttle the group to Boundary Creek
for the start of the trip. Our guests board an assortment of craft
and enthusiastically head downstream. It's an exhilarating day.
Spectacular scenery, breathtaking whitewater, sunny skies, and
a spirited group of friendly people. We get to camp around 4:30.
Folks find tents and change out of wet clothing, and we spend the
late afternoon visiting with each other, enjoying a glass of wine,
playing cards, and relishing just being in a a beautiful place. The
guides serve dinner and before dessert build a campfire which
nearly the entire group of guests and guides encircle.

I haven't changed clothes since we landed at camp and I am
still wearing my river attire, shorts, T-shirt, and sandals. As the
sun begins to descend I feel a hint of a chill in the air. Should have
brought a long pair of pants, but I didn't. My shorts and T-shirt
are a still a little damp, and the thought of slipping on a dry cap-
ilene or fleece top is appealing. But I didn't bring either. I've got a
cotton sweater in my bag and I fetch that. It handles the dipping
sun and related descending air temperature fine—for a while.
Scooting closer and closer to the campfire also helps to address
my creeping discomfort. My feet are cold. I wish I could slip on a
pair of warm, wool socks. But I didn't bring those either.

Borrowing some warm gear from one of the guides, one of
whom is my son Skip, would offer a simple and quick solution to my
thermal needs. But I'm hesitant to do that. I'm weighing the benefit of warmth versus the embarrassment of my "experience counts
when packing" rants. I endure my shivering as long as possible
before I feign fatigue and slink away towards the tent I'm sharing
with Skip. It's early June and the hills are lightly illuminated. In an

hour or so the cloudless sky will be star-studded. We're camped at over 5,000 feet at the northern end of the Rocky Mountains. The setting is exquisite, but the clear sky portends steadily dropping temperatures.

Back at the tent, I dump my waterproof bag on one of the sleeping pads and rummage through the contents. Must be more stuff in there. So I shake the bag again but nothing emerges. I know it's here somewhere, likely under the clothing I've piled on the pad. But it isn't. No sleeping bag. My personal warmth crisis has taken an ominous turn. The only sleeping bag in the tent is Skip's. For now I use it like a shawl and drape it over myself. The warmth gives me an opportunity to think through my options. Embarrassment is becoming less important, and is being over-shadowed by this new dilemma.

An option comes to mind, but I reject it. Skip isn't going to share his sleeping bag with me, so there is little sense in pursuing that one. The next solution seems ridiculous in hindsight. Our sleeping pads are thick and provide good ground insulation. I might be able to use one as intended, and the other as a cover. I drag both of the pads from the tent and try out my idea. The pads are so firm that the top one won't stay in place and just slides off my body. I lie on my back and realize that anyone who saw me could mistake me for an ice-cream sandwich.

The stars are starting to pop out. I watch a satellite streak near the horizon before returning the pads to the tent. Just like in one of those crime novels where the clue that solves the mystery comes out of left field, my sitting in the tent on a pad and looking up at the roof of the tent sparks a solution. I'll take the rain-fly off the tent, spread it on the ground and wrap myself in it by lying on a far corner flap and rolling to the opposite end. I figure that the multiple rolls that it will take to get to the other side should create enough insulation to stay warm. But I'll be wrapped like a burrito and unable to move. If I have to get up in the night, I'll never be able to re-encapsulate myself. I'm running out of ideas when I spot a flashlight heading in my direction. Skip arrives at our abode.

"We have a problem," I say. I proceed to explain that it appears that I don't have a sleeping bag. "We have a problem?" Skip responds, and mutters some comment about my packing skills. The solution we come up with isn't as draconian as I envisioned. We unzip Skip's bag and spread it out like a quilt. It doesn't fully cover either of us, but for one night it will be okay.

It's a chilly uncomfortable night. I finally sleep soundly from around 5 to 6:30 and awaken to an empty tent and the early light of day. I wrap the sleeping bag around me and manage another half-hour of warm dozing. There is a Patagonia jacket near the tent door, left for me by my son. I put it on and head towards the camp kitchen where our crew is prepping breakfast. I expect to hear a full ration of deserved sarcasm about my packing skills, but the crew says nothing. Rachael hands me a cup of coffee. We exchange "good mornings" and I join the few guests who are up and sitting around the morning fire. Everyone is talking about it being chilly. But no one even hints about my trip prep or bedding arrangement. I realize that they don't know about it.

After breakfast, the guests carry their bags and tents to our gear boat and Skip secures everything to the sweep rig. I'll be leaving the group at Indian Creek, a landing strip ten or so miles downstream. I hop on Skip's rig for the ride. The sun is rising, the air is warm, and it's going to be another spectacular day. We depart camp ahead of the group and make it to Indian Creek in less than three hours. Skip never mentions my packing misadventure or our sleeping arrangements. When we get to Indian Creek,

I jump off the boat as Skip unties my bag and tosses it to me. I wave goodbye and head to the waiting plane for the short flight back to Stanley.

As most dads will tell you, there is a never-ending game of one-upmanship between father and son. My youngest has kept quiet about my packing fiasco but he has silently stored the details for future retrieval. My leaving the group at Indian Creek will not be the end of the story.

Jerry, Carole & Colin Hughes

JERRY'S SECOND CHANCE

DICK LINFORD

THEY SAY THAT YOU AREN'T A TRUE IDAHO RIVER OUTFITTER unless you have a 4x4 crewcab pickup, a hunting dog, and a divorce. By this standard, Jerry Hughes, otherwise the prototypical Idaho outfitter, falls short. He has the hunting dog, and he has the pickup, but he doesn't have a divorce. In fact, he might not even be married in the eyes of the great state of Idaho.

Jerry and Carole had potential. They could have had successful careers in the real world. Jerry got an appointment to Annapolis but dropped out after a semester because he thought the hazing was bullshit. He zipped through the University of Idaho, where he played football, went right through law school, and immediately passed the Idaho State Bar exam. Carole meanwhile graduated with honors from the University of Idaho, earning degrees in economics, history and accounting. They were people on the move. But Jerry never practiced law for even a day. He wanted to run rivers, and Carole followed him on that seductive slippery slope from loving river running, to guiding, and finally to outfitting.

Jerry took his first river trip at fifteen. A Boy Scout trip on the Middle Fork of the Salmon. That did it. He was hooked. Another

BSA trip followed the next summer. This time on the Main Salmon. At seventeen he was paid $200 for the summer to work as a senior scout on eight BSA trips on the Middle Fork. He learned to row a raft. During one of those BSA trips, Jerry walked into a Hatch River Expeditions camp. The Hatch guides were cooking big ribeye steaks. The BSA meal that night featured canned beans and hardtack. Jerry was quick to notice the upgraded meal with the professional guides. When Jerry turned 19 he got a job with Hatch. He worked for Hatch the next several summers while he was in college and law school, guiding in Idaho, Utah, and the Grand Canyon. Don and Ted Hatch were great mentors.

Jerry met Carole Finley his first semester at the University of Idaho. For him it was love at first sight. For Carole it took a while, but when she finally decided to hang around with him, and to go rafting and backpacking, she was able to enjoy her love of camping, backcountry, hiking, and wild rivers. During her college and grad school years, Carole joined Jerry for as many river runs and outdoor events as possible. Carole found her way into the Hatch crew. Like most companies in those days, Hatch didn't have female guides, so Carole did everything else. She bought and packed food, drove trucks, and did warehouse work. In The Grand Canyon Jerry ran 10 day trips on motor rigs with up to twelve guests, and Carole worked as swamper. They lived out of a boat box on the motor mount on their 33 foot S-Rig Pontoon. As swamper, Carole did everything that Jerry did but steer the boat. (Carole actually did run the motor rig very well. and took it for long sections of the river.) Hatch didn't pay swampers in those days. Jerry and Carole were living together and they shared Jerry's pay and their tips. When Jerry worked on Idaho rivers the two of them lived in a tent (the Hughes family's canvas umbrella tent) pitched behind Bud and Stella Critchfield's amazingly cool old log cabin in Stanley the, same property where Hughes River Expeditions has its Middle Fork headquarters today.

After Jerry graduated from law school and passed the Idaho State Bar exam, he and Carole immediately went to work for Wilderness Encounters (Wild Rivers Idaho & Shepp Ranch Idaho), guiding on the Middle Fork, Main Salmon, Snake/Hells Canyon, Lower Salmon, and Owyhee. Jim Campbell owned the outfit, and longtime friend Cort Conley was river manager. Once again, Carole bought and packed food and drove vehicle shuttles. She was an ace driving a big crewcab dually, pulling a long overloaded 5th wheel trailer. Once in a while she got her own boat during the Campbell years. Jerry and Carole worked year-around for Wilderness Encounters, river guiding in the summer, doing raft maintenance off season, helping in fall hunting camps, and care-taking Shepp Ranch on the Main Salmon the winter of 1975-76. It was a great life, but it wasn't leading anywhere. Looked like it might be time to dust off their degrees. Look for real jobs. Yikes.

But, in 1976 Jerry, who could sell ice to Eskimos, raised some money from good river running friends, and he and Carole started Hughes River Expeditions. Jerry was twenty-nine and Carole was twenty-eight. Carole was at last a fully accepted guide and proved herself to be not only competent but fearless. They ran trips on the Middle Fork, Main Salmon, Lower Salmon, Snake/Hells Canyon, Owyhee, Bruneau, and Grande Ronde.

Jerry claims that he would have married Carole after the first date. Carole wasn't so sure. During the University of Idaho years, they moved into a basement apartment in spring of 1971. Living together worked great at the time. In 1975, Carole and Jerry set-tled in Cambridge, Idaho where, in the eyes of their parents, they were living in sin. Jerry always wanted to get married, but Carole was reluctant. Jerry figured that she was always looking for someone better.

In 1983, out of the blue and after eight years of sinful living, Carole said, "Let's get married."

Jerry responded, "Golly! When?" (Golly is about as strong as Jerry usually gets in his language in mixed company.)

Not wanting the thought to pass, Jerry said, "I bet my law school pal will do it on short notice. He's the district judge in Grangeville."

Jerry made the call. The judge, who will remain nameless for reasons that will become clear, was less than enthusiastic. It was a Friday and he had a tee time at the local golf course. Jerry wheedled a bit and the judge said, "I'll do it, but get here quick."

Jerry and Carole virtually flew the 140 miles from Cambridge to Grangeville.

They walked into the Judge's Chambers. After normal courtesies, the Judge asked, "Where is your witness?"

Jerry: "Witness? Golly. Nobody told us about a witness."

Judge: "You have to have one. It's the law."

Carole: "How about your secretary?"

Judge: "Nope. It has to be someone who knows both of you."

Jerry: "Shit!" (Sometimes "golly" just doesn't work, even in mixed company).

Carole: "How about Frogg Stewart?"

Frogg was a fellow outfitter and all-around bon vivant living in Grangeville who used to spell his name Phroggue, but no one could pronounce it.

Jerry called Frogg. "Carole and I need for you to be a witness at our wedding down at the District Court House." Frogg didn't want to participate. He had plans that involved a lot of beer..

Carole grabbed the phone from Jerry and told Frogg "We will buy the beer." Frogg was there in four minutes.

The Judge, anxiously watching his watch: "Do you want the long version or the short one?"

Carol, Jerry and Frogg looked at one another. Unanimously, "Short works."

The Judge looked at Jerry and Carole: "Do you want to be married?" They both nod approvingly. "I hereby pronounce you man and wife. That will be $90. Checks are fine."

Jerry paid the judge as he hustled off to his tee time. Jerry, Carole, and Frogg headed for the nearest of Frogg's favorite Grangeville bars. After beers, Jerry and Carole pointed the pickup truck for Cambridge, feeling completely and officially man and wife. Actually, not much different than "shacked up, or living with" but none-the-less probably an upgrade. When informed, both sets of parents appreciated the upgrade, but were pissed about not being invited. Can't please everyone. Along the way home Jerry and Carole took a detour to McCall for a celebratory Mexican dinner. Low key wedding for sure.

Remember that the wedding was in 1983. In 2009 the judge called Jerry to announce his retirement. Jerry congratulated him. The judge followed by asking Jerry how he and Carole were doing. Jerry said "Ok. We still enjoy being together, the business is good, and we have three wonderful kids. ." The judge said that he is very glad to hear that. He just wanted to check and be sure.

"I've been cleaning out my desk," he said. "I just wanted to let you know that I never filed those marriage papers for you and Carole.Totally my error. But if you want out, you might have a technicality in your favor." So they weren't officially married.

As he does with all big decisions, Jerry consulted with Carole about what to do. They decided to stay married. That night they celebrated their wedding one more time with friends in Cambridge. They have never bothered to check with the State of Idaho to make sure the judge did the right thing this last time. Would you trust a guy who played golf instead of filing the paperwork years before? Jerry and Carole have three adult children. They have owned and operated Hughes River Expeditions, Inc. for 42 years.

And does it really matter? Married or not Jerry doesn't qualify as a true Idaho outfitter. He may have a 4x4 crewcab pickup and a bird dog, but he hasn't gone through a divorce.

THE ACCOUNTANT

BOB VOLPERT

THE ACCOUNTANT LOOKED TO WEIGH a rotund 240 plus and wore a flowery unbuttoned shirt that showcased his exposed belly. A prominent gold chain and pendant dangled from his neck. He was leering at every woman who entered Perry's, the popular San Francisco watering hole on Union Street. Just a smarmy, creepy guy trying to look irresistible on a Sunday afternoon.

Our office was located in the Cow Hollow district, just a few blocks away. I'd made contact with the guy by some odd referral and he had invited me to join him for a beer to see if he could straighten out our taxes. A professional consultation on a Sunday and at a bar should have been a clue that things might not work out, but that hadn't occurred to me at the time.

We'd never met before, yet the first thing out of his mouth was "You pay too much in taxes." I hadn't filed taxes in about 5 years. His spiel presented the possibility of taking care of a lingering problem that was likely to deteriorate unless something was received by the IRS soon. He offered to trade the tax work for a Middle Fork trip.

On the bus back from the Middle Fork take-out, the accountant tells me the trip has been great and that he'd have my tax returns ready next time I got to San Francisco. And, by the way, "I'm going to stay in Salmon for a few extra days."

The extra days started out at the Stagecoach Inn, a motel just down the hill from our house. When our crew headed out for another trip, the accountant said staying at the guide house would be preferable to the Stagecoach and he moved in with us. So living at our two-bedroom house at 306 Broadway was Mary and me, our three young kids, guides between trips, and an accountant who showed no inclination to leave. He slept most of the day, got up and adorned his magnificent body with the gold chain thing, and went out around 9 pm every night, returning after the bars had closed.

Conversations that ensued:

Mary: "What's he doing?"

Bob: "I don't know."

Mary: "Get him out of here. Now."

Bob: "I'll try."

Bob to Accountant: "Probably time to head home."

Accountant: "I'm waiting for a phone call."

A few days later he got up early and announces that he is leaving. We rush to the Salmon airport but just miss the morning commuter flight to Boise. The next day, we got there in plenty of time, drop him off and celebrate when we hear the engine of the plane as it flew above our house.

We never saw the guy again. He simply skipped town. When I called my office to check if he'd dropped off my tax returns, I learned that no one had heard or seen him. The accountant was somewhat of a neighborhood fixture and his disappearance had sparked local gossip. Someone in our office had overheard a cryptic conversation about his being in the witness protection program.

As soon as I heard that, I made a beeline to San Francisco to retrieve my accounting records.

Steve Cutright worked with me back then. He was a former river guide and had joined our company to help straighten out our accounting and financial chaos. Steve was a big, strong guy and I asked him to accompany me to the accountant's office, located on the second floor of a nearby old Victorian building. He was to guard the stairway and block entry to anyone heading upstairs. I tried the doorknob to his office. It was locked so I kicked in the wooden panel of the door. I entered the office and slid open the top drawer of the guy's desk where stacks of pornographic photos greeted me. Then to the filing cabinet where miraculously I found my records and those of a friend I'd referred to the accountant. I grabbed the files. A full dose of adrenalin propelled us back to our office.

I'd gotten my records and knew someone who could complete the unfinished tax returns. I still wasn't sure what was going on but I was relieved to have recovered all my stuff. I had no idea what had happened to the accountant. At the end of that day, my bodyguard and I stopped at a nearby neighborhood bar to rehash events. It was a place where the accountant used to hang out. It was crowded and very noisy. We were seated on stools at the bar and I heard snippets of conversation from nearby patrons.

Pick-up lines, jokes, and sexual innuendos filtered to us. I caught words but not whole sentences: Dinner, Office, Idaho, Protection, Tequila, Screw, Steak, Friend, Dog, Pitrale, Gun, Hide, Chardonnay, Dice, Trunk, Belvedere, Missing, Belly, River, Feds, Hiding, Salmon, Witness. Others too. I'd heard enough to know that we would never, ever see or hear from the accountant again.

Eventually taxes were filed, I got a story out of the deal, Steve went on to a professional career as Fire Chief at a couple of Bay Area fire departments, my wife forgave me for housing a criminal, no one in Salmon ever mentioned him, and I was left with one regret.

I just wish I had been privy to that phone call he got in Salmon.

Mary Papale

THE JOE SLATTERY TELL

MARY PAPALE

WHEN JOE SLATTERY WALKED INTO THE KITCHEN we didn't immediately notice the red polish on his fingernails. Amy and I were at the table in our Broadway guide house in Salmon, Idaho drinking early morning coffee. It was the summer of 1994 and we were co-managing the day-to-day operations of Outdoor Adventures.

Joe was a big muscular guy. He had a happy friendly face and a laugh that would make you grin even if you weren't privy to what he was chuckling about. He was incredibly strong and way fun to hang out with. He grew up in Maine and was a polite. thoughtful person. Bob had met Joe when he bought boats and gear from us back when we owned Clavey River Equipment. In the early 90s Joe decided to become a river guide and went through our guide training.

The first time I met Joe was in 1989 when he walked into our Broadway house with his girlfriend, Helen, to go on a training trip on the Main Salmon River. It was early July in a busy river season and guides from California were pouring into our house to get organized for this trip. I was running on caffeine that day and was trying to fix the dryer that was in the middle of the kitchen. My handyman skills involved kicking and swearing at broken things. The old dryer was always wheezing along and ran day and night. Bob and I had two little boys at the time and the Idaho crew of several guides were there too, and were constantly doing their laundry between trips. My job for the river company was to round up food and other supplies for trips, keep the house organized, and handle all the stuff that moms are called on to do when raising two young boys. It was a waste of time to try to ride herd on river guides as they arrive in your life as a complete package. Joe gave me a polite "hello," noticed my frazzled look, quickly assessed the situation, and immediately started fixing the dryer. That about sums up Joe.

Helen walked up to me looking uncertain and guarded. She was doing her best to adapt to Joe's developing guiding career and all the river guides that she was meeting along his path. She looked me straight in the eye and the first words out of her mouth were "Oh no, are you another of those super cheerful guides that are always smiling and happy?" HA! There was little chance of me being a super optimist on that day or probably for the rest of the demanding river season. Helen was wary of Joe's new career/lifestyle and she was never one to mince words. We got along fine.

The next summer, Joe joined our Idaho crew and, as happens in river companies, the stories started and the Slattery legend grew. The crew would come back each week with stories of Joe's feats of strength on the river, packing for the river, loading boats, rigging, de-rigging, and of course his rowing. Joe had many facets to his personality. But probably the most outstanding trait was his stubbornness. I loved Joe's Maine manners and he became like a big brother to me. He knew the right thing to do in any situation and he set about doing it in his own Joe way. At the time we had four women on the crew and he about drove them crazy with his stubbornness about how to get things done. There is always jockeying on river crews about how to accomplish the many little and big details that go into a river trip. The best river guides are skilled and smart people with varying sizes of egos. There is lots of maneuvering on crews for the alpha positions of controlling how a trip is run or tasks are done. This particular crew would meet for hours on end after trips, beginning by discussing issues, then dissolving into arguing about how to accomplish tasks more efficiently, how to run certain rapids, how to deal with guest problem, and on and on. What all these discussions boiled down to was how they would meld together as a cohesive crew and get along. Joe would sit patiently in the meetings and would once in awhile make a comment or a suggestion that would immediately get shot down by one of the women on the crew. I would overhear the meeting dynamics from the kitchen but didn't get involved as the crew needed to work out their own issues.

Between trips Joe liked to camp in his truck because it was a lot quieter than a three bedroom house crammed with guides and a family with two young boys. He had a favorite site a few miles away on "the bar" above Salmon that was accessible by driving up a steep dirt road. It wasn't an official campground but it was away from the house chaos and afforded a magnificent view of the Beaverhead Mountains and the valley below. In the morning, he typically ate breakfast and showed up at our house somewhere between 8 to 9 AM to start packing for the next trip. Amy and I were both early risers and it wasn't quite 7 AM yet when he walked in that summer of 1994. We hadn't heard Joe's truck pull up and his arrival was a surprise.

"Joe, what are you doing here so early in the morning?" I asked.

"Oh my truck is stuck. I drove off the road and Bill Ricks is meeting me at 8 to tow it out," he answered in his Maine accent with as few words as possible. That type of brief response usually meant he was embarrassed about something.

Amy and I stared at him as he described how the truck had slid down a gulley, got stuck, and would need to be pulled out. As he talked we stared at his fingernails, but didn't say anything about them.

Bill Ricks was the local tow truck driver, a former Oregon State trooper who had moved with his wife and family to Idaho when his now-grown kids were teens. The joke around town was that Oregon was too liberal for Bill and that Salmon was a better fit. He joined the Marines at a young age and after completing his tour of duty, became a member of a competitive marksman team that traveled around the country. If anyone sported the image of a guy with a "crew cut and square jaw," it was Bill. He and his wife Bev drove bus shuttles for our company and Rocky Mountain for 26 seasons.

Bill always had a solution to any vehicle or shuttle problem. He would sometimes drop by, settle in a comfortable chair, and pontificate about the workings of the world. He liked our crew and frequently offered them life advice, even if it hadn't been solicited. And of course, he had plenty of driving tips. One time Bill had driven our bus to the Middle Fork takeout and I had followed in our truck. While we waited for the trip to come off the water he taught me two things. One: How to properly clean a windshield, and Two: How to make a "trooper-turn" on a narrow dirt road. I've never forgotten either.

"So ah Joe, how come you're here at the house and not going over to meet Bill?" Amy questioned.

Joe started to squirm and now Amy and I were totally engaged in the developing exchange. Joe stared at his red painted fingernails. "Well, these little girls on the last trip wanted to paint my nails and I let them. I need to get this stuff off before I meet Bill. I don't want him to see this." After his quick uncomfortable explanation he started to slowly move forward. "I figured there would be some of that stuff you use to take this junk off in one of the bathrooms."

Amy and I were both sitting behind an oval six-person dining table facing the windows and the sliding glass door that Joe had entered through. To my right and down the hall was the main bathroom. To Amy's left was a smaller bathroom with a shower that had a cabinet with tons of shampoos, shaving cream and plenty of nail polish remover.

Joe had been a running back when he played high school football and went on to play semi-pro ball for several years. From what I heard, five years later at his memorial, was that he was a tough hard-nosed, stubborn ball carrier. At the level he played Joe was good at reading "tells." If you were on defense and telegraphed a move, you gave Joe an advantage beyond his speed, athleticism and strength. Joe carried that quality in life too. You didn't have to be long-winded with him, he could read you quickly and figure out what was going on.

As Joe moved forward towards the table, Amy and I gave each other a look out of the corner of our eyes. We immediately understood what we had to do. We broke, me to the right big bathroom and Amy to the left smaller bathroom. Without saying a word we knew we had to get to the bathrooms and lock ourselves inside along with the nail polish remover. Why were we doing this? Because we had to torture Joe. Remember, he was like a brother to us.

Our "tell" was enough for Joe to precisely know our plans. Like the semi-pro running back that he was, he took a strong stride forward, sailed over the dining table, landed, pivoted, and was in the big bathroom with the door locked before Amy and I had taken two steps. We stood flabbergasted, mid-stride, staring at each other in astonishment. He had put a move on us that would have been in the highlight reel of any televised football game.

We could hear him chortling away in the locked bathroom as he took the red polish off his fingernails. Bill Ricks never knew.

Steve Cutright

OF NO RETURN

STEPHEN L. CUTRIGHT

Circa June 9, 1974

THE VACATION ROAD TRIP HAD BEEN PLANNED FOR MONTHS.
The Minishes would travel eastward from their home in Bellevue,
Washington, a suburb of Seattle, to visit longtime friends in the
Spokane area, then take their time driving south through western
Montana to the small mountain town of Salmon, Idaho. There,
they would meet a rafting group and float the Main Salmon River,
the "River of No Return."

Mervin was 61 and starting to think about retirement from
the civil engineering firm he had founded. Maxine was 60 and
energetic, a live wire in a group, but retirement from her position
as a floor supervising nurse at Bellevue Hospital was starting to
look attractive. This was to be an exploratory trip, a chance to get
away from their busy lives for three weeks, leaving work behind
and talking to each other about life in their retirement. Kathleen
and Karen, their 20-something daughters, would take care of the
house, Kathleen working at her job as a nurse and Karen, her
younger sister, still in school.

Kathleen fondly remembers her father as an avid engineer, who for a time had worked as a mining engineer in Peru, and who had his name on plaques at civic projects up and down western Washington State. He was continually fascinated by how things worked, tinkering with projects around the house, cerebral in his fascination about life. He was also deeply spiritual and introspective, not absorbed in material success, although his professional credentials were extensive. And he was quite bright. As a younger man, Mervin Minish had not been drafted into the military during World War II. Kathleen explains that, instead, he worked for Dupont Corporation at the Hanford nuclear facility as part of the team that developed the second atomic bomb dropped on Japan.

Her mother, she described, was the social glue in the family, with a warm personality, always looking on the bright side of life. But Maxine and Karen had their rough moments, a time of life when Karen chafed at her mother's direction, resenting Maxine's professional success and social ease, and perhaps somewhat frightened by the prospect of impending adulthood.

A lingering argument with Karen still pestered an otherwise amicable departure. Maxine joked over breakfast that maybe they'd like traveling so much they'd forget to come back. After all, they were going down the "River of No Return."

The station wagon was packed with Mervin's usual flair for physical space and Maxine had assembled a lunch basket and filled a thermos with coffee. As the Minishes backed out of the driveway on the warm Sunday morning, Kathleen and Karen watched from the front walkway. But Karen couldn't let go of the earlier verbal sparring with her mother over breakfast. Across the front yard she impulsively yelled out, "I hope you never return!" Kathleen noticed her mother wince briefly, then recover her smiling face and call back through the open car window, "I love you!"

Circa June 12, 1974, ARTA House in Salmon, Idaho

Daytime highs were climbing into the low 100s under bright cloudless skies and the rivers in Idaho were running high. A huge snowpack in the mountains was melting fast, and the forecast was for more of the same hot weather and clear skies for the next week. Area Manager Deane convened a meeting of the guides on the company's Idaho crew. Two rivers were already too high to run safely as commercial trips: the Middle Fork of the Salmon and the Selway. The Main Salmon, the River of No Return section, flows east to west and bisects the central mountainous area of Idaho's wilderness, or as it was called then, the Primitive Area. Reports from other river outfitters confirmed the impressions of the guides on two prior training trips in May that the Main Salmon's rapids would wash out at high flows. The worry was that paying passengers who came to Idaho to run whitewater would find the Main Salmon too tame.

Deane told the assembled guides that it was time to make several decisions about the upcoming trips. ARTA had cancelled previously scheduled Middle Fork trips due to high water and the company's headquarters in Oakland made it clear they wanted scheduled and booked trips to get on the water. First, Deane wanted to know if the guides were positive the Main Salmon could be run no matter how high the water. After the high-water training trips on both the Main and the Middle Fork, the mood of the guides was electrically charged with a "can do" attitude toward the river.

What no one knew, of course, was how high the Main Salmon would get. There was no publicly available river forecasting in 1974. The river at the Whitebird gauge below Riggins, Idaho, was reading around 100,000 cubic feet per second (cfs) on June 12th.

We guides thought we could safely navigate that level, but no one knew for sure whether much higher flows, if they were to occur, would "wash out" the rapids, make existing rapids bigger, or create new rapids with hydraulic violence much larger than anything we'd previously seen. In fact, the mindset of a washout captured the group's thinking.

Deane continued. The Selway passengers for June 16 had already decided to cancel. The June 16th Middle Fork trip passengers were scheduled to arrive in Stanley on June 15th from Florida and were already en-route to Idaho. These people would need to be met in Stanley and told their trip was being transferred to the Main Salmon. Since I knew this party from last year in Utah, I would make the presentation. The Main Salmon passengers were already arriving in Salmon for a June 14th launch and they were being asked to delay their launch to June 16th. The Area Manager wanted to have both trips—the Main Salmon group and the Middle Fork group—launch in tandem on the Main Salmon, separated by half an hour. This would provide group support in case anyone got into trouble downriver.

If anyone in ARTA had reservations about floating the Main Salmon, they weren't saying so. Even the Forest Service personnel thought positively. In retrospect, of course, estimations of a washout were not based upon realistic evaluation, but naïve belief.

June 16, 1974 on the Main Salmon Road

Leaving the little town of North Fork, the two school buses made their way on the dirt road alongside the river. The rafts—Rubber Fabricator Yampas and Green Rivers—and other equipment were loaded in a 1.5-ton stake-side truck. Where bridges crossed the river, the water level was just below the bottom of the girders. And the river was flowing fast, with debris littering the silty brown water: picnic tables, logs, whole trees, and an occasional part of a structure, like a barn. Mid-river islands present in lower water were now flooded, as were low gravel bars and beaches. The farther down river we drove, the more we felt that the river was high enough to wash out sections of the road ahead. We also noticed there were no eddies along the shore or at river bends; everything was flowing current, and that was moving very fast. What wasn't apparent from the road, but was obvious once we stood on the bank, was the way the river seemed to mound up in the middle, the water in center-river higher by three feet than the water level at the banks. Small waves could be seen on the water. But just as we'd been told by the old-time rafting outfitters and guides back in Salmon, there were no rapids.

Finally, above the small farm at Owl Creek, we stopped and decided this spot was as good as any to launch our two trips. With the river flowing this fast, we expected to easily make the miles needed to float the full Main Salmon in six days—about 100 miles to Spring Bar, upstream of the town of Riggins, Idaho.

We prepared lunch for both parties and each lead guide gave the safety talk. The safety rules were a bit different than for lower water trips. A spotter was assigned for each boat to watch for logs and trees floating down river faster than the boats. Boat spacing would be close, thirty feet or less. We announced that, due to the high water, the usual campsites would be washed out, so we'd have to scout for suitable places to stop for the night. Even though the day was hot, we advise the guests to dress warmly for the cold splash off the river. The truth of the situation was this: we had little specific knowledge of what we would be seeing down river in the way of whitewater.

Grant took the first trip of 18 passengers and four guides: Mark, Laurel, and Mike. Henry took the second trip with 22 passengers and five guides: Barbara, Tim, Guy, Roxanne, and me. Rena, my wife, was a trainee, her first time down the Main Salmon. Grant's trip left the shore 30 minutes ahead of Henry's trip.

June 16 —17, 1974 on the Main Salmon River down to Barth Hot Springs

We learned sometime later that the Main Salmon's flow at the Whitebird gauge on June 16th and 17th was 128,000 cubic feet per second, a full hundred thousand cfs higher than what we'd normally call "high water" on the river. Our flow at this point in the river canyon was perhaps half that level, but huge nonetheless. The first impression of floating this extreme high water was that there was no place to slow down, no small eddies to gather the boats and regroup the trip. All the shore beaches were washed out and instead we were looking at steep, rocky banks and talus slopes with no place to land. The second impression was one of speed. While we were in center river, we were floating downriver in excess of 15 mph. In a short time on the river, we passed the confluence with the Middle Fork. Shortly after, the Forest Service launch point of Corn Creek was passed, the end of the dirt road where our trips in lower water usually began.

Our first glimpse of whitewater violence on the Salmon at this high water level was in the large eddy on the right above Lantz Bar. Here the river's current clashed with a violent eddy which raced in circles and trapped at least an acre of driftwood. The beach at the head of the eddy was completely submerged and the eddy current so swift that landing inside the eddy was impractical. The "eddy fences"—the dividing line between main river current and the eddy—stood three feet high, enough to capsize a raft of the kinds we were rowing. Near the downstream end of the Lantz Bar eddy, the current boiled up in huge mounds of water, only to quickly subside and spin off to one or the other side of the river. Here again, the clash of moving and stationary water created large suckholes that could almost submerge the air tubes on our rafts.

The usual campsites down the river canyon were gone, flooded by the swift brown water. Where high benches along the bank provided the promise of campsites, the river flowed through tall trees, making landing difficult without impaling the rafts on the tree trunks protruding from the fast water. Finally, we found slack water surrounding a grove of trees partially drowned by the river. The camp up the hill was rocky with few areas of flat ground. Passengers were told to climb the embankment to find a spot where they could lay out a sleeping bag. Beware of the poison ivy! And rattlesnakes! Somewhere down river was Grant's ARTA trip, we assumed also struggling to make a camp in meager flat ground.

The nighttime camp reprieve from floating gave us time to reflect on what we were seeing on the Main Salmon and speculate on what might be downriver, where the canyon's gradient steepened, narrowed, and the river would crash around bends in the canyon.

The following morning we launched back on the river around 10:00 a.m. Our spotters noticed more logs and full trees in the river floating past us and we would row vigorously to stay away from their branches and root balls. A cadence developed for the group, staying to the inside of rapidly passing river bends, looking out for obstacles in the river, watching for whitewater down-stream. Opposite Barth Hot Springs we spotted heavy whitewater off the right bank: large holes and waves generated by submerged rocks near the shore. Rounding the next bend, we entered a long straightaway near Sandy Hole and saw people wearing lifejack-ets walking across a low bench on the right bank. At the end of the straightaway to the right Henry spotted slack water amidst a stand of trees and we pulled in to shore.

Laurel and five passengers walked into our landing area a few minutes later.

June 17, 1974, near Sandy Hole

Laurel had been walking at a fast clip when she met us and she paused a moment to catch her breath. Then in measured tones she explained that she'd let her boat drift into the heavy whitewa-ter opposite Barth Hot Springs camp and flipped her Green River raft. She immediately swam to reach the Minishes. Maxine was a non-swimmer, and she and her husband, Mervin, pulled Maxine to shore on the right bank about 400 hundred yards from the flip. Mik pulled his boat into shore at that point and told her that he saw Mark and Grant chasing after Laurel's overturned raft to bring it to shore.

Laurel told us that after their swim the Minishes were exhausted, particularly Maxine. So she and Mike concluded that the couple should ride in Mike's raft down to meet the other two boats. They were all concerned about Maxine's health after her exertion and fright in the river. A doctor on the trip agreed to ride with them. At this point, she said, Mike has been on the river about half an hour. "That swim to shore was very tough," she added. "The river is very cold and Maxine couldn't swim a stroke to help us out."

Perhaps another three minutes went by when into the group walked into Grant, holding a first aid kit. He, too, looked exhausted from his hike from far downstream, but there was something more ominous in his eyes. Laurel asked Grant if he'd pulled her raft to shore. Then asked quickly if Mike's boat had caught up with them. Grant interrupted, "Wait!" and paused for a few seconds to collect his thoughts. "Mark and I left our boats tied up to shore several miles downstream after giving up trying to pull your [Laurel's] raft to shore. We were walking high on the bank headed upstream, about a mile from our rafts, when we heard a shout from the river and looked down to see a capsized black ARTA Yampa raft and two swimmers wearing lifejackets in the river."

"What? No!" cried Laurel, her face instantly contorted in emotional agony. "The Minishes were on that raft!"

"There was nothing we could do to help them." Grant was shaking his head, his own eyes welling up with tears. "After seeing them, Mark headed back to our boats and I came up here to find you." Grant then added something we all were fearing, "I'm afraid Mike and the doctor might have drowned, too."

Sitting on the bank in the trees, amidst her sobs Laurel kept repeating, "They won't survive another swim!"

Henry, our lead guide, told Laurel and Grant that they could ride downriver with our group to pull everyone together. Laurel immediately said she was done with this river; she offered to lead a hiking party on shore to meet up with the rest of the group. Her passengers all agreed to follow her. Grant said that he should ride with Henry. The whitewater downstream is very serious and he should help guide us through it.

Laurel started hiking downstream a few minutes later, leading about five people. We all boarded our boats and worked our way back out through the trees and into the current.

June 17, 1974, down river from Sandy Hole to Bear Creek Bar

Reaching the main current, Rena took the oars. That lasted about five minutes. Rounding the bend at Nixon Creek we saw huge rounded waves in front of us, perhaps 20 feet or more in height. She would have none of this, so I started rowing again. Center river was smooth current into the waves, but off to either side was violent turbulence, breaking waves and boils of water welling up from the depths. The huge wave train subsided after about a quarter mile. Again the river made a bend to the left and on the outside of the bend was a huge hole which set up a continuously breaking wave that extended two-thirds across the river toward the left shore. We hit it mid-river, still a six-foot breaker. After Bear Creek on the right was a high bar with slower water near the shore, here were the two other rafts tied to shore, Mark waiting there with their trip's passengers. Laurel's overturned raft had gone downstream, to be recovered 81 miles later near the town of Riggins, Idaho.

Mike finally made it to the high bar downstream of Bear Creek after a harrowing experience. He said that he tried to cheat the big rolling waves starting at Nixon Creek by staying to the right side. Suddenly a hole opened up in the river, swallowing his boat and flipping it, throwing everyone into the river. Underwater for a while, when he surfaced he was being propelled to the river's left side, losing sight of his passengers. Struggling for over a mile, he finally gained the left shore and began walking back upstream in an attempt to find a better place to swim back to the right bank, where the guides had agreed to rendezvous if there were trouble.

Mike's scramble on the steep rocky left slope was tough and he paused many times, climbing over rock bluffs and near the water. Finally, his way was blocked by a rattlesnake and, rather than climbing higher to circle around the serpent, he decided to try swimming from that point. It almost killed him. He spoke of using the last of his strength to reach the right shore, crawling out of the cold river like a salamander slowly crawls out of the water. It was a terrifying and humbling experience.

The doctor riding with the Minishes in the front of Mike's raft swam out of the river to the right bank and eventually walked downstream to meet up with the rest of the group.

It was from the high bar downstream of Bear Creek that both parties were rescued by helicopter the following day.

June 17, 1974, the Long Journey

We don't know with any certainty the final minutes of life for Mervin and Maxine Minish as they floated down the Main Salmon in their lifejackets. But there are a few things we can deduce. First, Mervin was physically fit, an avid hiker and climber in the Cascades of western Washington. In all likelihood he could have physically endured the swim out of the Main Salmon at flood stage. Second, we know that he didn't try to swim out, choosing instead to remain with Maxine, perhaps consciously honoring the promise he made when he married her many years earlier. Kathleen was pretty adamant about this. Her father adored her mother and, as Kathleen said, it was simply not in his character to leave her and let her die alone.

Perhaps he spoke with her, trying to ease her fears and give her hope. Mervin probably tried to get her to talk, about what we can only guess. They were close, after all, and more than likely he used any number of the sacred words, the secret vocabulary that makes up the special language and deeply interpersonal knowledge shared by two people in a long and close relationship such as marriage.

Maxine may have urged him at one point to leave her, to swim for shore. She would have known he could make it. "Save yourself, Mervin," she might have said. To which he could have answered, "Sweetheart, I already am."

We'll never know the words Mervin and Maxine shared. We know this, however. When they floated in their lifejackets by the passengers waiting ashore, those who had been riding in Marcom and Pickering's boats, both Mervin and Maxine waved. No one ashore could have gone out and saved them. Perhaps the Minishes knew this. Perhaps their waves were a final gesture of hope and pleading. Or perhaps a simple goodbye.

The last anyone ashore saw of Mervin and Maxine, they were floating around a river bend, vanishing into the vastness of a wild river in flood stage, on their long journey to forever.

Only Two Tragedies

STEVE WELCH

In this world there are only two tragedies.
One is not getting what one wants, and the other is getting it.
—*Oscar Wilde*

PART I : NOT GETTING IT

I'M NOT VERY GOOD WITH DATES, but I remember the first time I met Tony Campagnone (rhymes with pepperoni) was in a Denny's Restaurant along Interstate-5 outside of Sacramento, California. I had just finished my junior year at UC Davis and I had signed on, sight-unseen, for a summer of guiding rafts for him on the Rogue River in southern Oregon. I didn't have a car, so a friend had dropped me off in the parking lot and I was going to get a ride up to Grants Pass with Tony. This was pretty much a one-way choice: if things didn't work out, my escape plan was to get a ride back to Sacramento with Tony at the end of the summer.

Before we get too far along, I should probably tell you that this was also pretty much my only choice. Just that morning I had broken up with my girlfriend, Liddie, when I found out that she had been sleeping with my best friend while I was studying abroad. I don't remember much about my final conversation with her, but I'm pretty sure that the last thing I said started with an "F" and ended with a "you." I wasn't too worried about my escape plan; not having a way to get back isn't so important when you don't have a back you want to get to.

I had asked my friend who had gotten me the job, how I would recognize Tony and he asked me if I had ever seen the movie *Patton*. I thought he was exaggerating, but when I saw Tony, sitting in a booth with a cup of coffee, all I could think was: "Where's the big American flag and the helmet?" Little did I know that the physical resemblance was the weaker part of the comparison. The voice, the glare, the presence, the top button of his shirt—everything about Tony screamed: *General Patton. Sir!* I wanted to look under the table to see if he was wearing those blousy jodhpur things but I was afraid to break eye contact.

I would come to learn that Tony had, in fact, been in the Army and that he enjoyed his Patton resemblance. And it was quickly obvious that this trait, this military disposition, was a big part of his identity; and I could tell that it was going to be a big part of my summer. And not a good big part. I thought about bowing out right there in Denny's, making up some excuse and heading back to Davis. But there was no back to Davis, so instead I started counting the minutes until it would be over. Given my escape plan, I figured I had about 11 weeks to go.

Tony and I small-talked our way north to the Klamath River where we would meet the rest of the crew and do some training. Another part of Tony's identity was that he believed that he could teach anyone how to row. Relying on that, he had recruited the rest of the crew from the music department at the local junior college. He had put up flyers looking for hard-working, outdoor-loving people and Deena Woods and Holly Wilson had applied and been hired. They were both healthy, charming, hard-working, sincere people with beautiful voices. They could play the guitar, sing, and cook. They had their own sleeping bags and tents. They were great human beings. But they could not row their way across a lake. And, we would discover, Tony's belief in his teaching abilities was highly inflated.

Our timetable for learning how to row was highly compressed. The summer before, a big rafting company had dismissed their entire Oregon crew over a labor dispute and then contracted with Tony, a small-time Klamath outfitter, to run their Rogue trips for them. Ready or not, an 11-week season was coming; trips were booked, people were on their way, the show must go on. It was the eve of opening night and Tony Campagnone and the Rogue River Misfits were rehearsing to stand in for Bruce Springsteen and the E Street Band. To say we were in over our heads would have been a compliment.

We spent the first few days on the very forgiving Klamath, and then, right before our first commercial trip of the season, we headed up for a training trip on the Rogue.

This would be a good time to tell you the difference between the Klamath and the Rogue. Amongst a bunch of other differences, the Klamath has a highway along it and the Rogue doesn't. On the Klamath, if things go wrong, you're pretty much a thumb away from help. On the Rogue, if things go wrong, you're pretty much on your own.

So, the Rogue was a step higher and a leap deeper. Tony drilled us and we got better. Tony drove us and we got tougher. Tony pushed us and we pushed back. He got headaches; we got blisters. We all questioned our summer plans. But by the end of the Rogue training, we had found a tense truce and a fake confidence built on our mutual unwillingness to admit weakness. We were a floating house of cards but we weren't ready to admit that we couldn't pull it off.

And if it weren't for Blossom Bar, the Rogue's notoriously difficult Class IV rapid, we probably could have pulled it off. The rest of the Rogue is pretty merciful; we were good cooks; and Deena and Holly had that music thing going for them, so even our roughest days would always end with full stomachs, campfire songs, and passenger-forgiveness—or at least passenger-forgetfulness.

But you can only fake it so far. And you can't fake it through Blossom Bar. Blossom is as forgiving as the DMV. For us, "Blossom Day" (day three of our four day trips) was always an adventure and usually a disaster. We never blossomed on Blossom Day.

This is probably a good time to tell you a little bit about Blossom Bar. The thing about the rapid is that the better you get, the worse it treats you; the closer you come to having a good run, without actually having a good run, the further up the creek you are. It is like doing a backflip: a full rotation is a smooth success and zero rotation is embarrassing but not that painful; but if you rotate anywhere between say, 10 percent and 80 percent, it's really bad, it really hurts. That's Blossom. Because of the way it lays out, (a hard pull from left to right in front of a minefield sieve of big boulders into a safe slot on the right), it is better to completely swing and miss than to foul one off; it is better to go down the left shoreline into the "catcher's mitt" than it is to only make it part—way across and go into the middle of the "picket fence." If you can't make the full back-flip, well, it's less painful to not start at all. In other words, there's not a lot of gray area with Blossom; it is do or die, hit or miss, clean or very, very, dirty. So, as we slowly kept getting better, things steadily kept getting worse.

The first time we ran Blossom, on the training trip, we sent two rafts down the left side without even sniffing the eddy, let alone the desired right-hand slot. We spent that afternoon hiking along the left bank, unloading gear, and trying to pull the rafts back upstream far enough to be able to get them out of the catcher's mitt and back into the main current—the debut of what would become a fairly common production for us.

The second time, which was our first commercial trip, was an encore performance.

The third time we got a little better, but as I said before, that made it much worse.

And so it went, week after week, our backflips progressing from embarrassing but manageable bail-outs into ugly and painful back-flops. Every week we would move steadily across the fence, stuffing a raft between new pickets. Getting closer, but not really getting better. We spent a lot of afternoons yelling to each other and pulling on ropes with each other and listening to Tony tell us what to do and then we spent a lot of evenings drying out sleeping bags and salvaging dinner. It sucked.

This is probably a good time to mention that Tony had had quadruple bypass heart surgery the winter before and wasn't in any shape to do anything other than tell us what to do. But, to his credit, he was good at that.

This is also probably a good time to mention that Liddie had gotten a job guiding on the Tuolumne and had apparently launched into a wild and very public love affair with the company manager who was a legend inside the world of California raft guides and famously virile beyond that.

And that Holly and I had started sleeping together.

The other commercial trips that paralleled us would make a supreme effort to get ahead of us on Blossom Day. They knew that we were a floating time-bomb, a wrap waiting to happen.

To be behind us meant an extra hour or two waiting for us to pioneer new lines through Blossom's boulders and to engineer new methods for extracting rafts from pretty much everywhere in the rapid.

To be ahead of us meant watching the river during lunch for various items that were likely to come floating downstream.

More than once, after we gathered our belongings, dusted off our prides, and resumed our journey below Blossom, we would find some piece of our rescued gear piled conspicuously along the shoreline along with a ceremonial offering to our survival: a loaf of bread, a bag of apples, a six-pack of beer; generous and sympathetic invocations from our fellow rafters for a speedy recovery and better luck next time.

Needless to say, as the trips and wraps went by, there was tension in the ranks. There was a lot going on: My youth and ill-warranted confidence running into Tony's stubborn age and dominance, Tony's conservative military rule running into Holly and Deena's liberal arts tenor, Tony's opinion of his teaching abilities running into reality, and our rubber rafts running into all those rocks in Blossom. Outside, we were a cheerful and intrepid band of troopers; but inside we were a mess.

And then we would get to Blossom and, for a moment (well, actually, usually for way longer than a moment), we would unite around the shared peril and we'd work together to get through the rapid. But those moments were the exception; Holly, Deena and I thought that we would be better off on our own. We thought that success was just a trip without Tony on it.

Be careful what you wish for.

Trip number six was the turning point. Trip number six was the halfway point of the summer and trip number six was where the shit hit the fan. Or, less colloquially, trip number six was where Tony's raft hit the "Gumdrop Rock."

This is probably a good time to tell you about how the difficulty of a rapid is determined. There are two systems. There is The International Scale, that well-referenced Roman numeral system that everyone knows, and then there is The Guide Scale, the long-winded, myth-laden system that river guides know. One of the many tenets of The Guide Scale is: the more named rocks a rapid has, the more difficult that rapid is. Blossom Bar has a lot of named rocks. There's the "Volkswagen Rock," the "Wave Rock," the "F-U Rock." There's the notorious group of rocks known as the "Picket Fence." And there's the "Gumdrop Rock."

This is also probably a good time to tell you Tony's strategy for getting us through Blossom. Like all things Tony, it was rigid. The first rule was that you always did what Tony told you to do and you never did anything until Tony told you to do it (think: chain of command). In the morning, Tony would assign guests into boats (think: lifeboat and Titanic) and when we got to Blossom, Tony would lead everyone down to scout the rapid (think: omen of horror). And then Tony would always make us wait at the scout rock and watch him row his raft through (think: setting an example). And then we would always run the rafts through in the same order (think: military precision—but maybe without the precision part). Tony first, then Deena, then Holly, then me. Always. This usually meant Tony was through the rapid and conveniently out of the way for most of the excitement and that we were left to deal with whatever happened to the rest of us (think: Oh, shit. Not again).

"Gumdrop Rock" isn't Blossom's signature rock or its most ominous threat Those distinctions clearly belong to the Picket Fence. But Gumdrop is significant. It sits in the middle of the river, exactly where you want to go after successfully making it into the critical right-hand chute, and it comes at exactly the moment when you think the worst is behind you. Running Blossom, navigating the left-hand entrance, the eddy, the picket fence, the chute, and then Gumdrop Rock, is like speeding along in the far left lane of the freeway and then making a last-minute exit across five lanes of dense traffic onto a tight off-ramp on the right. And then finding a desk in the middle of the off-ramp. On trip number six, Tony made the exit but hit the desk. And he wrapped his raft around it. Solidly. As we watched from the scout rock, obeying the first rule of Tony, (never do anything until Tony tells you to do it), Tony and his raft and the father and son who were riding in it, slowly fused and became one with the Gumdrop. Despite our intimate familiarity with Blossom, despite our numerous hours spent staring at it from every angle, this was new. We had never seen this before.

And what we saw over the course of the next 30 minutes was nothing short of jaw dropping. Tony, without once looking up towards the rest of us on the rocks, took out his knife and began to cut everything loose from the raft. Everything. While the father and son were perched on the rock, occasionally looking up at the rest of us in wonderment, Tony worked his way back and forth through the boat cutting lines and jettisoning gear. Dry bags first, sent bobbing down the river. Then bigger, less buoyant boxes, sent to the bottom of the river. Then the cooler, with Tony's treasured personal ammo box perched impossibly on top of it, sent adrift like a Norse funeral pyre. Then, incredibly, his oars tossed defiantly into the current. Throughout, Tony was methodical and efficient and surprisingly nimble. It was not an easy undertaking. The whole spectacle was simultaneously heartbreaking and inspiring. If it hadn't been so backwards, it would have been noble. And it was a visual Siren: we knew we should look away, but we couldn't.

And then it got more incredible.

Tony got on top of Gumdrop with the father and son and huddled with them for a moment and we could tell from the scout rock that he was coaching them on how to swim the rest of the rapid. He was pointing downstream, signaling where to go, and giving encouragement. Even from the scout rock, you could feel Tony's conviction and reassurance and you could feel the father and son's hesitation and disbelief. It was mesmerizing. And then Tony coerced them into the water and watched them drift downstream following the line of abandoned gear.

Now, you should know that swimming the bottom part of Blossom isn't that big of a deal. It's not fun, but in the end, it's pretty benign; it's exciting, but not terrifying. And, by this time, Al from Paradise Lodge had been alerted to the wreck and had driven his jet boat up the short distance from the Lodge and was idling in the eddy below the rapid, so abandoning the rock wasn't reckless, it was probably a relief. But still, most people wouldn't want to do it.

And then things got even more incredible.

Tony finally turned and looked at us. He made direct eye contact and then he waved at us and jumped into the river. Well, wave and jump aren't really the right words. It was more ceremonial than that. More of a combination of a Nazi salute and that Black Power pose that Tommie Smith and John Carlos struck at the 1968 Olympics. I don't think Tony bowed his head or clicked his heels together, but if he had, it wouldn't have seemed out of place. The best way to describe it is that he saluted us and then goose-stepped off of his raft. Directly into the river. I'm pretty sure that this is when the expression "WTF?" was born.

I wouldn't see Tony until two hours later after we had made it through the rapid, peeled his raft off of the rock (with the help of what seemed like everyone), retrieved a few no-longer-dry bags, picked up some floating produce, and floated down to Paradise

Lodge where Tony and the father and son were sitting around the big fireplace eating lunch and drinking coffee with Al.

The first thing Tony said to me was that we should have lunch at the Lodge on all our trips.

He never mentioned the incident. Never asked about his raft. Never let on that anything out of the ordinary had taken place.

But he didn't go on any more trips that summer. He left them to us, green, but no longer innocent.

I want to say that that is the end of the story. I want to tell you that the rest of the summer was smooth and without incident. But that wouldn't be true, that wouldn't be life. There's a reason you have to be careful about what you wish for. All summer long Holly and Deena and I had been wishing for a trip without Tony. On trip number seven we got it.

PART II: GETTING IT

This would be a good time to tell you that between trip number six and trip number seven I had heard from mutual friends that Liddie and her new boyfriend, (let's call him Adonis since everyone else did), were taking a week off from the Tuolumne and heading up to do a private, two-person, one-boat Rogue trip. And this would also be a good time to tell you that a private, two-person, one-boat Rogue trip is to river guides what a week in Paris with roses and chocolate covered strawberries and champagne is to everyone else: it is whatever is beyond romantic.

Trip number seven started off beautifully. The weather was gorgeous, the guests were easily entertained, and Look, no Tony! In his stead, Tony had sent one of his long-time Klamath guides, a jovial, older gent named Bill Hemmit who was quite possibly the most positive person I had ever met. He was even less familiar with the Rogue than we were, so he went along with our suddenly liberated itinerary. By default, I took Tony's mantle of Lead Guide and By Jove, we did all of the things we had always wanted to do: we hiked places that had been deemed a little too sketchy; we swam rapids that had been judged a little too risky; we took off our shoes in camp. It was everything we thought it was going to be. Until we got to Blossom.

When we got to Blossom, we missed Tony. Or at least we missed something about Tony. His rigidity had given us structure and that structure had given us a way forward. Without him, we were less committed, less sure; the way forward was up to us. Naturally, we fell into our old routine: assign the passengers, scout the rapid, watch from the rock. And naturally, we reverted to our appointed boat order. Bill went first and he nailed it. Hooray! Deena was next and, for the first time all summer, she made it. It wasn't pretty, but it was gorgeous in comparison to her portfolio of prior misadventures. Hooray! Holly was next and she worked harder than she had all summer and squeaked across the lip of the picket fence and made it into the right-hand chute. Three for three? Us? Three for three! Hip, hip, hooray!

And just as I was turning to head back upstream to get my raft and attempt to complete our improbable Grand Slam, I heard a groan. And without looking, I knew: Gumdrop Rock. Ugh.

There was Holly's raft, along with two moms and their two pre-teen daughters, draped in exactly the same place Tony's raft had been exactly one week earlier. Call it irony. Call it Karma. Call it simple, unconnected bad luck. But whatever you call it, it wasn't good. But, at the same time, it wasn't as bad as some trips. In fact, it wasn't any worse than last week. We've seen this before. We're not novices anymore. We can do this. Again.

To Holly's credit, the first thing she did, after getting everyone up on Gumdrop, was look up to the scout rock and make eye contact with me. I don't think she was smiling, but she definitely made eye contact. And in that moment of eye contact, I realized that everything was up to me; that the weeks of pretending and wishing were over and that the moment of independence was here. And I realized that I had no idea what to do. I headed back to my raft racking my brain for a plan.

This would be a good time to tell you that as I was coming up with my plan, as I was walking back to get in my raft, I passed Liddie and Adonis walking up to scout Blossom. I didn't say a word. She didn't say a word. Two ships passing in the middle of the day.

What happened next was pretty incredible. Not incredible in the Tony goose-step way, but incredible in another, maybe more mythical way. I got in my raft, my fully-loaded oar raft with my four fully-grown adult passengers in the front, and I had the best run of Blossom of my entire life, before or since. And when I got to the middle of the rapid, when I had made the freeway exit and was barreling down on the desk, I rowed harder and more beautifully than I have ever rowed in my entire life, before or since, and I caught the eddy behind the Gumdrop Rock. I glided right in and tossed the stern line to Holly like I was pulling in to camp. It was one of those lift-a-burning-car-off-a-pregnant-woman moments.

*Now, if you've seen Blossom, if you've rowed it, and especially if you are young and courageous, I wouldn't fault you for trivializing this feat. It doesn't look that hard. And it really isn't. It's just an eddy. But if you were in my position, the position of **having** to catch the eddy, of having placed your entire rescue plan on that one move, and of having to execute that move with your best-friend-sleeping ex-girlfriend and her bronzed God of a new boyfriend watching, (and I hope you never are—but, let's admit it, the chances of that happening seem pretty slim), if you are ever in that position, you will know how hard it is.*

And then the work began. The two moms and their two pre-teen daughters climbed on to my raft while Holly sat on the rock and held it. Then together, over the course of the next hour or so, we untied everything from her raft and transferred it to mine. Bags, boxes, coolers, oars. Everything. I was adamant that nothing and nobody would swim the bottom of Blossom. (Sweet redemption doesn't offer itself up every day, right?) And when we had everything we could salvage, everything except the rubber and the rowing frame, I climbed in my raft, grabbed the oars, and Holly jumped back in and we headed downstream. My raft was ridiculously overloaded and I was ridiculously out of adrenaline, but all that was left was the bottom of Blossom (and hey, you can swim that, right?)

The afternoon was a blur of lunch (wet), gear inventory (also wet), people redistribution (remarkably happy), a trip back up to see if Holly's raft was salvageable (no), and a short drift down to the first camp we could find, followed by an afternoon and late evening of moving wet sleeping bags up the hillside chasing the sinking sun. We'd been at it for seven hours and we were about one hour of river time downstream from where we had woken up and about two hours short of where we wanted to be. Somewhere in the incident, Holly had strained her shoulder and sometime in the afternoon, a doctor on the trip had given her a combination of too much muscle-relaxer and too much pain-killer, so she had her arm in a sling and was loopy. If you've ever wrapped a boat and soaked someone's sleeping bag and then had to hang around with them in close quarters, you know how nice it could be to be loopy. So Holly was crushed and embarrassed and loopy, but probably in better shape than if she hadn't been.

On the other hand, Deena was rising to the occasion. She and Bill and our intrepid passengers masterminded a meal out of what was left of our dry food and we ate a very late but quite respectable dinner. The sleeping bag situation resolved itself with everyone stepping up and offering to suffer but no one really having to. And there were enough dry clothes to go around so no one was cold. We were on the side of the hill, in a crappy camp, eating salvaged food in the dark, and looking forward to soggy sleeping bags, but then Deena played a few songs on her guitar and it didn't seem all that bad.

But there was a significant problem: we only had three rafts left and we had a lot more gear and people than would conveniently fit in them. This was a problem. But this was also when, for the first time all day, Providence turned in our favor. Al, of Paradise Lodge and the jet boat, had heard of our latest misfortune and had come up river to see what was going on. In his self-appointed role of Keeper of the Rogue, Al had apparently spent his afternoon driving his jet boat up Blossom to the Gumdrop Rock and removing our raft and frame for us.

You should know a little bit about Al. Al is a character, a book of stories unto himself. He is a man of many skills; skills of strength, skills of courage, skills of toughness, skills of generosity. But not skills of finesse.

Al's method for removing our raft and frame was to drive his jet boat up into my little eddy, toss his claw anchor into the raft, then retreat to shore and retrieve his anchor using a cable and winch. When we left Gumdrop, there were only two things left behind: the raft and the frame. But it took Al many more than two trips to retrieve everything, despite rarely pulling in his anchor empty-handed. At dusk, when Al was returning to Paradise, he stopped at our inclined village to tell us that he had our raft and frame.

And true enough, he did. There they were in the back of his jet boat. A pretzel of tubing that was once our frame and a surprisingly small pile of rubber strips and scraps that was once our raft. Um, thank you?

This would be a good time to tell you that seven of the passengers on our trip were scheduled to fly home the following evening and that we had therefore arranged for an early take-out time: 1:00 p.m. instead of our standard 3:00 pm. This would normally be a manageable arrangement; just spend an hour longer on the river on day 3 and get on the river an hour earlier on day 4. Easy; if there aren't any glitches. Of course we were looking at the mother of all glitches: we were two hours behind a normal schedule, it was almost dark, we were down a raft, we had a loopy guide with a bum shoulder, and we had way too many people and too much gear to fit in our remaining rafts. The prospects for our guests catching their plane seemed highly unlikely.

But wait a minute, Al. Is that a jet boat? Um, thank you!

We arranged to meet Al at the lodge early the next morning and give him seven early-departing passengers and all their gear, plus one loopy guide and all her boxes and coolers . He would transport them, along with our pretzel of a frame and door mat of a raft, to take-out in his jet boat. They would have no problem getting there by 1:00. The rest of us would double-time it downriver, make a quick stop for lunch, and hopefully make it by 2:00; 2:30 at the latest. The first group could leave in one of the vans and tell the other van that we were on our way. Great plan. I went to bed thinking my troubles were over.

They were not.

We got up early as planned. Rushed through breakfast, hurriedly loaded the rafts, and had Holly and the "early seven" and all their gear on the jet boat right on schedule. As they jetted downstream, all we had to do was double-time it through the many miles of almost all flat-water that remained, have a quick lunch, and then sprint to take-out. What could go wrong?

This would be a good time to mention that Bill was a diabetic. A jovial, positive diabetic, but a diabetic nonetheless. I didn't think it would matter and it shouldn't have mattered. But it would and it did.

We headed downstream, pulling steadily and trying to make up time. Bill lingered behind and eventually fell out of view. Then Deena, rowing her heart out, fell out of view as well. I kept going, thinking that being one hour late to take-out instead of two hours late would somehow salvage the dignity of my first trip as a lead guide.

Now, you should know that being out of view on the river is not good boating practice. And you should know that I knew that. But you should also know that this stretch of the Rogue is pretty much all flat-water. And that it was sunny. And that it really didn't seem like there was that anything that could go wrong.

Somewhere, about four hours into the day, I pulled over to make lunch. And to keep looking upstream, and looking upstream, and looking upstream, waiting for Deena and Bill to come back into view.

On the river, fifteen minutes is a long time to be waiting for someone. So is twenty. So after twenty-five minutes, when Deena rounded the corner, there were hearty cheers from my passengers and from hers and sighs of relief from the two of us. She hadn't seen Bill for a while, but it's flat water, it's sunny, what could go wrong?

On the river, thirty minutes is a long time to be waiting for someone. So is forty. So after forty-five minutes, when Bill rounded the corner, there were more hearty cheers and more sighs of relief. But as I watched Bill make those last strokes towards our lunch spot, something didn't seem right. He was a little loose with the oars and his passengers looked alarmed. As he pulled in, Bill got up and stood on the back of his raft with his arms over his head and gave a big whoop. It looked like he was happy to have caught up with us. Until he fell forward flat on his face. On a rock. In about six inches of water.

*You may know that severe hypoglycemia can result when some-
one with diabetes exercises more than usual and eats less than
usual. And you may know that it is exacerbated by dehydration and heat. Like if someone were to have an early breakfast
and then row across flat water for four hours and forty-five
minutes on a sunny day to a late lunch; their insulin-glucagon
balance would go out of whack and they would become hypo-
glycemic. You may know that, but I didn't know that.*

But, I knew that if Bill was acting drunk, I was supposed to give
him a spoonful of jam. I knew I was supposed to do that because
Bill, bless his diabetic, positive heart, had told me that when I first
met him. He told me that all I really needed to know about his diabetes was this: if he acts drunk, give him jam. I'd never seen Bill
drunk, but it seemed pretty safe that this is how he might act if
he was. So I helped him get up out of the water, grabbed a spoonful of jam, stuck it in his mouth, escorted him into the shade, and
propped him up against a tree. When I turned back to all of the
passengers, there wasn't a single mouth that wasn't gaping.

Bill had also told me that even with the jam, he still might go
unconscious; but as long as he got the jam, eventually he'd be fine.
"If you give me jam and then I go unconscious, don't worry about
it," he said, "eventually I'll be fine." (I told you he was jovial). But I
was worried about it. I didn't want him to go unconscious.

It was at this time that Providence again turned in our favor.
One of the big commercial jet boats that cruise the lower part of
the Rogue came screaming around the corner headed downstream
for the coast.

On the Rogue, the relationship between the jet boat world and the raft world is tenuous. We're cordial, but we try to stay out of each other's way. It would not have been uncommon for this jet boat to continue past us without a glance, a courtesy in fact, to minimize the contact time. But at this moment, for some reason, the jet boat pilot looked over at us and immediately dropped the throttle and turned his boat into our lunch eddy. Maybe it was the look in my eye, maybe it was the 10 gaping mouths, maybe it was Bill propped against the tree with a spoon sticking out of his mouth, but for whatever reason, the jet boat pilot knew to stop and offer assistance. In a flash he somehow grasped the situation and offered to take Bill downstream to takeout.

Remembering Bill's footnote about going unconscious and figuring that it would be a lot better if he went unconscious at takeout or at least on the jet boat, I concurred and together the pilot and I roused Bill and hustled him on to the boat. As the pilot was climbing back in, he asked what he should do with Bill when he got to takeout. I told him to just leave him with the loopy guide with her arm in a sling who will be sitting on a pile of rubber next to a big metal pretzel. I swear to God that's exactly what I said. I didn't even think about how pathetic it would sound. The pilot just sort of looked at me, (to this day I have never seen a more sympathetic face), and then he revved it up and headed downstream.

This solved one problem but, of course, created a new one: three rafts, two guides, and five more miles of river to take-out.

Now if I told you that Providence once again turned in our favor, you might begin to think I was making this whole thing up. But I'm not. And when I tell you what happened next you might not think it was Providence; you might think it was The Prince of Darkness.

As soon as the jet boat rounded the corner heading downstream, Liddie and Adonis rounded the corner coming from upstream. Now, I'm no math major, but I was quick to see that they had one more guide than raft and we had one more raft than guide. This was quite a fortuitous circumstance.

This was also quite a painful moment. All I could hear were my last two words seven weeks ago. All I could think of was my best friend. All I could see was Adonis's girth and grace. All I could feel was pathetic and helpless. But shit, this was quite a fortuitous circumstance! Figuring that the chances of another spare river guide coming down the river anytime soon were pretty low, I swallowed my pride, waved Liddie into the lunch eddy, and asked if she would be willing to row one of our rafts to take out for us. Without asking why, Adonis said sure.

The rest of the trip was pretty much uneventful.

We were two-hours late to take out and by the time we got there Holly and Bill had improved dramatically. Neither was 100 percent, but at least they were both mobile and acting sober. We hugged our shell-shocked passengers goodbye, gathered our wits, and turned to loading the truck.

Liddie didn't come over and say goodbye at take-out, but Adonis did. Liddie sat in her Subaru while Adonis came over and helped me load a cooler into the truck and then he shook my hand and said he didn't think anyone could ever catch that eddy behind the Gumdrop Rock. I told him I hope I never have to do it again and then he got in the Subaru and drove away. Nice guy.

We finished loading the truck and then, as planned, drove to the store at Cougar Lane so I could call Tony from the phone booth out front.

I must have spent an hour on the phone. Holly and Deena and Bill sat patiently in the truck as I tried to explain everything. And even though I left a few parts out, it still took a long time. There were a few hearty laughs and a few suppressed tears and I promised I'd drive home safely. When I got back to the truck, Deena was in the driver's seat and wouldn't budge. I climbed in the back and I think I was asleep before she started the engine.

I don't remember the rest of the summer. Five more trips, no more catastrophes. My escape plan with Tony was replaced when Holly drove me back down to Davis to start school again. She stayed for a few days, but we both knew what we knew: that ours was a summer, rebound, romantic, river fling and that it was now fall and we weren't on the river. I went to class one day and came home and she had left. No closure, but no uncertainty either.

I would see Liddie around campus, but we never spoke. Two ships.

I have no idea what happened to Adonis, but if I ever run into him again I hope he remembers me. Maybe we could be friends. Maybe he would tell the story of me catching that eddy.

I went back to the Rogue the next summer and worked for Tony. He stayed on the Klamath and let Deena and me run the Rogue trips for him, along with two guys he recruited from the athletic department of the local Junior College. Twelve times in a row through Blossom without incident; including the last one with Tony. Lunch at Paradise Lodge every time; including the last one with Tony. And still no mention of trip number six.

I had a car that second season, but I talked a friend into driving it back to Davis at the end of the summer so that I could help Tony close up the warehouse. Then I got a ride back to California with him and when he dropped me off at Denny's in Sacramento I told him I was looking forward to seeing him the next summer and he said he was looking forward to it too. We both meant it.

But there wasn't a next summer. Tony went in for more heart surgery that winter and died on the operating table. He never made it back to the Rogue.

I've been luckier. I still go back to the Rogue every summer.

And I can't look at Gumdrop Rock without thinking of Tony.

Emerald LaFortune

Barry Dow

EMERALD LaFORTUNE

YOU NEVER FORGET THE SOUND OF A WOODEN BOAT HITTING A ROCK. As I drop into the entrance of Elkhorn rapid, the transom of this dory older than me dips into the wave beneath the water and makes contact with granite.

"DNNNK."

I've hit rocks in metal boats plenty of times. A metal boat meeting rock mid-rapid creates a loud, CLANG that even your coworkers can hear below through the whitewater noise. Hitting rocks in a rubber raft is expected and often, and holds the sound of an airplane landing. REEEEK.

But here in Elkhorn Rapid, the early July sun baking my shoulders, is the first time I've hit a rock in a wooden boat.

It echoes in my ears.

"DAMNIT!" I exclaim. My guests look back at me.

"We're okay, We're okay," I grimace. I start to feel the back of the boat fishtail, heavy with the weight of the Salmon River entering through the crack.

Even at this mid-range water level, Elkhorn is the longest rapid on the river and I still have two distinct drops to run. The waves and rocks race by the sides of my boat but my thoughts have slowed and I'm thinking of... Barry Dow, of all guides.

The first summer I worked as a commercial guide for OARS, I worked with Barry frequently. Barry's reputation preceded him. He was known for his 1980s style short shorts, his early morning a coyote-is-dying howl of a coffee call, and for getting irrationally angry at non-functional kitchen utensils and tossing them into the river. In a true mark of a legend, guides who have never met Barry Dow still refer to hucking something into the river as "Bdowing" it. (Note: this is not the Leave No Trace policy endorsed by my outfitter.) Most of all, Barry was notorious for being hard on new baggage boaters. On my first commercial trip, Barry pulled his dory into the eddy and slowly back rowed, watching me struggle to strap the last of the toilet supplies to my big yellow balloon of a raft. I was assigned to work trips that Barry lead because Barry was thought to be easier on female guides than on the younger, sometimes arrogant males.

I'll note now that I consider Barry a friend and a mentor. Any stories I share here I would gladly share with Barry too, cocktail in hand, snickering and teasing each other across the deck of a wooden boat.

I learned about wooden boats first from Barry. At the top of a drop, Barry would bring his boat to a complete stop, back rowing and surveying the river for rocks. He insisted that I run close behind him, so I would frantically pull back on my oars, trying to stop my two-ton poop raft from colliding with his delicate Briggs wooden boat.

Following Barry that first summer, I saw his good lines and his bad lines. I watched his teal and white dory float effortlessly through waves and around boulders. I watched him dip an oar into the water and let the current draw him horizontally into his line.

I also watched him botch rapids and explode oars out of his oarlocks. I learned from Barry that running a rapid one hundred times before is no guarantee of a good line. I watched him ruthlessly berate new guides for making innocent mistakes. I also watched him pass off his beloved boat to a third year guide and grin ear to ear, watching her nervously take the oars.

Sometimes, white hair drooping over a grill full of teriyaki chicken, Barry would get a far away look in his eyes. We all knew his time guiding was coming to an end. We didn't know if he was guiding because he loved it or guiding because he didn't know what else to love. Some nights he would drink one too many Steel Reserves, the only adult beverage he brought on the river, and slip, cursing, off the wooden deck of his boat into the river. A senior guide would offer him a hand and he would pretend as if nothing had happened and crawl under his sleeping bag under the Idaho stars.

The first time I helped repair a wooden boat it was the Copper Ledge Falls. Barry's boat. Barry, ignoring the advice of the other trip leader on the water, had run center in Black Creek rather than left. Coming through the rapid close behind him I thought I heard a hit, but couldn't be sure. As we came through the rapid, he shot ahead of us, not looking back. Confused, the rest of the guides followed him, at break-neck dory speed, down river four miles to a lunch beach.

With the guests distracted with their sandwiches, he showed us the hit. A gaping crack showed daylight through the chine. At camp that night we took turns entertaining the guests and helping Barry repair the boat. By the time we had pulled the wood rot away, the hole was big enough to fit a 24-pack of Steel Reserve cans through.

I learned that with some sawing, sanding and duct taping, a big hole could be made smaller. He limped the dory down to Whitewater Ranch and, for the first time in my boating career, I ran Elkhorn in lead while he stayed back to exchange his boat.

Five years later, Barry rarely guides trips. He's moved on to his next adventures. Amber, nn up-and-coming dory guide, bought his boat, The Copper Ledge, and is rebuilding it, learning the art of wood rot and fiberglass and sanding. I lead trips now and, as a rule, always stay firmly parked on shore until all my guides are done rigging. Occasionally, I still chuck a ill-functioning can opener into the riffle below camp.

And five years later, here I am, rapidly approaching the giant domer know as the elephant rock, my boat getting heavier by the second. With all the adrenaline I have left at the end of a 25-mile day, I pull over to a micro sandbar. I toss crates of fruit and rolled umbrellas onshore until I can run my fingers over the split wood. Damn. I feel a knot of regret in the pit of my stomach that I've done such an ugly thing to such a beautiful boat.

But the thing about guiding is there's no time for self pity or reflection. We pump water out of the hatches, make a quick epoxy patch, and cover it will plastic and duct tape. I pull over at the first halfway adequate camp I can find, already an hour behind on dinner. I'm exhausted and for the first time, wondering if I'm here because I love it or here because I'm not sure what else to love.

As dusk turns the river pink, I wade out into the eddy to wash the day's sweat, epoxy and sand off my body. There, bobbing in the eddy next to me, is a single Steel Reserve. None of the other guides on my trip drink Steel Reserve and there are no other camps in sight.

(This is a true story!)

I grin. I crack the tab and pour the potent, metallic beer into my mouth. I know that somewhere, Barry must be laughing.

Anyone who rows these wooden boats will tell you —the sickening crack of wood against rock is the price we pay for the glorious feeling of wood sliding over water. Anyone who has guided long enough will say —it's about more than just the water and the wilderness and the boats and the paycheck, it's about the tribe. That day in Elkhorn I learned something about Barry and about the dory boatmen that came before me. I had felt, cracking through the wood, what we all feared most.

By running the same rivers, over and over, in the same boats, battered and bruised, guides weave together time. Older guides look wistfully toward young guides with their long, tanned muscles and indefatigable backs. They don't miss being twenty two, but they do miss the way that an Idaho river was just a place of beginnings, shiny with promise. The best of these guides slowly pass on what they know, understanding that most of the mistakes a river holds will be made over and over again. To me, Idaho sounds like a wooden boat on water and tastes like a sip of Steel Reserve. I want to share that with those who come next.

Sue Cawdrey

GREY'S GRINDSTONE
SWIM TEAM

SUE CAWDREY

AFTER 30+ YEARS OF CREATING AND IMPLEMENTING PR campaigns for the likes of Chevron, Porsche, Nextel, Ghirardelli Square, and MJB Coffee and Rice, I can now say with confidence that I have never had more fun and been more enthusiastic about a client as I was during those many years when I represented river rafting outfitters in California, Oregon and Idaho. Let's face it, what better product or service is there to promote than a whitewater adventure, connecting with family and friends, sharing delicious meals by the river and reveling in nature's glory?

To that end, I was fortunate enough to float many a river in the name of duty, including California's Kern River, Oregon's Rogue River, and Idaho's Main and Middle Fork of the Salmon River. But it was a media trip on California's mighty Tuolumne that provided the best fodder for a river story.

It was the early 90s, and I had scored the PR person's equivalent of the Big Kahuna—a media trip with San Francisco's "Dan,

Dan the Anchorman" from KGO-TV, ABC Channel 7. Picture a more robust Ted Knight from the Mary Tyler Moore Show—the silver fox, not a hair astray, teeth as white as a fresh pack of BVDs, and little to no outdoor adventure experience. It was a Big Water Year, so the adventure ahead was like nothing he'd ever seen. And it was spring, so the weather and the water were not so warm. Alrighty then.

After a Class V bus ride featuring some gnarly switchbacks on a narrow dirt road leading down to the canyon floor, we convened with the other guests at the Meral's Pool put-in. Once the safety talk was complete, we discussed boat assignments. It was important to the station that we not alter our trip in any way for the news team—they wanted to report on the river, the trip and the overall experience in an objective and unbiased fashion. Dan and his producer Eric decided that it would be a great angle for the segment if Dan were to ride with the only female guide on the trip, sweet Wendy, a critical care nurse by weekday, and a bad ass river guide by weekend. Wendy and Dan hit it off immediately—she was charming and knowledgeable about the river and the region, and had years of experience guiding this and other rivers in the West. Perfect.

Once Dan was settled into the bow of Wendy's oar boat, and the cameraman securely stationed in the bow of another that would shadow Wendy's, Eric and I were assigned to a paddleboat skippered by the legendary river guide "Animal" (so named early on in his guiding career when he misidentified the ammo cans as "animal cans"). It wasn't long before our paddling skills were put to the test—Rock Garden, Nemesis and Sunderland's Chute, followed by Hackamack's Hole, Ram's Head and India were what we had for breakfast. Feeling exhilarated and confident for having

successfully tackled a slew of Class IV+ rapids, we eagerly anticipated the numerous challenging rapids to come. The lunch stop
was full of play-by-play recounting of the morning's adventures,
riddled with laughter and fist pumps celebrating our athleticism,
and of course, our admiration and accolades for our outstanding
guides. From a PR perspective, things couldn't have been going
better. I was certain that this was going to be a killer segment,
sure to drive in a ton of business for my client.

Then along came Grey's Grindstone, a 1000-yard maze of
rocks, boulders, big holes, standing waves and at high water,
a bunch of hidden danger. Luckily, our guides knew this, so we
stopped to prepare. The cameraman packed away his gear, straps
were tightened and resolves were bolstered. And we were off—like
lambs to the slaughter.

The lead boat entered, dodged the big hole at the top with a
stylish spin, and continued on, successfully dodging and weav-
ing the seemingly endless obstacle course. Then came Wendy and
Dan but—alas—not so fortunate. Just when we thought Wendy
was clear of the hole at the top, the waves came down on her bow
and flipped her boat completely, and—again alas—Dan, Dan the
Anchorman was tossed into the drink. Shit.

With no time to ponder this unfortunate circumstance, our
paddleboat followed closely behind. Animal managed to zag right
at the last moment, successfully avoiding the same fate. However,
the left side of the boat, not so much. We dipped (and would have
flipped if not for the expertise of our guide) and the two port side
paddlers—KGO Producer Eric and I were ungraciously tossed
into the chilly waters. Eric and I immediately assumed the "swimming" position, feet downstream, knees slightly bent to ward
off rocks and other obstacles, arms out to the sides for steering.

Once I caught my breath, I looked downstream only to realize that there was no place to attempt to swim to shore or to a boat for a long, long time. Crap. After many bumps and lumps, and several mouthfuls of the Mighty T, my swim, which felt like 10 minutes but was probably less than one, was finally done. Animal pulled me to shore and set me down next to Eric, who was still in shock. No sign of Dan. Shit.

Once I realized I was safe and still breathing, nothing broken, my mind immediately turned to how this was going to play out from a publicity standpoint. It had the potential of ruining the client's entire season, if not their whole business, if the reporter perceived this to be a horribly dangerous sport, suitable only for the extreme athlete. I had some spinning to do, and fast. Once we reconvened with the rest of the guests and guides, and I realized that Dan and Eric were okay and in fact, kinda stoked about surviving, I knew it was salvageable. Remembering the "swimming position," Dan had made it through the bumpy maze that is Grey's Grindstone, and was rescued downriver from us by none other than Wendy, his trusty guide. And fortunately (thank you lucky stars), none of it was on film, so Dan's recounting of his tale on camera would have to be all verbal, and in the form of a lead-in or closing to his segment. Whew. Thank God for small miracles.

Immediately upon our return to the Bay Area, I put my plan into action. I went to the embroidery kiosk at the mall, bought two navy blue baseball caps and had them stitch "Grey's Grindstone Swim Team" on them in bright gold lettering, then had them delivered that day by messenger to Dan and Eric at KGO. I knew I had to act quickly, as they would be editing the footage to air that night on the six o'clock news. Lo and behold, the hat not only made it into the segment, but Dan proudly and ceremoniously placed it upon his head after the incredibly beautiful footage of the Mighty T, accompanied by the Chariots of Fire theme song. He was almost CHALLENGING the audience to go on the trip so they could earn a hat and a place on the team! And the footage was so spectacular and plentiful, they turned it into a two-part segment, running about five minutes each on two consecutive nights. Sheesh! Needless to say, the client was ecstatic, their phones rang, they booked some trips, and my job was saved. Whew.

Will Volpert

Tales from the Rafting Center

WILL VOLPERT

OUR RAFTING CENTER IS LOCATED NEAR DOWNTOWN ASHLAND, Oregon and if you've visited town in the summer you may have seen our rafts, trailers, vans, guides and customers wandering around between Pioneer and Oak Street. The location serves multiple purposes —the first being our meeting location for trips, second being our "warehouse" where we store our equipment, and the third being our reservation office where the phone rings and emails are hammered out. Being in the middle of town on a somewhat busy road is an odd place for a rafting operating base and over the years we've had some bizarre, hilarious, and entertaining things happen at the Rafting Center. We do get walk-in traffic but it's normally just people who are lost or totally confused as to why there are rafts on the sidewalk. The most common question we get is "is this the Ashland Food Co-op?" It happens so frequently that we've joked we should just change our building sign to "Not the Co-op."

One time, a rough and tough and somewhat bedraggled guy walked in and said he wanted to go rafting. But, there was a catch:

He didn't want to pay. "That makes things tough," I told him, "because the typical transaction is that people pay us and then we take them rafting. It's really the only way to run a successful rafting company." He responded that there was surely something he could trade us for a rafting trip. "What do you need?" he asked. I told him that we really needed money, but I'd be open to trading for a computer. He didn't have a computer, but he had a TV. "Do you have a photo of it?" I asked. "Even better," he replied, "I can draw it for you." He proceeded to draw a rectangle. "I don't think I'm interested," I told him.

He appeared flustered, but then I could see a light bulb go off in his head. "I know," he started, "how about I let you ride in my car?" It took me a few seconds to realize that he had completed his sentence. "You want a space on a rafting trip and in return I get to ride in your car?" I asked, completely baffled. "Yes, it's a really nice car —a classic [something or other]..." I spend enough time on the road and politely turned him down but gave him a company hat to encourage his departure.

A couple days later, as I returned from a Rogue trip and headed up Oak Street in our van with boats in tow, there was an obvious commotion of fire trucks and sirens. We continued up Oak Street and passed the firefighters spraying down a car that was engulfed in flames. Next to the remains of a battered Chevy Nova—and with a look of total despair—stood my friend from the other day. He was wearing his new hat.

Noro Madness

BOB VOLPERT

THE FIRST HINT THAT A CONTAGIOUS ILLNESS was heading towards the Middle Fork of the Salmon came via a story on NPR in early June 2013. More than 200 visitors and employees at Yellowstone and Grand Teton National Parks, only 300 or so miles from central Idaho, had reported suffering gastrointestinal illnesses assumed but not confirmed to be norovirus. The initial outbreak had occurred when a tour group visiting a famous hot spring region experienced symptoms typically misdiagnosed as stomach flu. "Those heading on a camping trip this summer might want to be just as wary of crossing paths with the wrong bacteria as they would a hungry bear," was the oft repeated wording in articles and social media posts about the incident and the perils of vacationing in the western United States. With 10,000 people from across the U.S. expected to float the Middle Fork that summer, it was a given that some would arrive with the contagious disease.

For Idaho river outfitters, the warning ushered in a summer of concern and diligence towards the goal of avoiding similar illnesses that would affect guests and crew.

We were hoping that our trips wouldn't be viewed in the same light as some cruises, many of which had experienced noro incidents in recent years. The outbreaks had become so commonplace that at our pre-trip meeting the evening before a trip departed, we always admonished guests to "be diligent about washing your hands. We don't want to become a cruise ship."

When we heard about the virus outbreak in Yellowstone National Park, our crew made an effort to learn how the illness spread and how it could be avoided. We were relatively certain that it was noro and washing and sanitizing common areas, particularly those in the kitchen and toilet areas, became the first mantra of defense. If it wasn't noro, those steps wouldn't hurt and might provide some protection from whatever it was. The next three trips went off without incident.

Like June, the first half of July was uneventful with no verified outbreaks. We heard periodic rumors that someone had gotten sick on the river but lots of things could cause that and they were all individual, unrelated occurrences. Towards the latter part of the month, things changed. There were verifiable group incidents involving outfitter guests and guides, private boaters, Forest Service crews, and the employees at local motels and restaurants. With each outbreak a new set of questions and concerns arose.

With river flows low, most Middle Fork groups opted to start their trips by flying to Indian Creek instead of driving to Boundary Creek. This necessitated a flight to the river, but it allowed avoidance of upstream low water and rocky channels. With this shift there was an increase in noro incidents in groups that launched at Indian vs. those that continued to launch at Boundary. Could something at the Indian Creek launch site be a contamination factor? And, why did the sickness disproportionally affect women?

The answer seemed to be that women arriving at Indian used the toilet facility but men, out of convenience, just urinated in the river. In what was to become a weekly exercise of identifying a never-ending list of possible sources of contamination, we started requiring all our guests to vigorously wash their hands before boarding our rafts. Each week brought more awareness. Noro was spread by touch, air, vomit, and water and the sources of infection seemed to be everywhere. Stay out of the local bars, avoid fire fighter crews, wash everything in a bleach solution, isolate anyone who is sick, don't eat at local restaurants, sanitize beer and soda cans, don't dance with strangers, and avoid petting stray dogs were just some of the warnings to our staff. Local stores were finding it difficult to keep Clorox items in stock. On a weekly basis, those products were flying off store shelves and landing in the bed of outfitter trucks.

"Holy shit, this stuff won't work," bellowed one of our guides when she read that only sanitizing products with bleach eliminated the virus. We had just discovered what the 99.7% effective statement on the Clorox bottles meant. The missing .03% was noro. Every week brought new noro awareness and education as news spread from outfitter to outfitter about outbreaks. With so many sources of contamination, only two factors seemed to afford any protection. The first was luck and some of us adopted peculiar habits that we thought might be fortuitous, like lovingly smootching and whispering sweet nothings to every bottle of bleach.

The other factor involved avoiding camps that seemed to foster the illness. If multiple people had been ill and vomiting at a certain camp, that camp was likely infected. People staying at Pool (mile 61) and Johnny Walker (mile 60) seemed to get the illness frequently.

But not as frequently as those who stayed at Survey (mile 75).

"We don't even look at Survey camp anymore," proclaimed one of our guides. "We just tell our guests to close their eyes when we get close and just float by."

By the time mid-August rolled around, our post—and pre-trip routines had become marathons of anxiety. We were sanitizing every piece of equipment that went out on a trip. Boats, tables, chairs, kitchen items, and because cruise ships claim to sanitize even the Bibles they carry, we disinfected the covers of books in our trip library. Another precaution my wife Mary and I took was to leave Salmon for Stanley three hours earlier than usual so we would have time to wipe down the table and counter surfaces in the rooms our guests would be using the night before departure.

It was too early to declare victory in the noro battle, but the end of the season was in sight and so far we had miraculously avoided the illness. Our last few trips would be structured for fly-fishing and the groups would be smaller. The crew would do a two-day deadhead from Boundary Creek to Thomas Creek, a launch site downsteam from Indian Creek, and I'd meet our guests in Boise the evening before departure to brief them on conditions, check fishing licenses, and answer the usual myriad of questions about boats, meals, and fishing. They would fly to Thomas the next morning. This particular trip had some issues that I'd deal with in Boise, like helping the guest whose fishing gear and luggage hadn't arrived with his flight from Texas.

A two-day deadhead means that we have to get to Boundary early enough to rig boats and get on the river that afternoon with the goal of bagging at least 10 of the 35 miles to Thomas that day. We use extra boats on fly-fishing trips, so the rigging is a little more time consuming and complicated than usual.

For our next trip we got to Boundary in plenty of time. We were the only group there and unloaded all our gear near the ramp. As we began the process of rigging and sliding the boats to the river, we could hear vehicles on the road, and shortly a number of trucks pulled up near us. It was a private group with boats on trailers. One guy didn't look happy with how we were dominating the ramp space. He was probably right that we shouldn't have used so much of the immediate rigging area, but no one had been there when we unloaded. I apologized and promised to get our stuff out of the way as quickly as possible. He seemed OK with my assurance but began to pose questions about our company, the allocation of private vs. commercial permits, and other stuff that didn't have anything to do with our rigging.

"Where are you guys from?" he asked, followed by "Are you the outfitter?" followed by "Do you live in Idaho?" followed by "How many trips do you get to go on every year?" followed by "Where are your guides from?" My responses were brief and meant to avoid a discussion about my California residency or the permit system. I don't know why I said it but I mentioned that I paid more taxes in Idaho than I paid in my home state. The questions pointed to a discussion that I wanted to avoid. I just wanted to get going as soon as possible.

He mulled my responses for a little while and then said, "Your company is based in Idaho and you are running a river in Idaho and your guides are mostly from Idaho. Don't you think you should be using boats made in Idaho?"

I responded with "Aire and Maravia make terrific boats but for this trip we are using boats made by NRS. Last time I checked NRS was still based in Idaho."

The Questions Guy didn't have more immediate queries and sauntered away to his group. He glanced in our direction a couple of times but the inquisition seemed to be over. Our crew continued to rig boats and slide them down the ramp. I was anxious to hit the road and get to Boise. The drive would take three hours and the litany of stuff I had to do before meeting the group the next day was extensive. I wanted to plot out those chores but the conversation I'd just had bothered me. I understand the excitement that boaters have at the ramp and usually don't mind answering questions or helping them. But this interaction had been unpleasant and I couldn't figure out why it had occurred or why Questions Guy had singled me out. Nate Moody, one of our guides, spotted my consternation and as he walked by told me to ignore what had just happened. "Forget it," admonished Nate. "The guy is just excited." I kept my mouth shut and tried to focus on getting away from Boundary Creek without insulting anyone or causing a problem that could be avoided with silence.

I walked over to our rig and settled in for the drive. It took me awhile to clear my head and regain my focus. A few minutes by myself brought relief and I started the engine. All the truck windows were down and the crew was standing just beyond the passenger side. We were exchanging goodbyes and last minute reminders when Mr. Questions Guy wandered over to the driver side of the truck and posed a final query. My response was met with smiles from our guides. I drove away from Boundary Creek feeling elated.

The question he posed was this: "You guys are out here every week. If you had to pick one camp that was an absolute must for any trip, which one would it be?"

THE TUOLUMNE GRIDDLE

STEVE WELCH

IF GEAR COULD TALK, IT WOULD ALL LISTEN to the Tuolumne griddle: "I was born in 1992. Custom-designed and custom-built to replace my grandfather, an aging and warped World War II military surplus field-kitchen lid that had seen too much heat and too little attention. I was made of quarter-inch thick anodized aluminum, with welded 12 gauge round-stock handles, perfectly-sloping sides, and special anti-rocker bars on my bottom. I was the cat's meow, cutting edge, one-of-a-kind. The griddle of the future."

Well, '92 was a high water year and on my virgin voyage, the Tuolumne was flowing at over 8,000 cfs at put-in. I was in the Assistant Guide's drop bag with Pete "the Bomb" Propane, Freddy "the Bastard" Firepan, Quicksilver Jones and the Chicky Pail Sisters. They were veterans, and they wore their dents and chipped paint with honor, but I could tell even they were scared. This was big water and a young guide A sketchy combination. We were in for quite a ride.

The first day went smoothly enough. We got jostled a bit and we bounced around down there in the drop bag, but we stayed upright and made it to Indian Creek in good shape. Not to brag, but I was a huge hit at dinner, handling the spaghetti sauce with ease and cleaning up afterwards with no scrubbing. At breakfast I churned out golden brown griddle cakes without breaking a sweat. Things were looking good and I could tell I had the attention of the Chicky Pail Sisters, if you know what I mean.

But things didn't go so well on the second day. Seems the Assistant Guide was a little nervous and lost his focus when it was time to strap Tommy the Table down on top of the drop frame. He did fine with the back bars, but in the front, instead of passing the cam strap around the top bar of the drop frame, his fingers got confused and he simply went around Tommy's bar. Without the front secured, Tommy was just sitting up there like a giant hinge and we were just sitting down below like little popcorn kernels, ready to pop out should things get too hot and the raft flip.

And flip it did. In the big, gnarly-ass hole at the top of Gray's. We didn't get far enough left, typewritered across the lateral and, Whammo!, we're flat-side up and there's Tommy flapping like a sheet in the wind and the rest of us visiting the Moss Lady.

I went down fast, straight to the bottom, and I saw something go by upside down and in a bad way; it was Freddy, God rest his soul.

Jonesy didn't have a chance, he blew his lid and they're still finding pieces of him along the shore.

Pete fared better; he had a wee bit of air and managed to stay near the surface and eventually got pulled into another raft.

The Chicky Sisters had quite a ride, tumbling and banging along the bottom, spinning in and out of eddies, puking up the soap and the Clorox. Hell, it must have been a nightmare. They made it to shore, though, and eventually found their way home.

But me, I wasn't so lucky. I stayed down. Took some big hits. Lost both my handles. Eventually I wedged down deep between some big chunks of granite and I just lay there, exhausted, beaten, thinking I was a goner. Well, it's a miracle I'm telling you this story. A miracle. I was down there for four months. FOUR MONTHS! before Curtis, God bless his soul, came looking for me.

He left camp early one morning in August before the water came up with a dive mask and a heart full of compassion and he pulled me from my watery grave and into the glorious sunlight. Sweet holy Dutch Oven did it feel good. Not to brag, but Curtis even did the Fajitas on me that night down at North Fork and hell if I didn't nail it. Took the Olive Oil like I was a full-blooded Italian, if you know what I mean.

True story. Look, here, on my side, you can still see the scars from where my handles used to be.

Bryce Whitmore

Bryce Whitmore

DICK LINFORD

IF BRYCE WHITMORE WERE A BOASTFUL MAN, he could claim to be the father of river running in California. There were a few other crazies kayaking California rivers with Bryce in the 1950s, but they're all dead. And there is no question that Bryce pioneered whitewater rafting. He was offering rafting trips before people knew they wanted them, and with rafts that he designed and made himself because no one else was making them.

Bryce was born in a small town in Ohio in 1926. Upon graduation from high school he was drafted, and spent his Army career on a hospital ship in San Francisco Bay. While his fellow soldiers were plying the bars and fleshpots of the Bay Area, Bryce got out of town. He came to love the California countryside.

When he was discharged from the Army, he returned to Ohio. It was February and freezing. He lasted a few days and headed back to California. With no training or education in the field, he got a job as a chemist at a paint factory in Berkeley, across the Bay from San Francisco. At first he spent his free time skating and sailing. Then he discovered car racing. He found himself spending most of his spare time driving racecars at various race tracks in

Northern California. He bought a Panhard, a French two-cylinder vehicle that was ahead of its time. It could hit 90 miles an hour, and had front-wheel steering. He won a lot of races. He was actually arrested for speeding on the highway. Unable to pay the fine, he was sentenced to a week in jail.

Even though he was winning races with his French car, Bryce was frustrated that America wasn't producing anything that could compete with the foreign cars made by Porche, Panhard, Ferrari, etc. He decided to change this by building his own car in his garage.

But then his life took a new turn. A neighbor invited him on a river kayak trip. The river bug doesn't bite everybody, and some who are bitten aren't affected strongly. Bruce was not only bitten. He was smitten. He had found his true love. He threw himself into kayaking and soon joined The River Touring Section of the Sierra Club.

Several members of the Club had just returned from Europe, where they had found out about kayaks. Europeans at the time were using kayaks based on the Inuit model, but where the Inuits made their frames of whalebone and stretched animal skins over the frames to make them water-tight, the Europeans made their frames out of wood and their "skins" out of canvas. Klepper, a German company, made what it called The Foldboat, so-called because it could fold up into a package that made for easy carrying. The company is still around, is and still making Foldboats.

The one problem with these boats was that they were fragile. Bryce bought one, hit a rock head-on on his first trip, and destroyed it. He decided to make a boat that could handle whitewater and take at least a minor beating. He applied the technical smarts and quiet self-confidence he had been applying to building a better racecar to building a better kayak. After studying both boat design and materials for some time, he decided that the best boats should be made of fiberglass. He built a mold and made himself a kayak.

History gets fuzzy here, and again Bryce—Mr. Modest-—won't make the claim. But this could well have been the first fiberglass kayak in the world. If there is evidence to the contrary, I would like to see it. Bryce still has that first boat.

When he tried it, it worked so well that several of his kayaking buddies asked him to build them one. He built twelve. At the time, the life jackets available were too bulky for kayaking. Bryce and his friends got a surf shop owner to make them special short-sleeved wetsuit tops that provided both flotation and warmth. The shop owner was so impressed with the fiberglass kayaks that he asked Bryce if he could buy the mold to make more. Bryce convinced him that the kayak market was saturated, and he threw the mold away. While this might seem short-sighted now, remember that this was 1956 and kayaking was limited to a very few crazies. It would take another fifteen to twenty years for kayaking to really catch on. But building the kayaks filled both his time and his garage, so he sold the parts of the car he was building to make room for his new venture.

From then on, all of Bruce's spare time was spent kayaking. He and his friends started doing multi-day trips, packing their gear into their boats. He had a black lab named Charlie Brown. He had a wetsuit made for Charlie, who would ride in his lap. Charlie especially enjoyed it when Bryce rolled his boat. In 1959 they ran the Rogue River in southwest Oregon. They ran the forty-five or so miles from Galice to Agness, and Bryce and Charlie both loved it.

1960 was a pivotal year. First, Bryce took first place in a down-river race at an international kayak event held on the Arkansas River near Salida, Colorado. Later, he and friends did the first descent of the Upper Kings River in the California Sierra. But most important, when he returned home after that trip, he found that his house had burned to the ground. Only the garage had survived.

Most people would have seen this as a tragedy. Many people would have been scarred for life by such an event. Bryce saw it as an opportunity. When his insurance company paid him a grand total of $5,000, He figured he had enough to live on for at least a year, so he quit his job and dedicated all his time to boating.

Coincidentally, Lou Elliot, an Oakland printer and fellow Sierra Club boater, had just started a river running company. The company was to become The American River Touring Association, or ARTA, which at its peak was the largest company of its kind in the world. ARTA still exists, though somewhat diminished. Lou was a dreamer, but not a detail person. He painted with a broad brush. He needed a nuts-and-bolts man, so he hired Bryce.

The summer of 1960 Lou, Bryce, and some others took off and ran rivers around the West. Among others they ran the Rogue in Oregon, the Middle Fork and Main Salmon in Idaho, and the Columbia and Canoe Rivers in British Columbia. They finished the summer with a trip through Glen Canyon in Utah.

A brief digression. In 1954 the Sierra Club, with David Brower as executive director, had won a major battle against the U. S. Bureau of Reclamation, stopping a dam that would have flooded Echo Park, a beautiful canyon on the Green River in Colorado. Basically, to save Echo Park, Brower agreed that Reclamation could build a dam in Utah's Glen Canyon, a place he had never seen.

David Brower and nature photographer Eliot Porter went on the Glen Canyon trip with Bryce and Lou. Brower was stunned by the beauty of the place, and appalled at what he had traded away six years earlier. Thereafter he referred to the trade-off as "America's Most Regretted Environmental Mistake." He and

Porter published what was to be the first of many Sierra Club Books coffee table books, The Place No one Knew, a paean to the canyon, with Porter's photographs and Brower's text. The book became a classic and is still in print.

The Glen Canyon experience radicalized Brower. It gave him the outrage, the will, and the staying power to stop dams planned in the Grand Canyon. Brower became president of the Sierra Club, increased its membership tenfold in three years, and transformed it into the nation's premier advocate for the environment.

Back to Bryce. There was no whitewater in Glen Canyon, so to run this trip Lou and Bryce used 20-foot aluminum skiffs with military surplus seaplane moorings from World War II strapped on the outside. Each mooring consisted of four 24-foot inflatable neoprene tubes welded together. They gave the skiff protection from rocks and additional floatation.

At the end of the 1960 season Bryce figured he wanted to have his own company. He bought a skiff, found two surplus seaplane moorings in a surplus store and built a boat similar to Lou's. In 1961 he ran weekend trips on the Sacramento river below Redding. The trips were fun, but they lacked scenic beauty and whitewater excitement.

The Stanislaus River in the central Sierra foothills was the answer. It offered a wonderful two-day trip with solid Class III rapids, a beautiful canyon, great camping beaches, and a lovely tributary, Rose Creek. Bryce kayaked the river in 1962. He fell in love with it and saw its potential for commercial trips.

His first challenge was boats. His 24-foot pontoons were too long for a small, technical river like the Stanislaus. Nobody was making rafts in the 1960s. The only rafts available were military surplus. The best were assault rafts, 14 to 16 feet long, incredibly tough but also incredibly heavy and incredibly rare. People combed surplus stores and distributorships looking for them. These assault rafts came with ribbed, rubber cone-shaped devices, to be plugged into bullet holes when they got shot up.

Meanwhile. pioneer outfitters on the Colorado River through the Grand Canyon, a big water, non-technical river, found that the surplus 30-foot inflatable pontoons, shaped like elongated donuts, that the Army lashed together to make bridges, worked with motors.

The least satisfactory rafts were those made to be rescue rafts for planes crashing at sea. These were called "basket-boats" because they were made of two ovular tubes, one on top of the other. They were fairly available but very flimsy, and overly flexible. They folded like taco shells in small waves, and they tore if you looked at them hard. The floors were so loose that, when they filled with water, you could stand up yet still be submerged.

Bryce needed rafts, but all he could find was three basket-boats. To round out his fleet he bought more 24-foot seaplane moorings, cut them in half, and had the world's first self-bailing rafts. They were so maneuverable that Bryce dubbed then "Supersports." The only problem was that they tended to flip end—over-end. But they and the basket-boats got Bryce through his first season. Of course he had a grand total of 20 passengers that summer. It was 1962, and he named his company Wilderness Water Ways.

That same year he tried to enter the national kayak championship races on the North Fork of the Feather. The American Canoe Association disqualified him, saying that his rafting business made him a professional. He ran the course for kicks anyway, and had the best time by far.

The number of passengers on his trips increased to 200 in 1964, and Martin Litton, who was travel editor for *Sunset Magazine*, became one of his weekend boatmen. Bitten by the river bug, Litton would go on to found Grand Canyon Dories, the only Grand Canyon company to run with wooden boats, and become a major force in preventing dams in the Grand Canyon. By the time of his death, at 97 years of age, he had become one of the most eloquent environmentalists of his time. But he got his start with Bryce.

In 1964 Litton published a four-page article about Bryce's trips on the Stanislaus in Sunset Magazine, and Bryce's numbers rose to 564. They peaked at 715 in 1968. To get these numbers Bryce needed a second fleet of boats, so he could run overlapping trips. He was tired of the basket-boats tearing and the Supersports flipping. He needed a better boat.

Coincidentally, Rubber Fabricators, the Maryland based company that made the seaplane moorings and other military inflatables, was looking for new business. Their military contracts had dried up. They had somehow seen what Bryce was doing, and asked if they could build a boat for him. Bryce asked if they could build 14-foot versions of the seaplane moorings. They said they could. These new boats, two feet longer than the Supersports, could carry a lot of gear and people, and they didn't flip end-over-end. Plus they were maneuverable and bombproof. Bryce named them "Huck Finns." Marty McDonnell, who went to work for Bryce when he was 15 and later bought his California operation, used these original Huck Finns until 2010. And he never wrapped one, even on the Tuolumne, a river that flips and wraps a lot of boats. In retrospect it's amazing that the boats didn't become really popular, but only Bryce and Marty used them.

Actually what happened was Rubber Fabricators, hungry and sensing demand, came out with three rafts modeled after the assault rafts: The Green River was a tank of a boat, maybe 17 feet long. The Yampa was 15 feet long and made of lighter neoprene. The Salmon

River was 17 feet long and with bigger tubes. The year was 1971. In 1973 Avon, an English tire company soon followed, with the 16-foot Professional, and then the 18-foot Spirit. These boats opened the doors for exponential growth in river running. Without them, the Huck Finn might have become the raft of choice.

While his bread and butter business was on the Stanislaus, Bryce had time to explore other rivers. He was the first person to run commercial trips on the Klamath, Eel, Trinity, East Fork of the Carson, South Fork of the American, Illinois, and Tuolumne.

In the 1970s rafting was quickly moving from an esoteric sport for the lunatic fringe to a mainstream recreation. Explosion is not too strong a word. For example, in 1961 around 100 people ran the Colorado River through the Grand Canyon. In 1965 around 500 ran it. In 1969 that number was 1,000 and in 1972 the number was *17,000!* The Park Service capped use at 23,000, but has now increased the cap to 29,000.

In California there were eight river outfitters in 1972. By 1982 there were 74 outfitters on the American River alone.

Many of the new companies expanded fast and offered trips on rivers all over the West. Bryce chose to focus on California and Oregon, and to remain small. He wanted to run rivers, and not be tied to a desk. His second wife ran his office for a while, and when they divorced, his mother retired from her Post Office job in Ohio and moved to California. Bryce built her a house in Port Costa, an artsy town on San Pablo Bay. She ran his office from there.

As far as Bryce was concerned, eight outfitters on the Stanislaus was seven too many. He felt crowded. In late 1972 he sold his California business to his long-time employee, Marty McDonnell, who is still operating, under the name Sierra Mac. Bryce concentrated on the Rogue River in southwest Oregon.

The Rogue was among the first eight "Charter Rivers," declared Wild and Scenic by Congress in 1968, and people were just discovering what a summer rafting trip the Rogue provided. It had long been known as a great salmon and steelhead river, but was virtually unknown as a rafting river until 1970. There are a few rustic lodges in the canyon, but they opened only for fall and winter salmon and steelhead fishing. Bryce convinced two of them to stay open in the summer, so he could run three-day trips where people stayed in lodges at night. With the crowding of California rivers in mind, he also started pressuring the U. S. Bureau of Land Management (BLM) to limit use. In the fall of 1972 BLM did just that, limiting the number of outfitters, the number of trips each could run, and the number of people that could be on any given trip. Each outfitter's allocation was determined by the number of trips he had run that year plus fice additional trips.

Under the new allocation Bryce was allowed to run three trips a week, with starts on Saturday, Sunday, and Wednesday. This made him by far the largest outfitter on the river. To start trips on both Saturday and Sunday, he needed a second crew and set of equipment. From 1973 until 1986 he personally ran the Saturday and Wednesday trips. He was on the water Saturday through Monday, and Wednesday through Friday. On Tuesday, his only day off the river, he bought and packed food, repaired equipment, ran errands, etc. That's seven work-days a week, and river days are at least 14 hours long. A brutal pace by any normal standard, but he loved being on the water, and he was far from normal.

Winters were easier. He was still busy, but in a different way. He liked real estate. He was always on the lookout for an empty lot or a fixer-upper. He built five houses from scratch over the years, and fixed up at least that number. He would do all the work himself, including plumbing and electricity. He would live in each for a while, and then sell it. He also bought acreage in what is now downtown Grants Pass. He made good money and he didn't spend it foolishly. Some would say he was more than frugal.

He sold his Rogue River business in 1986. He was 59 years old. He bought a house on 50 acres outside of Talent, Oregon, and went back to enjoying what he did before running rivers: Skating, sailing, and working on cars.

He rollerskated several hours a day, on a rink he built himself, on the second floor of his barn, and earned several certificates of achievement. One day, while skating, he realized that his sense of balance was gone and his skating days were over. He was in his 80s.

So he bought a small sailboat and sailed on the lakes in southern Oregon. That ended when he capsized and nearly drowned his fourth wife.

As of this writing Bryce is 92 years old. He lives in his house, on his 50 acres, with his two dogs, Georgia and Raven, who adore him. When he goes to sit in his easy chair, Georgia gets there first and lies across the back so that Bryce can lean on her. His only heat is a wood stove and he cuts his own firewood. He drives to town less than once a week. He is a contented man. He lives modestly, and is in good shape physically, mentally, and financially.

Bryce has never borrowed money or bought anything on time. He paid cash for all his vehicles, his river equipment, and his many houses. He never insured his houses and never had collision insurance on his vehicles. He figures that insurance companies have it figured out so that they always win. He has no credit record because of never having borrowed money, so when he tried to get a satellite dish the company refused him. His daughter had to put the dish in her name.

He is good company. He is also very generous. When he recently heard that the Medford, Oregon Humane Society was going to close because of lack of funds, he wrote them a check for $75,000.

He never had trouble attracting women. He was less successful maintaining relationships. As he says, "Outfitters don't seem to make good husbands." He met his first wife, Betty June Currier, at a skating rink when he was 21. She was still in high school. That marriage lasted about three years. In 1960 a teacher named Mary Ellen Brody came on a Middle Fork trip when Bryce was working for Lou. She was smitten both by the river and by Bryce, and immediately signed up for the following Main Salmon trip. Bryce married her the following March. When he started his own company she ran his office until they divorced. The marriage lasted ten years.

In the early 1970s a woman named Kathy Eicher came on a Rogue trip with her ex-husband and son. Romantic sparks flew and Bryce invited her on another trip. This time she came without her ex-husband and son. She and Bryce were together for a few years. In 1986 he met Caroline Bach at a singles club in Ashland. They were soon married. That marriage lasted fourteen years. He is now single, but has a girlfriend.

His love of cars remains. He buys old ones, rebuilds them, and sells them as classics. He has a hoist, and can pull engines for major work. Not too long ago he had 15 old cars. He is now down to five.

Bryce doesn't fear death, but he worries about what will happen to his dogs. He has a dog door set with a timing device to open twice a day. When I asked him about this he told me, "I plan to die up here. Hopefully in my sleep. I often go a week to ten days without contact with the outside world. I don't want the dogs trapped in the house with me when I go. First, the poor things would drink the toilets dry. Then, after a few days, they would probably start gnawing on old Bryce here. They wouldn't like that.

Neither would I." When my business partner Joe Daly called him recently Bryce said he was out cutting firewood for this winter, and was wondering how much to cut. No sense in cutting more than he can use before he dies.

His favorite car is a 1953 MG TD. British Racing Green and in mint condition. When he dies he wants someone to come up with a backhoe, dig a hole big enough for the car, put him in the driver's seat, put the car in the hole, and bury it.

Bryce is a man of deeds more than a man of words, but in my short time with him recently he got off some great one-liners. Here are the ones I recall:

"Woman guides? Heck (Bryce doesn't swear) women shouldn't even be allowed to drive. Put that in your book, Dick." (Bryce actually had two woman guides. That ended when one of them had a river accident in which someone died.)

"Dick, you're 75? Heck, that's not old. I was just starting on my fourth wife when I turned 75."

"When you can't pee off your front porch, it's time to move."

"If you can't make it a tax write-off, it's not worth buying."

Words to live by. Except maybe his comment about women.

THE CARSON JINX

BOB VOLPERT

WE WOULD HAVE CALLED HIM AN INDIAN BACK THEN. He was the only patron and was perched on a stool near the end of the bar, fairly close to a sign painted on the wall with an arrow pointing to the Ladies Room. Big guy around 50 years old, maybe 250 long-ago fit-pounds. He was hunched over the dark padded bar staring at his large hands that cupped a glass. A whiskey something. George Jones was crooning. The only other sound was the air conditioning unit that was struggling to overcome the 110-degree afternoon Nevada dessert heat.

He might have looked at us when we came in but we hadn't seen him. The transition from bright sun to bar-darkness blinded us, and it wasn't until we were seated at a nearby table and our eyes had adjusted to the dimness that the place and all its charms and its only customer became visible. Unless he had glanced our way when we entered, he didn't look at us, which seemed odd given that one of the crew was Desi, a young women whose stunning good looks would have stopped traffic on any thoroughfare in America that day.

Our crew of guides had just come off an overnight East Carson River trip through scorching, high desert terrain concluding in a torturous two-hour take-out. After cramming our sweating bodies into the cab of our aging pick-up truck, we sought relief in the first place that looked like it had air conditioning and cold beverages.

We ordered a pitcher of beer, sat silently at our table relishing the coolness and listened to the jukebox. George. Tammy. Merle. We weren't planning on staying long. One beer, water, some bar snacks, use the restroom, splash water on our faces and start the three hour drive back to our headquarters in Angels Camp on the opposite side of the Sierra Nevada range. We'd done all of that and had started to get up to leave when the bartender strode over with another pitcher of beer. "Cochise wants to buy you this," he said.

We sat back down. The Native American guy turned in our direction, acknowledging our "thank-yous" with a quiet nod. We couldn't help noticing the T-shirt he was wearing, its front a beautiful western graphic of a bucking horse and rider, and the back a collage of big, bold colors. A spectacular garment.

Desi got up and glided over to personally thank the man. She placed a hand on his shoulder, bent down, whispered something in his ear and then headed to the Ladies Room. Shortly after that Cochise got up and headed in the same direction. They weren't gone long. Maybe a couple minutes. Desi came back swimming inside the bucking horse and rider, while Cochise was scrunched into her small river-company shirt, his arms barely squeezing through the sleeves, his neck tightly pinched by the collar.

About fifteen pleasant minutes passed. Then a blinding glare of sunlight and a stream of hot air rushed in as the front door was flung open. It took a moment or two for the big women's eyes to adjust to the change in light but when they did she was not pleased. She stared at Cochise in his new attire. She surveyed the bar and since we were the only other folks there, she glared at our table. When she saw Desi sporting her man's T-shirt, her anger flooded the room. A swift pivot and she was stampeding towards Cochise. He tried to rise off his barstool but she was too quick, pummeling his head with her fists and purse before he could duck for cover. A pool table was nearby and she lunged for the cue stick resting on the felt. The chorus of "Let's get out of here" was all I heard as our party of four careened out the front door.

As we escaped, one of the crew screeched "can you believe what was playing on the jukebox when she swung that cue stick? Tammy Wynette was singing "D-I-V-O-R-C-E."

• • •

Most of the rivers on the eastern slope of the Sierra Nevada Mountains don't glide towards Nevada; they plummet. The Carson is an exception with a steady and swift descent fueled by spring snowmelt. The rafting stretch from Hangman's Bridge near Markleeville, California to take-out, 20 miles east near Gardnerville, Nevada, drops a brisk 25 feet per-mile through cowboy country full of jaw-dropping western movie vistas. Much of the territory looks the same today as it did when Kit Carson explored the region for John Fremont in 1848.

• • •

I attribute our encounter with Cochise and the series of bizarre episodes that followed, to a curse picked up from a guy who stopped at our office wanting to talk about the Carson River. He had one of our old trip schedules jammed into the front pocket of his western style, pearl-buttoned shirt. He was in his 70s, with the weathered look of someone who had spent the better part of his life outdoors. He told me he lived in Reno but for most of his life had wrangled at ranches between Tahoe and Winnemucca and had ridden every trail in the territory including those near or above the Carson River. Back in Reno he had a stash of historic photographs, some he'd taken, some he'd acquired, and he asked if I'd like to see the photos next time he came to San Francisco. I said, "yes." He promised to bring them. It was a couple years before he returned.

When he did show up, he had a strange collection of tattered, worn pictures bound with rubber bands. Some were scenic shots, others of old ranches, a few of cowboys, and a bunch he claimed to have taken years ago inside burial caves near the Carson River. He told me the images of the burial caves "really captured the spirit of the deceased." I found them nearly impossible to decipher. Each had an indistinguishable central subject that looked eerily like an out-of-focus marshmallow. He was intent on selling me the collection but I could think of little use for it and declined. Like most guys who peddle tall tales, he was difficult to move along but after an hour or so he left.

In the cultures of many indigenous peoples, it's believed a photograph can steal the pictured person's soul. Photographing without permission is spiritually disrespectful. I hadn't *taken* the photos but I had *looked* at them and much like the guy who drives the getaway car from a hold-up, I was implicated. For the next few years our East Carson trips experienced a spate of weirdness. Nothing terrible happened, just disruptive stuff and oddball events like the encounter with Cochise. It seemed like a jinx had descended upon us for my looking at the photos. Not a full-blown dose, just enough to cause continuing mild chaos.

There was the case of our helping an outfitter with his shuttle, leaving passengers' cars where the trip ended and transporting the drivers back to the put-in. The shuttle vehicle we were using, left momentarily unattended and idling, somehow slipped into gear and accelerated directly at the assembled drivers who could only leap out of the way. The vehicle continued to speed up and then plunged into the river…Another time, we were the only group on the river, camped a couple of bends upstream and on the opposite shore of a popular hot spring. In the morning, one of our boats was missing. After numerous countings and recountings of the boats at camp, a frantic search ensued. The missing raft was spotted tied up at the hot spring, across the river, a quarter-mile from our camp. No one was there…Well after dark one evening, a guy walked into our remote campsite, grabbed a few beers from our drink cooler, joined us around the campfire, and introduced himself as Frank Sinatra…And on and on and on…

We ran one more commercial and one private trip before rolling up our Carson boats and calling it quits in June 1985. The Carson just didn't fit into our marketing scheme anymore.

The commercial launch was with a longtime client who had left his executive position with an advertising agency to start his own specialty travel company. He called himself "The Ol' Proprietor" and organized groups that primarily took weekend outings. John had a loyal clientele that returned to the Carson annually for a charter trip. He understood that rafting trips were theatre and although the river was the stage, the theatrics took place at camp. An "Ol' Proprietor" trip entailed designating a person as royalty. The River King or Queen got to sit on a high camp chair that was supposed to represent a throne, wore a crown and was attended to by John and the crew who brought food and drink and pillows or anything else that made royalty happy. There was always music, the other guests (peasants) were given odd hats to wear, and a roaring campfire enhanced the evening festivities and story telling.

This curious scene, a person on a throne and a group wearing odd hats rollicking around a campfire, caught the eye of a lone rafter floating past our camp at dusk. Lured by the revelry, he landed his boat, promptly tripped getting out of his raft, and stumbled in our direction. The guy was feeling the effects of too much sun, too much beer, and too many hours by himself. We guardedly welcomed him to our gathering.

One of our guides got a line and secured the raft while the others prepared a plate of food and made room for him with our group. Our goals were simple: feed him, keep him away from booze, don't let him near our group and put him to bed. We failed on most counts. Food energized the guy and he found a beer.

He slowly surveyed our group, took in the merits of a campfire, and, somehow, getting up from the log he was sitting on, announced he was going to build a river sauna. This would entail building a structure, heating large rocks, moving the rocks into the tent, pouring water on them to create steam and rounding up people to sit in the shelter. A river sauna is akin to a sacred, ceremonial Native American sweat lodge. We weren't going to go there.

My wife Mary offered to help him gather rocks. With a sly hand, she picked up a long length of webbing and headed away from the group with our uninvited guest. When he had tottered about fifty yards beyond our gathering, she asked the guy to sit propped against a giant pine while she looked for suitable rocks for the sauna. She told him to hold the end of the webbing. He did. She circled the tree several times, securing our guy firmly to the trunk where he soon fell asleep. Before retiring for the evening, we cut the line and our guest slumped forward to the ground where he remained until morning.

Our final East Carson trip was with a couple of friends, just before Mary and I headed to Idaho for the summer. It was a mid-week, low water trip in June and no one else was on the river. We camped at the hot spring, stayed up late staring at a spectacular star-filled sky and enjoyed each other's company. Nothing weird happened.

Had the jinx run its course? Perhaps our torpedoing of the sauna had done the trick or maybe the spirits had just gotten tired of tormenting us. We needed to cement the deal. Nine months later, our first son was born. His middle name is Carson.

Jenner Fox

FLOW WITH ELEPHANTS

JENNER FOX

RIVER FLOW IS MEASURED BY HOW MANY CUBIC FEET of water are passing a given point each second. The term is cubic feet per second or cfs.

A cubic foot of water weighs 62.4 lbs. A big African elephant weighs 14,000 lbs.

Flow is a volume of water on the clock. If you stand in one place looking at a river, a certain volume of water will flow past you every second. It is a continuous action and the time component is important. Second after second, the volume keeps rolling by.

On the Tuolumne River in California (the "T"), very low flows can be 700 cubic feet per second. So this means that every single second at low water on the Tuolumne, 43,680 lbs. of water are flowing by—the equivalent poundage of 3.12 large elephants. Or for you math minded folks, nearly π large elephants.

For the majority of the 2015 T season, the river flowed at roughly 1,200 cfs, that's 5.34 big African elephants with great memories.

High water flows on the T can be 10,000 cfs. That's 624,000 lbs. of water going by every second or 44.57 elephants.

Rounding up, at high water on the T, the weight of 45 elephants is stampeding through any given point of the river every second.

We are stampede surfers, hanging ten on the backs of watery elephants.

Flow is a nebulous word. Hockey players use flow to describe the hair that sticks out the back of their hockey helmets. In the field of experimental psychology, flow is a state of consciousness in which the difficulty of a task is challenging enough to test but not exceed the limit of our abilities; perhaps, what a skilled guide experiences when rowing the Tuolumne for the first time. It is a pleasurable feeling. One that demands all of our mental capacity, forcing us into the present moment.

Flow has little to do with elephants and a lot to do with rivers. Perhaps not in the hockey hair sense, but hair does stick out the back of whitewater helmets too. The following quotation is peripherally related to all of it:

> *"Have you also learned that secret from the river; that there is no such thing as time?" That the river is everywhere at the same time, at the source and at the mouth, at the waterfall, at the ferry, at the current, in the ocean and in the mountains, everywhere and that the present only exists for it, not the shadow of the past nor the shadow of the future."*
> *—Herman Hesse, Siddhartha*

So, the best way to navigate a river is being in the moment and going with the flow. Not in the hippy-dippy sense of naked dudes on a beach, but in the sense of water going down stream. You want the elephants on your team.Use the elephants.

THE FORCE THAT
RULES THE WORLD

While the other guides were spending their tips

on beer and chips for the long drive over the mountain,

you and I wandered out behind the Agness General Store.

There, a knotted rope and tire suspended from the giant

cottonwood. I climbed on and we didn't dare speak

as you pulled me back as far as the rope would go,

one hand on my hip as you pushed me   out   out   out

I sailed over the gulch, the dappled stones, until I was

midriver, feet skimming the sky—that wide shock of blue—

the summer air humming. To the west, the river's silver sinew

rushing to the ocean. Below, in the shallows, shadows

of steelhead winnowed the current, summoning the force

for the final swim. The rope and I entwined, illumined,

a hot, gold filament. I hung there midair— minutes,

hours, days—then pendulumned back to you,

my body ripe   sweet   willing.

—*Moira Magneson*

Bob Rafalovich

WE CAN'T SMOKE 'EM WITH ALDER, BOYS

BOB RAFALOVICH

IT WAS SOMETIME IN THE MID 1990s. I'd just gotten off of one of my four-day fishing lodge trips down Oregon's Wild and Scenic Rogue River. When I arrived back at the warehouse, and while the guides unpacked the trip, I sat down in my office and my wife appeared and handed me a letter. Myrna said, "You better open this and see what's going on." The letter was a certified, registered letter with return receipt from the legal office of the Bureau of Land Management, Portland, Oregon.

There really wasn't much to the letter. It simply stated "Cease and desist all harvesting of Alder products." It left me scratching my head and wondering what the hell this was about?

At this point I need to digress and give you'll a little background information before I continue with my story.

My name is Robert Rafalovich (aka Bob) and I've been an outfitter and guide here on the Rogue River for over 40 years—43 to be exact—and I'm still working, but only as guide and only part time. Guiding is more fun and relaxing than outfitting.

SMOKE'M WITH ALDER: A ROGUE RIVER TRADITION

This alder-smoking tradition dates back to the early days of outfitting and Glen Woolridge, the first guy to run the Rogue River from Grants Pass to the Ocean and the very first commercial outfitter. At lunch time every day on the fishing trips, the guides pulled over, cleaned fish, built a fire and cooked and smoked the morning's catch with fresh picked Alder leaves. They then serve it to the guests as part of a "LONG" lunch break —not to mention the fact that the lodges wanted nothing to do with cooking fish for the guests when they arrived. Alder-smoke salmon and steelhead is delicious.

Second generation Rogue fishing guide Willard Luca, who had been guiding since the mid 1940s and retired about a year or two after I started, told me that the tradition started because the guides were so dead-ass tired from running back to back five day trips with no "turn around" day off, that they really needed to take a nap every day after lunch. Of course their excuse was that the middle of the day was bad fishing because "the sun's on water, so let's take a little nap and wait for evening shade to come before we start fishing again."

You see, back in those days there was no road up the Rogue River from Gold Beach, so once you started at Graves Creek, the only place to end the trip was Gold Beach. It was a five—day trip on a five-day turn around, with four lodge nights along the way. Once the guides got to Gold Beach, they stacked their boats, drove north up 101 to Coos Bay, cut over to Roseburg, shopped for the next trip and by the time they arrive to Graves Creek it was dark. They would sleep in their rigs and wake up the next morning to start the next trip. The typical season was 10 to 12 of these five-day trips. So you can imagine how tired these guys were. Thus began the tradition of the "Long Lunch," with alder-smoke fish. It was really the only way the guides could grab some much needed rest.

ENTER THE NEW BLM DENDROLOGISTOR: OR DO WE REALLY NEED THIS MUCH GOVERNMENT?!!

The next day, after getting the letter (on my day off because new the road out from Agnes cuts the trip to four days and shortens the shuttle) I called the BLM office in Medford and talked to Jim Leffmann, BLM River Program Manager. Jim was a really likable guy and probably the best bureaucrat that the BLM ever had. He was a level-headed, reasonable guy, and besides that he wasn't personally interested in river running. We were on good terms and had become good friends. I read the cease-and-desist letter and I said, "Jim what the F*** is this about?" Jim began to explain. I could tell he wasn't happy about the whole thing. He explained that the River Program" had hired a dendrologist (tree scientist), and on a recent trip down the river he had seen the fishing guides pulling leaves off the Alder Trees and using them to smoke their fish.

The dendrologist was concerned that we might be having an "impact on the Alder population along the river." My response was, "You gotta be kidding!" I told Jim that Alder Trees were everywhere along the river, and besides that, it was now fall and in a month all the leaves will fall off the trees anyway. He agreed, but because the dendrologist had raised the issue, the agency needed to take a look at this practice. He went on to say that because the issue had been raised they needed to do an EIS (environmental impact study), and according to regulations, we (the outfitters) should have to pay for the EIS (environmental impact statement. He happily said though that the new dendrologist had filed for a grant to pay for the study so we might be off the hook paying for it. The grant application was $50,000.

So I asked "what does all this mean?" Jim explained that while they were doing the study, we could not remove any leaves off the Alder Trees in the canyon. I think my response was "what the F***!" Jim suggested a solution: On our way down to the put-in, we should simply stop along Jump Off Joe Creek, take a plastic bag, and pick all the leaves that we needed for smoking our fish. That's county property and BLM has no jurisdiction, he explained.

So, for the next two years on our way to the put-in, we stopped and gathered the Alder leaves we needed.

At the end of the second year, the study was finally completed and Jim sent me a copy. It was about 120-page document. It included the purpose of the study, the design of the study, how the study was implemented, and how the data was gathered, all in scientific jargon.

What I really loved about the study was its conclusion (the last two paragraphs). The next to the last paragraph stated that the Alder population was in excellent condition and that we probably weren't having an impact. The best part was the final paragraph that stated because the harvest was taking place in the fall, the leaves were about to fall off the trees anyway. So there wasn't an impact on the Alder population. All of this for a mere $50,000 in tax payer's money. What a deal!

I called Jim and thanked him, but before we got finished the conversation he said that, "there's one more little problem."

WHEN IS ENOUGH ENOUGH?!!

Jim went on to explain that because the legal office in Portland had been involved, they had reviewed the situation, and had concluded that we were "harvesting Alder" as part of a commercial operation on Federal Lands. Therefore, a "Special Use Permit" would be required. So, every year from that point on, I had to fill out a "Special Use permit application" and send the BLM $20 to get the Alder Harvesting Permit which I had to carry down the river, just in case they ever wanted to check. I shit you not.

A FINAL NOTE:

In 2008 I took Laura Bush and four of her friends on a four-day wild section lodge trip.

Of course I had to tell her my alder story." Her response was to ask, "Whose administration was that in?" I had to think for a minute. I finally said I believed it was the Clinton Administration. She looked at me and said, "Imagine that."

CONCLUSION: THEN THEY FORGOT ALL ABOUT IT

Several years later, after I had I sold my business, BLM was changing Rogue River Program Managers about every six months. One day I met up with the newest River Program Manager at the Rand Permit Station while I was filing a permit for a commercial trip. I was guiding for my old company. After introducing myself we talked for a few minutes, and I just had to inquire how the Alder Permit process was doing. Her response was, "What permit"? I said, "You know the Alder harvesting permit." She said, "Never heard of it."

ONE FINAL NOTE:

About a year, or so, ago I ran into one of my fellow outfitters who was still in the business. We got to talking and he mentioned the BLM was requiring "Alder Harvest Permits" again. "Really" I said. I sure wasn't going to tell him I was the one who spilled the beans!!

APPARITION

High in the Sawtooths the wind   the wind
    tugged me from sleep and I slipped
from the skein of my down bag.

I walked to the river   crossed the wild
    alphabet of scattered stone and sat with back against
the scratch of a driftwood pine. Stars salted the sky.

The campfire's orange embered eye   watching.

I nodded off   then woke   shivering to see the antlered crown
    break the water   enormous muscled shadow rising
slowly   slowly into his own weather.

Huffing white clouds of steam   water rivering off
    the dewlap he ascended the bank to the meadow   past
the miners' cabins   the scabbed orchard where

he nosed the fallen apples but did not eat.   I saw him
     move up   and up   a shaggy darkness parting the trees
disappearing into the forest. I saw

and though I was left cold and alone   and though I would walk
     to the campfire   feed it   till it burned hot and furious
though I would make breakfast go on with my life

some part of me was gone   surrendered to that form
     vanished with him into the wild dark.
That much I understood.

—*Moira Magneson*

Michael O'Malley

Ursus Among Us: Black Bear Triptych

MICHAEL O'MALLEY

FROM CRATER LAKE TO THE COAST OF SOUTHERN OREGON, the Rogue River descends through a steep, pine-clad canyon. In 1969, Congress designated thirty-five miles in the middle as one of the original Federal Wild & Scenic Rivers. That stretch is home to superlative whitewater and excellent black bear habitat (where no hunting is allowed), and this convergence has led to thousands of human/bear encounters over the years. Here are three of them.

THE DELILAH WARNING SYSTEM

In the fall of 1981, my wife Lauren and I joined a private rafting trip organized by Bob Volpert. Though we had rafted for several years, this trip was her first foray into bear territory and only my second. We were excited and nervous to camp three nights in country that was likely to bring a bear sighting.

Joining us on the trip was Delilah, Bob's German Shepherd. She was a river veteran, having spent her life riding rapids in California, Idaho, Oregon and British Columbia. And though she couldn't row, she could discern a rower's capabilities quite quickly. She once jumped out of one boat and swam to another when she determined the first pilot's skills were not up to her exacting standards. Her awareness was not limited to evaluating a guide's rafting skills. Her canine senses detected, assessed, and calibrated the precise threat level of camp intruders.

On night one, we camped on river left on a flat, sandy bar backed by brush. The incline of the tree-clad canyon slope was well back from the river. Lauren and I pitched our tent closer to the kitchen area than usual. Our desire was not to be the first line of defense if a bear decided to investigate our camp.

In the early evening October darkness, we sat around the campfire eating spaghetti. Delilah stretched out near the fire's envelope of warmth. Suddenly the conversation stopped as her ears pricked up and she emitted a low "grrrrr."

Our forks stopped between plate and mouth, and we glanced to and fro. I looked at Bob. Without taking his eyes off his plate, he murmured, "Deer."

Delilah rose to all fours and looked to the hillside. A long tense moment later, there was a crackling of leaves. A few seconds later, a buck picked his way through the brush. Phew, we breathed. A few barks by Delilah sent the buck rushing away, branches snapping.

On night two, we camped on river right, and the scene replayed itself. Delilah stiffened and grrrr'd. Lauren and I looked at Bob. No reaction. He continued eating. We looked at each other and nodded. We knew the score now. "Deer," I said, and sure enough, moments later a doe and fawns picked their way around the edge of camp.

On night three, we were in the lower canyon. Lower Solitude is a beautiful, multi-level, rock-and-sand camp on river right. On river left was a steep hillside that slanted straight into the river.

A riffled stretch of fast water separated the banks and provided a continuous murmur beneath our conversations. Smoke from grilling steak hung like mist in the narrow canyon.

As we laughed and joked and relived the day's runs, Delilah once again straightened and brought conversation to a standstill. "GRRRRRRR," she thrummed deeply.

Bob bolted up, and said, "Oh, shit!"

A minute later, a black bear worked his way down the steep slope on the far bank, nose testing the air. He reached the river, splashed in the water a bit, sniffed longingly at the steak smoke, turned around and disappeared into the trees up the slope.

We had seen our bear, and knew it could swim across the river, but we slept easily, knowing that Delilah's early warning capabilities were on high alert throughout the night.

BEARS ARE LIKE BUILDING INSPECTORS

Barry Smith was a part-time Rogue guide throughout the 1990s. His real-life job was general contracting in Point Reyes, CA. He had a special affinity for kitchen remodeling projects. If you wanted something dovetailed, his high standards and sense of detail made him the man for the high net-worth crowd in West Marin County.

Barry's accent and attitude tended to stray between the New Jersey cynicism of his youth and the California mellowness of his middle years. The beret he often sported leaned toward the "Hey, man" hippie, but when it came to running a raft trip, his demanding East Coast edge came to the fore. He had clear expectations of the guides on his crew, and he wasn't shy to share his opinion if the crew's efforts were sliding to the sloppy.

On a July trip, I was crewing with Barry, and we found ourselves at Lower Solitude camp…bear country again. Dessert was served, guests were slipping away to their tents, and he and I were cleaning the kitchen area for the night.

Post-dinner bear prep is a detailed and precise exercise. Wash all the dishes, pots and pans. Check. Store all food in the coolers and commissary box. Check. Wipe down the tabletops and coolers with bleach. Check. Scour the sand for those little bits of zucchini ends and carrot shavings. Bag the trash and strap it down in the boat coolers. Wipe down those in-boat coolers. Eyeball the area one last time. Check and recheck.

I was returning from the boats, ready to call it a night. Barry was finishing up in the kitchen area. He turned away from the table, and began to peel off his apron. Behind him rested a paper plate holding a slice of moist chocolate cake, topped with a rich buttery frosting.

"Okay, amigo, we're done," Barry said.

I gestured at the chocolate cake. Pretty sloppy of him, I thought. "Barry, what the hell . . .?"

Barry glanced back. "Ah, not to worry. Bears are like building inspectors. They have to find something, and you've got to plan for it."

Sure enough, the bear showed up at 2:00 a.m., knocked over the table, ate the cake, and ignored the coolers and commissary box. We had nothing to clean up but some shredded paper plate, thanks to our detail-oriented resident contractor.

Is the Dessert to Your Standards?

River guides consider ourselves to be resourceful, athletic, and erudite exemplars of talent. Oh, we are natural-born chefs too, able to produce gourmet meals, with a pair of tongs in one hand and a beer in the other.

In the late 1990s, Lauren and I once again joined a commercial trip led by Barry Smith. The afternoon before put-in, the crew met in Grants Pass, loaded the equipment, and headed to the supermarket to execute a $1,200 food buy for the four-day trip.

Barry assigned distinct segments of the menu to different guides, and we dispersed through the store in a Teva-shod version of the 1960s TV show, "Supermarket Sweepstakes." We reassembled at the check-out line with multiple carts and began the long process of bagging the food.

We packed the sturdy 150-quart coolers for each boat out in the supermarket parking lot. Then we headed for put-in camp, just under an hour's drive away and a few miles downstream of the "blink-and—you-miss-it" town of Galice.

At put-in, Lauren was quietly arranging her gear in our tent. She couldn't help but hear various conversations wafting around the campsite. Some of the talk centered on the food buy, and the good meals that lay in the days ahead. Lauren sifted the information; something didn't gibe. About 9:30 p.m, she lifted the tent flap and asked an innocent question.

"Barry, who bought dessert?"

"Michael did," Barry responded.

"Nope, I was lunch and juice," I said, digging the paper with food-buy assignments out of my back pocket as proof.

Barry snatched the paper from my hand and glared at it.

"No way," he said.

"I'm not going on this trip without dessert," Lauren said.

After quickly interrogating the other guides, Barry determined that indeed there had been a catastrophic failure in the food buying process.

"By the time we get back to Grants Pass, the supermarket will be closed," he said.

"Don't panic," I said. "The Galice General Store doesn't close until 10 p.m. Let's jam down there and improvise. We're river guides, man. It's what we do."

Barry fired up the crew cab and we lead-footed down the winding road to the general store. The lights were still on as we kicked up gravel and skidded to a stop in the parking lot.

The Galice store is a mishmash of picnic tables for the breakfast crowd, stacks of T-shirts and baseball caps, fishing gear, propane cans, junk food, canned food, and other boxed food items that had been set in the shelves sometime during the Carter Administration.

The counter clerk was a mousy young woman in a yellow, ketchup-stained "I survived Blossom Bar" tank top. She eyed us cooly. "Make it quick," her body language seemed to say. "We're not staying open after closing time."

"Miss, could you hand me that box of Hershey Bars, those Graham crackers, and a bag of marshmallows please?" Barry asked sweetly, all trace of New Jersey edge gone. One dessert down.

I scanned the cake mix shelves and grabbed the last two boxes of gingerbread mix, pausing to blow the dust off. Another dessert taken care of.

Then our luck ran out. Short of serving Pleistocene-Era Gummy Worms for the last night's dessert, we were out of options. Barry knitted his brows.

This was a challenge, I thought. To succeed would yield a culinary miracle in the wilderness, worthy of campfire tales for years to come. I was confident, I was ready.

"We have grapes, right?" I asked.

"Yeah."

"Brown sugar?"

"I think so."

"Sour cream?"

"If we hold some back from the baked potatoes, yeah."

"All we need is brandy," I said. I had in mind a splooge of grapes in a sweet brandy sauce. "We serve this on the American River all the time," I said. "Somebody on the trip will bring some brandy. I can make this happen, Barry. Trust me."

"Let's do it," he said, yawning.

I reported back to Lauren when we returned to camp. When I described the plan for night three, she frowned. "The grape thing? Really?"

"It'll be fine," I said.

Night one. We rolled out the s'mores. Maybe not as high-end a dish as we usually like to offer, but it seemed to work due to the nostalgia factor. Mmmm, just like camping when we were kids, the guests said.

"That went well," Barry conceded.

. . .

Night two, the gingerbread steamed as we served it out of the hot Dutch oven. So moist, the guests said. Better than a bakery.

"Who knew that stuff doesn't go stale," Barry said.

Night three. About two pounds of grapes were cleaned of stems and carefully rinsed. The bowl was ready. The ½ cup of sour cream…the sour cream was gone. It had been all used up on the steak night baked potatoes. I must have been heavy on the beer and light on the tongs that night.

Improvise, improvise. Ah, yogurt! That should work. Add the brown sugar. Hmmmm, no brown sugar in the commissary, but white sugar and a little honey is pretty much the same, right? Fold it all into the bowl.

Now for the brandy. Brandy? Anyone? No one? Nothing?

It was down to leftover Chardonnay or Schnapps. Ooookaaay, Schnapps it is. Let's give it a go.

I mixed the conglomeration in the bowl and sampled it. A little odd, but hey, don't they say that being outdoors is the best seasoning?

Guest after guest warily scooped a sample, tasted it, and set it aside.

"This sucks," Barry said.

I was crushed. To divert the downward spiral of my self-esteem, I focused on bear prep, and cleaned the kitchen with extra care. I scooped about two pounds of untouched dessert from the bowl into the trash bag. The congealing lump looked too organic, like seeing someone's spilled intestines. I tied the bag up, carried it down to my boat, and stowed it in a cooler that already had a ripe bag of BBQ chicken night trash taking up half the space. I wiped down the cooler and re-secured with a stout cam strap.

"I don't even like that dessert when it's done right," Lauren said when I dropped onto my sleeping bag.

I didn't sleep well that night, so when in the wee hours, a thumping and bumping rose from the boats, I was instantly awake. I sat up, and peered out of the tent. A large dark shape was moving about my boat.

I fluffed my pillow, turned over, and lay down again. They don't pay us enough to go toe-to-toe with a 300-pound black bear. I set my internal clock to get up before dawn to do whatever clean-up was necessary.

A few minutes later, Boom! The cam strap broke. I put the pillow over my head and ignored the further huffing and snuffling that spoke of ursine pillage. Eventually the noise stopped and I drifted back to sleep.

The sky was turning a rose tint when I crawled out of the tent. The good news? The bear hadn't punctured the boat. The bad news? The cooler was shredded. There were dozens of tooth and claw marks spotting the thick plastic lid, which was now torn in half. The cam strap was in tatters. I stood in silent awe of the bear's power.

The bottom of the boat had two inches of bilge gently rocking with the river's pulse. I trudged back to the kitchen and grabbed a colander to scoop the skanky swill. On his tarp near the kitchen area, Barry sat up, stretched, and nodded at me.

As Barry started the campfire and put on the big pot of cowboy coffee, I spent 20 minutes ankle-deep in a swirling miasma of bacon grease, coffee grounds, and lettuce rinds. The chicken bones and scraps were virtually gone. The bear had been particularly interested in them.

Everywhere there were grapes. They were jammed under the edges of the tubes, stuck under the rowing seat, tucked under the thwarts. Grapes, grapes, grapes. About two pounds of them.

Barry appeared at the side of the boat and handed me a cup of coffee.

"Even the bear didn't like your dessert," he observed.

The 1969 Wild & Scenic River Act is a wonderful piece of legislation, one of the country's finest. But like all complex laws, it has had unintended consequences.

"These bears are spoiled," I said. "They ought to allow hunting in this canyon."

Moira Magneson

In Marble Canyon

for Beth and in memory of Grif

In the big river's blue-green
tumble, in the nave of late light,
you are embracing your beloved,
leaning into her. Her hair golden,
unruly, wild. You are doing
what humans do so well—
your mouth on her mouth,
filling her up with your life,
its long blue-black music.
You are filling her with beauty,
and therefore sorrow, though
it cannot feel like that because
the two of you are entangled,
limned in light like a brightedged
thundercloud, charged,
electric, swollen with rain.
Caught in the circle
of your arms, holding
but not spilling a tin
cup of red wine, she is
surrendering to the pressure
of your kiss, the lengthening
dark, a night of falling stars.

—*Moira Magneson*

Dick & Suzy Linford, circa 1978

Our First All-Woman Crew

DICK LINFORD

JUST BEFORE SHE FELL ASLEEP, Teri Drabec said to Barb Birks, "I feel like I forgot to do something." Then she was asleep.

She had good reason to sleep well. The day had been perfect. Most days on a wild river are, but this one had been special. The river was the Stanislaus, at the time the most popular whitewater river in California. The year was 1979, and the guides had all been women. As far as we knew it was the first commercial whitewater trip anywhere with an all-female crew. A lot of people had doubts about women working as raft guides, and an all-woman crew was really pushing the envelope. Especially on a multi-day trip like this one, where all the food and camping gear had to be packed in rafts and carried downriver. Here, a flip or wrap could really mess up a trip. Food and equipment is often lost and what isn't, is probably soaked.

With the exception of Georgie White in the Grand Canyon (Georgie broke all the rules) river guiding was a man's work until the early seventies. The first women to break into this man's world were tough, and they had to work twice as hard as men did to prove themselves. There was a lot of resistance. Women were considered too weak, too emotional, and too timid. In other words, too feminine. As far as I can tell the first company to hire women was The American River Touring Association, or ARTA, in 1972. Joe and I started our company that year, and hired our first woman in 1974. As far as I know, we were the second company to do so.

We were pretty smug about hiring women. We were based in Berkeley then, and it established our reputation as a sexually liberated company. At the same time it was used against us by Idaho and Oregon outfitters. When competing for clients they would tell people that we were a California hippie company who didn't know their rivers, and hiring women was evidence of just how far out we were.

Looking back I have to admit that I wasn't all that liberated by today's standards. While I didn't insist on it, I strongly suggested that women run paddle rafts and not oar boats. That suggestion was pretty much ignored. Around 1975 I started putting women on the Tuolumne, California's solid Class IV river, but I didn't put them on high water trips. I didn't think they had the strength to avoid the big stuff or power through it. When pressed on the issue, I told the women that I wasn't sexist; I was "sizeist." I would be glad to put any woman on the crew who was at least six feet tall, weighed at least 180 pounds, and could do 50 pushups and ten chin-ups. I thought that was pretty clever until the women pointed out that most of my male crew would fail on one or more of my criteria. I conceded that I was exaggerating to make a point and changed the subject.

I also remember being on a Middle Fork trip in 1979. After watching Moira Magneson slam into the wall at the bottom of the rapid named Tappan Two, I thought, "Women just don't belong on the Middle Fork. They just aren't strong enough—at least for oar rafts." Fortunately I didn't say this out loud. The next boat through was Davy Burke. Davy was built like a Greek god—only his shoulders were wider—and had been goalie on Stanford's water polo team. When he slammed into the same rock, I was forced to re-assess. And when Danny Bolster, one of our all-time best guides, flipped three times in one day on the Tuolumne, I laughed and suggested that we outfit his boat with a gyroscope. It never entered my mind to take him off the crew. When Patricia Stow told me that, if she had flipped three times in one day, I would take her off the crew, I strongly denied it. But she was right.

So in 1979 women were still not totally accepted as guides. And an all-woman crew? Unthinkable. Even now, when I started writing this story, I polled eleven Idaho Outfitters, asking what they thought about putting an all-woman crew on a multi-day trip. Here is how they responded.

Three said that they never had and never would.

Two said that they had done it, but only for all-woman groups who demanded it, and would continue that policy,

Three said that they had never done it, and would be nervous about doing so, but wouldn't rule it out.

One said that he had done it for a lesbian group but never would again because the women bickered with each other too much.

One said he had done it and would do it again but preferred mixed crews.

One said that he did it regularly, and gender had nothing to do with his scheduling.

So only one of the eleven was totally fine with all woman crews. The reasons against them included : 1) the guests expect men and would be nervous without them, 2) Women can't fix broken equipment, patch boats, or change tires, 3) Without men around women don't get along with each other, 4) Women don't know how to deal with wraps and flips, and 5) It's just a weird idea.

As for us, in Idaho we have used all-woman crews only for all-woman trips. In Oregon gender is not an issue.

In 1979, if anybody could conceive of an all-woman crew, convince me to do it, and pull it off, it was Teri Drabec. Teri didn't fit the image of a woman breaking male barriers. She was five feet five inches tall, maybe 125 pounds, quite feminine and soft—spoken. But in her quiet way she demanded respect, from women and men alike. She managed our California operation in 1980. She went on to law school, where she was vice-president of her class, and became a deputy district attorney in Alameda County in California. The county includes Oakland, often the murder capital of the United States, and that was right up Teri's alley. She successfully tried many homicide cases, putting people on death row.

She hand-picked her crew too, choosing very competent women. Barb Birks was almost six feet all and very athletic. Sylvia Hoekwater had a model's slimness, but was fearless and—as far as anybody can remember, our first female Tuolumne guide. Sue Wissler was the youngest and was in her first year of guiding, but had the general competence and confidence that came from being a Stanford student and diplomat's daughter.

The guests for this Stanislaus trip were somewhat apprehensive at put-in, but Teri won them over by singing the praises of the women and telling everyone that they were about to make history. By lunch everyone was into what was happening, and by camp everyone was ready to celebrate. Camp, at Duck Bar, was below the most significant rapids on the river, so the tough stuff was behind them. An added plus was that Teri had just found out that she had been accepted to law school. There was a lot to celebrate that night, and celebrate they did. Many batches of sangria were concocted and consumed, each one stronger than the last.

Duck Bar Camp had a big sandy beach and a huge old fig tree. It was along a stretch of slow moving water, about fifty yards above Razorback Rapid. At Razorback the river narrowed, forcing boats toward a barely submerged and very sharp rock. It was usually easy to miss, but if you hit it just wrong, it could slice your floor from bow to stern. Hence the name.

At about 2 a.m. Teri woke with a start, thinking "The boats!! I forgot to make sure the boats were all tied up!" She grabbed a flashlight and ran to the beach. No boats. Not one. Nada. Zero boats.

Nothing is more maddening to an outfitter than boats floating away at night. The best of guides can flip, rip or wrap boats. But to fail to tie a boat up properly at camp—or anytime for that matter—is sheer carelessness. To fail to tie up ANY of the boats is carelessness of almost unheard of proportions. Our rule is that everyone is responsible for securing his or her raft. If there is significant current at camp, safety lines are used to tie the rafts together and secure them to a big tree or rock. In calm water this extra precaution might not happen, but the lead guide is supposed to check the ties at least once. In this case, not one of the four women had tied up her boat, and Teri had not checked. Heads should have rolled.

She ran back and woke the other guides. They all grabbed flashlights and headed downstream, expecting the worst. Teri was thinking, "We're screwed. This is the first and last all-woman trip ever, and Dick isn't going to send me to Idaho next summer." They quickly spotted one boat bobbing thirty yards downstream, with its bowline snagged on a rock. Below that and just above Razorback another boat had run into rocks and was safe. They shined their flashlights on Razorback rock itself, and were hugely relieved that no boats were skewered on it. They scrambled fifty yards farther downstream and found the paddle raft nicely eddied out on shore, paddles all in place. And fifty yards downstream from that, the last boat was inching its way along, in the very slow water that we called Stanislaus Lake. Sylvia, still feeling the effects of the sangria, swam out, climbed in, and rowed the boat ashore. All was well —or at least better. There was no way to get the two boats back upstream through Razorback, so they tied them up well and returned to camp. Teri told them, "We'll laugh about this some day. But when Dick hears about it . . ." And then it hit her. Dick didn't have to hear about this. He tended to get overly stressed by things like this, and he and they would all be better off if it never came out.

The next morning they confessed to the guests that two boats had gotten away, and explained that some people would have to walk down to them after breakfast. Before breaking camp, Teri got everyone together and explained that, if I were to find out what happened, women's lib would suffer a monumental setback, and she swore everyone to secrecy.

And secret it was. I didn't hear about it until years later, at a company party. My memory is that Teri told me. She swears that she didn't. The others deny telling me too. These women could really keep a secret. At least from me.

So the trip was historic in two senses. It was the first all-woman crew trip, and it was the first trip where ALL the boats had floated away during the night. We had lost boats before, but never all of them.

But it wasn't to be the last time it happened. In 2007 two very experienced males guides, Brad Hahn and Travis Staple (now himself an outfitter) ran a trip on the Rogue. They camped at Horseshoe Bend the first night. They swear that they tied the boats up, but for some reason Brad woke up around 3 a.m. and checked just to make sure. Not only were the boats gone, but they were WAY gone. Brad and Travis ran for miles with their head-lamps showing the way before they found them. They grabbed the breakfast food out of the coolers and hiked back. After an awkward breakfast conversation they had to stand at the river's edge and ask people floating by to help them out by carrying equipment and people downstream to the boats. You can't imagine how totally embarrassing this was for them. It was embarrassing for me too. It still is.

But did I fire them? No. And did I take all-male crews off the river? It never entered my mind.

Joe Daly

THE TALENT

JOE DALY

PART I

We, "The Talent," were five river guides struggling to adapt to our newfound title. At first, we felt awkward and self-conscious about our recently anointed status, but if you are a principal in a national TV beer ad, that is what the Hollywood people call you—"The Talent." Being humble river guides, we adapted quickly when the director ordered, "The Talent, grab your paddles," "The Talent, get in the raft," "The Talent, give me a big smile." The title has a nice ring to it, don't you think?

It all began in the spring of 1979 in Angels Camp, California. Angels Camp is located in the foothills of the west-sloping Sierra Nevada. The announcement went forth to the local river community that a national brewery was about to produce a rafting beer commercial and wanted to audition local river guides because the Hollywood production company was unable to find Hollywood actors who knew how to paddle a raft through raging whitewater. If interested, we were to show up at the hotel in downtown Angels Camp in a week.

Seven days later, when my business partner, Dick Linford, and I came through the front door of the hotel, we were greeted by a swarm of about 100 guides eagerly filling out forms listing their attributes and skills, as well as the usual identifying information such as date of birth, address, and telephone number. Hmm. Maybe this was going to be tougher than we first thought.

But being the veteran guides we were, we did not panic. Dick and I began working the room and discreetly discovered that the vast major of guides were going to be eliminated simply because they were too young. The family who owned the beer company did not want anyone in the ad who looked remotely close to the minimum drinking age. Without publicly announcing it, what they wanted were people between the ages of 25 and 35. That was great news for us, except for one small fact. We were outside the age range on the high end. I was 36 and Dick was 37. Before turning in our forms we struggled with the truth. I ended up lightly writing "36" on my form and hoped my baby face would carry the day. Dick flat out lied and wrote "35."

Polaroid pictures were taken of each guide and then a general announcement was made. Everyone was told a decision would be made in a week and a second "audition" would be held in the town park near the hotel. The lucky candidates would be invited to a callback interview. And by the way, the number of guides ultimately needed would be five, which sent a chill through the hotel lobby. The final edict of the day was, "Don't call us, we will call you," which caused the initially enthusiastic crowd to head home in a subdued mood.

Step one of "Don't call us, we will call you," was about to unfold. No call for a week made the week very long, even discouraging, because after the hotel lobby interaction, both Dick and

I felt we had a good shot at being invited to the park audition. By Thursday we were not feeling very sure at all. Most likely our advancing years had done us in. Then Friday afternoon a call came to our office saying that both of us were to go to the park next Wednesday for an informal chat and walkabout. We were not sure what that meant exactly, but we knew nothing, absolutely nothing, was going to stop us from being there.

On Wednesday, as we walked toward the small park in Angels Camp, we could see there were a fair number of people who clearly were not river guides. They turned out to be two sub-groups. Personnel from a world famous ad agency from Chicago made up one group, and the other group had people from Venice, California representing the filming company. They were distinctly different from us and from each other. Let's call one group "the suits" and the other "the Hollywood people." They were about to determine our fate.

The river guides standing in the park numbered about 20. They were wholesome looking, robust, broad-shouldered, and tall. Tall was what got my attention first, because I am not. Doubt crept into the edges of my brain. Imagine Woody Allen walking among the Redwoods. Fortunately, at my moment of greatest creeping despair, someone called all of us to attention. That someone was Jeff De LaSalle, the film director. He outlined how things were to go. The ad agency and film people were to spread out across the park, and we, the river guides, were to go mingle with them in any manner we saw fit. It was an awkward and lurching beginning, but off we went.

After about 20 minutes of small talk and walking about, I realized two things. First, the suits and the Hollywood folks were drawing conclusions fast, and second, I was in big trouble. Of the

20 guides who were there, all were six feet or taller, except me. I am well under six feet. Most weighed 200 lbs. or more. I may have topped out at 155. No one was wearing glasses except me. I was desperate. Suddenly I made a panicked, pathetic move that I cannot explain.

As the meeting was obviously coming to a close, I casually walked fast (ran) over to Jeff De LaSalle, shook his hand, looked him in the eye, and said, " Jeff, if I am not selected for this ad, millions upon millions of American men who are five feet seven inches tall, weighing 155 pounds, and wearing glasses, will not be able to identify with this ad."

Jeff blinked a couple of times, smiled slowly, and walked away. I thought, "I am dead in the water." He probably thought, "What an obnoxious jerk."

Again, we were told, "Don't call us, we will call you." But this time the wait would not be days; the lucky five would be called by 6:00 PM that day. Dick and I had a mostly silent three-hour drive home, because we concluded it was unlikely that both of us would be chosen. Ego-wise it was going to be tough for the loser, and after my desperate comment to Jeff De LaSalle, I was feeling less than confident, except for one key fact. Jeff was about five feet seven, weighed about 155 pounds, and wore glasses very similar to mine.

Upon arriving home and with an outwardly cool demeanor, I told my wife, Sue, we had to make a few changes in how our home was arranged for the next few hours. (Remember now, in 1979 there were no cell phones, only hard wired, clunky telephones and no such thing as call-waiting.) Directive # 1 was NO out-going calls were to be made, again stated in a cool, nonchalant voice. Directive # 2 was that only I was to answer the phone, and # 3, I am casually going to move the telephone line across the den and kitchen floors and rest the phone itself on the kitchen window sill while I casually go into the garden to do some yard work. Sue's eyebrows went up, but she wisely said nothing. To keep occupied, I snipped and clipped some bushes, talked with a neighbor, and strategically hung close to the back door. At 5:00 no call, 5:30 also no call. The crusher was that no call came at 6:00. Dick was going to be in and I was going to be out. Then at 6:15 the phone range, and I bolted.

I said, "Hello?" The woman's voice said, "Hi, Is this Joe Daly?" I instantly recognized the woman's voice from earlier in the day as that of the director's assistant, Alice. At that moment I knew I was going to be a Hollywood star. Well, not quite a Hollywood star, but a fun time was about to begin. Alice said, "After this experience, you will never view a TV ad the same way."

PART II

Two weeks later, five of us were standing on the bank of the Merced River, which flows out of Yosemite National Park. The five were Jim Segerstrom, Marty McDonnell, Kevin Clark, Dick Linford, and yours truly. Jim was an independent rafter, Marty owned a rafting company, Kevin worked for the Bureau of Land Management, and Dick and I also co-owned a rafting company. The common thread among us was that we were "can do" people. We were roaring to make this ad happen. But to our surprise the production company did not want us to do anything.

Under normal circumstances in readying for a river trip, all of us would blow up rafts, tie down gear, and carry bags and boxes of food from the equipment truck to the rafts. Not now. Dozens of extra people had been hired to attend to "The Talent." We were not to lift a finger. We were so dumbfounded all we could do was stand there and smile. We knew many of the extras. We all had a good laugh about the situation.

Director Jeff De La Salle's first executive decision reinforced my light-hearted spirits. To my delight, he made me "captain of the ship." Here I was Mr. Four Eyes, the smallest in the group, and a lightweight in more ways than one, and suddenly I was paddle captain. I was the one who will be shouting orders and steering the raft.! This definitely was going to be fun.

But our light-hearted mood did not last long. As the director and his principal film man Max got to work, a multitude of problems came up, ranging from minor to major. There was the low water crisis, the mustache crisis, the failure to buy the concept crisis, the too-good-to-be-real crisis, the schizophrenic eyeballs crisis, the "point of view" crisis, the tooth abscess crisis, and the how to hold a beer can crisis. But the production people were real pros. Each crisis was handled with ingenuity, diplomatic aplomb, or blunt force, depending on the situation. Here is a rundown of what we faced:

#1. Major Crisis. Low Water. The Merced is a free-flowing river and the spring run-off had been below average. Each day the river was getting lower, and the director was worried that the scenes would not be exciting enough. Max (the cinematographer) solved that problem by saying he would change camera angles and do a number of close-up water shots. He was confident he could make the water exciting. In retrospect, Max performed a small miracle with his cameras.

#2. Virility Mini-Crisis. Too Much Facial Hair. Of the five of us, two had full beards, two had mustaches, and one was clean cut (yours truly). The director said he needed one of the four to cut their facial hair. There was a long pause. He next said, "O.K.

then one of the mustaches has to go." The mustaches belonged to Marty and Dick. Both paused too long. The director barked, "Look, you have 30 seconds to decide, because if you can't, I have 40 people standing over there who can take your place with the snap of the fingers!" Dick did not need 30 seconds. In two seconds, he said his mustache would be gone.

#3. Major Crisis. Failure to Buy the Concept. Once all the gear was ready, the director gathered us around him in a close circle to announce the underlying theme for the story line. He was very excited and in a hushed tone, he announced the theme was *"Go For It!"* None of us said a thing. We just nodded our heads and stared straight ahead. I knew the others were thinking the same thing I was. I had heard the term a million times over the last five years. It was a yawner of a phrase; no one in America was going to get excited about "Go For It." In a few hours, we would realize our know-it-all attitude almost cost us the whole project.

#4. Irony Crisis. Too Good to Be Real. The equipment was ready; the cameras were ready; it was time to jump in the raft to run a long series of rapids. Our attitude was, "We are the pros." We know how to get through this section of whitewater without hitting a rock or dumping anyone overboard. We were out to prove to the director he had picked the best five for the ad. The first run was beautiful, even graceful. We eddied out, happy with our moves. We climbed up the river bank to get confirmation from the director that our flawless run was to his liking.

Shockingly, it was not. He was stone-faced and wringing his hands. In short, he said the run was too good to be believable in the eyes of the average guy out having some weekend fun. What we had done was dull and boring. He walked away saying over his shoulder that the project was off to a bad start. We were speechless.

At that point, we looked like whopped puppy dogs. Marty, who had done a previous beer commercial, took a deep breath to begin a pep talk. He said we probably had one more chance to do it right before the director would start making big changes. We listened closely. We had to change our know-it-all attitude. We had to imagine we were with "Joe Six-pack," out yucking it up with a bunch of friends. We were to exaggerate every move, paddles in the air, shouting at the top of our lungs, even slamming into a few rocks. Go big and get wet.

The second run was a beautiful, chaotic mess and the director was thrilled. He was beaming as we reached the top of the river bank. However, there was one complication, Crisis # 5.

#5. Major Crisis. Schizophrenic Eyeballs. Our desire to overdo every action produced the most serious problem of the whole experience for me. We were well into our second run, thrashing and paddling like crazy, when we hit the biggest drop in the rapid. The front of the raft plowed into the hole, basically stopping the raft's momentum. But I, in the back as paddle captain, kept going forward, slamming into Marty's paddle. For a moment, we all became a pile of humanity. Then we burst up out of the hole and the raft continued downstream. But something big had changed for me. With one eye, I could see way downstream, but with the other, life was a massive blur. The top of Marty's paddle had bashed into my face knocking the left lens out of my glasses frame. I had schizophrenic eyeballs!

The lens was not to be found, and stupidly, I had forgotten to bring a backup pair of glasses. I suggested to the director that I simply go without my glasses for the rest of the shoot. He said no way. Everything had to remain exactly the same. We were too far along to make any changes. So we worked it out that I would stay in the same position in the back, with my glasses on, but Marty, just in front of me, would actually call the commands. Somehow it worked for the remaining runs.

#6. "The Point of View " Crisis. Without most of us common citizens realizing it, almost all ads have a moment where a "point of view" shot is presented. It is a subtle technique to draw us into the ad, to make us feel as if we are there. At first you see the person (the paddler), then you see a view as if you are seeing things through the eyes of the paddler. The next time you are having a couch potato day try finding the "point of view" moment in each ad.

For us and Max, the film man, the point of view shot was going to be a big challenge. The decision was made that the perspective was going to be through my eyes in the back of the raft. That meant adding one more person and his camera to the back of an already crowded boat. Most of the credit for making the shot work goes to Max. He was a genius at building a small oil derrick-like stand on the back of the raft. We ran a part of the Merced that was exciting, but not too exciting. Max got his "point of view" shot, and the five of us kept most of his very expensive equipment dry.

#7. The Tooth Abscess Crisis. Early on, both Dick and I said nothing, absolutely nothing was going to keep us from being in this ad. I stayed off of ladders and looked both ways before crossing streets. Sadly for Dick, about a week before we arrived at the river, he developed an off-and-on pain in a tooth. The dentist was not sure what to do, but a root canal was clearly an option. Two days before departing home the decision was made to do nothing. Because of an early start the first day, we all had to be in the area the night before. The big hurt began in the night and would not stop. Dick refused to take codeine for fear of looking glassy-eyed and being dopey acting. He simply gutted up for two days, got through the shoot, and then vomited on the way home.

#8. How to Hold the Beer Can Crisis. This was not really a crisis, more a lack of knowledge on our part. When each of us was tossed a can of beer we failed the test. But now I know how a real man drinks a real can of beer when on a real river. There is a particular grip, with fingers placed just so. Of course, the label had to be just right, too. Most of us do not think about such things as "left tab," "right tab," and "center tab" openings. But on this shoot, we had 40 cases of beer and a specialist who judged which were the right cans for us to hold.

The next time you watch a beer ad, notice how the hand and fingers are placed.

In the end we had worked hard for two days. And when all was said and done, amazingly, we each made, in today's terms, the equivalent of $46,000.00. That was because during the next two years, 30-and 60-second versions of our ad ran locally, regionally, and nationwide, and even during the Winter Olympics and 1980 Super Bowl. Almost every Monday we received a "T and R" (a Talent and Residuals) check. I loved walking to the mailbox on Mondays. It was a sweet time for us. Embarrassingly, I admit sometimes to having a ridiculous entitlement pout if the check did not arrive until Tuesday.

Then one day a different envelope came in the mail, formally saying the ad campaign was over. They were stopping the commercials! "The Talent" was no longer needed. I was crushed. It was like being a pitcher standing on the mound during the World Series, and suddenly, the manager comes out and takes the ball away from you. New pitcher, please.

Just the same, it was great fun being a part of the whole experience. Each of us still has vivid memories. To this day, Dick can

recite every word of the ad with emphasis, and I am in heavy nego-
tiations with the Mrs. to see if the term "The Talent" might end
up on my tombstone.

Green Room, Havasu

naked   we hurried upriver   before the afternoon monsoon
rolled in   leaping over rocks   loose lariats of rattlesnakes.

bold lizards—janizaries leading the way—suddenly broke
rank.   along the bank   cottonwoods and willows

gathered their green dresses up wading to their knees.

five miles we ran   dust clouds swirled
in the air like ash.

at last we reached the falls

where thunder hollowed a deep wide pool
in the limestone travertine.

so loud we had to shout

watch me   he yelled   *I'll guide you.*
I shivered   as he dove down

swallowed in the river's booming blast.   I gulped a breath
finned behind   into a corridor emptied out of light.

blind   my heart ticked in its shell   until

we bobbed into a cave   quiet   save our breathing.
unmoored weightless asphodels   we floated.

below the fathoms opened their turquoise doors

and like little gods we flew or fell
into the broken sky beneath the world.

                                        —Moira Magneson

Dick Linford

CAMPFIRE TALES

DICK LINFORD

FOR MY FIRST TEN YEARS OR SO OF GUIDING, I felt that we guides were the most interesting people on any trip. We had great stories, we were witty, and we were ever so cool. But somewhere along the line I realized that I was listening to the same stories over and over again, and the most interesting thing about them became how they evolved over time. The rapids became bigger, the weather got colder, and the characters changed. Guides would tell stories as though they were there when it happened, when I knew that they weren't.

That's when I started really listening to our guests. They often told much more interesting stories, and I only had to hear them once.

People who take multi-day river trips are a small and special segment of the population. First, they are financially successful. Our trips aren't cheap, especially considering that people sleep on the ground. But our guests are also adventurous, well traveled, world-wise, and articulate. And nothing loosens the tongue like a day on a wild river, a good meal, and a glass of wine or three, to be followed by sleeping under the stars. Here is just s smattering of the interesting stories I have heard from our guests.

One guest had been the lead prosecutor of John Mitchell, President Nixon's Attorney General, who eventually spent 19 months in jail for his complicity in Watergate. I hated Nixon and thought that everyone connected with Watergate was evil personified, but this client, who had helped put him behind bars, told me that Mitchell was a delightful human being. Warm, witty and self-deprecating. Go figure.

Another guest told about walking on a secluded beach in Portugal. A stranger casually joined him and the two struck up a lively conversation as they strolled along.

The stranger eventually asked our guest what he did for a living. Our guest told him he was a corporate lawyer in New York. The stranger seemed duly impressed, and they discussed law for a while. The stranger asked good questions. Then the guest asked the stranger what he did. The stranger said, "Oh, I'm a king." It turned out that he was King Juan Carlos of Spain. Many of our guides have met people on river beaches, but none of them a been a king.

A Japanese sake exporter talked about growing up in Japan during WWII. He was sent from Tokyo to the mountains as a child, to be saved from our fire bombing of that city. His mother was killed in the firebombing of Tokyo. His father perished on Iwo Jima. He told of the terror that he and the other children experienced when the Americans were approaching the village. They expected to be killed and eaten by the white devils. And here came these strange giants with red faces who smiled a lot, gave them rides in jeeps, and handed out candy. There was an elderly man who had been the village's English teacher his whole life, and proudly told everyone that he would serve as translator. Much to his embarrassment, the teacher couldn't understand a word of the English the GIs spoke, nor could they understand him. He had learned and taught the language without ever hearing it spoken by English or American people, and had had no feedback. Kind of like my college French.

A man whom we were told to call Martin (pronounced *Martaa*) introduced himself as a rice farmer in Italy. Late one night, around the campfire, his friends got him to admit that he was one of the richest men in Italy and would be the King of Austria if the monarchy had not been abolished after after WWI. Another man was made *Knight of the Realm* by Queen Elizabeth the same day as Paul McCartney. Two of our ex-guides guides are related to the Norwegian royal family, but no guide has been made a *Knight of the Realm*.

Some stories were harrowing. One man was the son of the German ambassador to Rome during World War II. The father had married into a prominent Italian family. He was involved in the 1944 attempt to assassinate Hitler in the plot named Operation Valkyrie. The plot failed, and the father was executed along with all the other conspirators. Our guest's mother was sent to prison for her husband's crime, and he and his younger brother were sent to a camp for the children of convicts. They got separated in the camp, where they were malnourished and lived a feral existence for the duration of the war.

After the war the allies had no idea whom the kids belonged to, so they just kept them locked up—albeit under more humane conditions than under the Germans. At the time, Austrian farmers had been devastated by the war and lost most of their labor force, so were pressuring the allies to allow them to adopt the children. This was not altruism. The farmers were looking for cheap labor. The kids were to become basically slave labor.

Meanwhile, their mother was released from prison, but had been so traumatized by her experience that she was quite helpless, so her mother, a powerful woman in every sense of the word, prevailed on Eisenhower himself to give her a car, a driver, and carte blanche to find her grandchildren. After months of searching, she found them in a camp in Austria. She and her grandson— our guest—immediately recognized each other. They thought they recognized the younger brother, but the child they thought might be the right one didn't recognize them, and so they weren't positive.

The grandmother didn't have much time to decide. The day she arrived was the day that the kids were to be divided among the farmers. She begged the American Army sergeant for time, but he told her it was too late. Then he winked and told her that he was taking a coffee break and would be back in ten minutes. She decided to take a chance on the one she thought might be her grandchild, thinking that, if he weren't hers, she would still be saving him from a life of serfdom. She grabbed both kids, put them in her car, and drove off. When they arrived back at the family estate the younger child pointed to the photograph of a horse and called it by name. She had made the right choice.

Our guest went on to an illustrious career as a diplomat.

One of our guides got lost in a shopping center when he was three, but he was found after an hour.

Then there is the tale told by a woman who suffered from acute bends, or de-compression sickness, while SCUBA diving at a Club Med in the Caribbean. First she experienced a severe headache. So acute that she was bed-ridden. Then she went blind. When Club Med finally realized how sick she was they decided that the only way to save her life was to fly her to Miami, where she would be placed in a de-compression chamber and slowly returned to normal. As they carried her to the plane she requested that her eight-year-old daughter be allowed to fly with her. They told her that they expected her to die on the flight because it would create even more de-compression problems, and it would be better if the daughter remained at Club Med. She survived the flight and spent a week in the de-compression chamber. Only then was she re-connected with her daughter.

But the story that haunts me the most was told by a most ordinary man. When I met him on a Middle Fork trip he was a big, somewhat overweight guy in his fifties. I don't remember his name, so let's call him Bob. In college Bob had been six feet, six inches tall, weighed 220 pounds, and played varsity basketball for a Big Ten university. This was during the Viet Nam War. Upon graduation, filled with misguided patriotism, machismo, or whatever you want to call it, he enlisted in the army. He had a chance to go to Officer Training School, but turned it down. He wanted the true grunt experience. He wanted action.

He was outstanding in boot camp. He was a head taller than anybody else, he was blond and blue eyed, he was in great shape when he arrived, and he was smart. Therefore his drill sergeant hated him. He singled him out for extra pushups, give him extra miles to run, and blamed him for other people's screw-ups. In every way possible, Bob was singled out for abuse. One day Bob had had enough. He knew that if he confronted the sergeant in front of the other men the sergeant would feel cornered and need to strike out to defend his authority, so he waited to catch him alone. The sergeant told Bob that he was way out of line, but if he wanted to settle the matter man-to-man, they should meet privately, in the shower room, when the others had gone to the mess hall for dinner.

Bob was nervous waiting for the confrontation, knowing that the sergeant was expert at hand-to-hand combat. But he also figured, "What the Hell. I outweigh him by forty pounds, my reach is at least six inches longer, and I'm in great shape. I was a Big Ten basketball star. How much damage can he do? Even if I lose, he'll respect me enough to leave me alone from now on."

At the chosen time, Bob steeled himself and walked into the shower. He caught a blur out of the side of his vision and everything went black. He came to several hours later in his cot. He couldn't see out of one eye, had a hard time breathing, and noticed that some teeth were missing. He hurt all over and slipped in and out of consciousness during the night. The next day he couldn't get out of bed. Friends covered for him. The sergeant let them. Twenty-four hours later he was no better, and his friends, afraid he might die if untreated, took him to sick bay. The doctor told him that he had a skull fracture, broken nose, broken jaw, several broken ribs, a punctured lung, ruptured spleen, and bruised liver.

When he told the doctor what had happened, the Army moved fast. They court-marshalled the sergeant and gave him a dishonorable discharge.

It took Bob several weeks to recover, and his injuries precluded combat duty. He was shipped from the East Coast to a posting in California where he pushed papers. In his bed one night, close to a year after the incident, he was awakened with a knife on this throat. A voice whispered, "You motherfucker, you ruined my life. The Army was all I had and you took that from me. I'm going to kill you. Not tonight, but some time when you least expect it. I found you here and I'll always know where you are. You will never be safe." Bob hoped it might have been a dream, but when he dared move he went in the bathroom and turned on the light. There was a slight cut on his throat.

Bob is a lawyer now. He is married and has two sons and a daughter. He has an elaborate security system in his home, he sleeps with a gun under his pillow, and he wakes with a start at the slightest sound.

Guides have taken some epic swims through rapids, but I doubt that any of them feel the need to sleep with a gun.

Mark Palmer

HIGH WATER AND LOW CULTURE ON THE MERCED

MARK PALMER

I AM ON HOLD WITH THE AUTO CLUB, standing at a dented black pay phone bolted to the cinderblock wall of Jack Bass's living room in Briceburg, California. Our truck wouldn't start. Again. Most people wouldn't have a pay phone in their living room. But here, it makes sense. While this is Jack's home and the nerve center of this seven-person town just outside of Yosemite, it's really just an old gas station with some carpet on the concrete floor. I put Jack at 75 years old. But it's hard to tell. He's wrinkled and toothless and speaks in a raspy grumble. Given the evidence of good living that fills the room: empty beer cans, cigarette butts, biker magazines, and cereal boxes, Jack could be 45 and I'd never know. I can see him on his porch sitting on a vinyl car seat he pulled out of some junked sedan, his face to the morning sun. Jack is sandwiched between a pair of sausage-shaped teenage girls in tube tops and cut-off jeans. One girl slaps her naked thigh with the business end of a wire flyswatter.

Across the room, heavy metal music pounds out of a stereo I am afraid to turn down. Cardboard boxes serve as side tables for a thrift shop couch and chair. And there are copies of *Easyrider Magazine* draped over the arms of the furniture. On the walls hang fake oil paintings of a handsome, sinewy Jesus suffering so passionately that they seem vaguely pornographic. Large shutters open onto a patio to one side of the repair bays. There, unattended, is a boy of about eight. He stands there without emotion, rhythmically squeezing lighter fluid from a rectangular red can onto a fire he's got burning in the little cast iron grill. The lighter fluid pulses from the can with the regularity of a heartbeat, exploding into a ball of fire each time it hits the grill. I am not in hell, but you can definitely see it from Jack's house.

Welcome to the Merced River, where I am halfway through a two-day commercial trip. But there isn't going to be a second day. I have just sent our 17 passengers home.

It began the previous morning when I met the passengers in the parking lot of the Cedar Lodge motel. In 1982, the lodge still had the picturesque faux-alpine quality of a movie set. Still, you couldn't shake the sense that things weren't quite right. As if the guy who was repairing the riding mower at the far end of the parking lot might be a serial killer or something. (Sadly, 15 years later that's exactly what happened. A Cedar Lodge handyman would be found guilty of multiple murders.)

That morning the place was lit by the rays of the rising sun and smelled sweetly of wood smoke and pancakes. Our passengers waited in small groups, standing by the trunks of their cars, ready and excited. My hopes for the trip were high and bright as the morning sun.

This had been a wet, cold winter. But the warm spring had melted a lot of the snow and the river was running high. On the

Merced that presented a unique challenge. Near the end of the usual two-day trip was a large rapid called Quarter Mile. Just below it lay the unrunnable North Fork Falls. At lower flows, there was enough slow water between the two that a trip could pull to shore well above the falls. Then it was simply a matter of portaging North Fork Falls and heading on downriver. But at this water level, there was no place to eddy out between the rapid and the waterfall. So for safety's sake, no one ran the bottom stretch. But our trip had been sold as a two-day, so we planned to go downriver as far as we could, camp just above the last chance to takeout, head back upstream and run the same stretch again on the second day. It wasn't ideal, but it was the only safe option. The passengers would miss out on Quarter Mile rapid. But the high water let us begin the trip upriver of the usual put-in, adding a mile-long string of class three and four rapids to the trip.

The gods of weather and water were on our side. My crew—Myles, Mike and Del—were good company and great boatmen. The only wild card was the beach where we planned to camp. The large sand bar was the only decent camp below Briceburg, but none of the guides, including me, had ever seen it. We'd all done one-day trips or camped downriver at lower flows. Still, it was a beach on the left side of the river. Below the bridge. We could find it.

Our passengers were a combination of couples, old friends, co-workers and one or two adventurous folks who'd come alone. Strangers, really, having had only fifteen minutes in the parking lot of the motel to get acquainted. But from the moment we pushed the boats off shore and into the moving water they began to work as a team. There was a reason this stretch had been named Miracle Mile. One rocky rapid spilled into the next one without a break. We picked our way through narrow chutes and ran holes that stalled the boats and got everyone wet. By the time we reached the first calm stretch of river—a mile below put-in—these strangers were laughing and shouting like they'd known each other forever.

Below Miracle Mile, the river quieted and we caught our breath. After congratulations all around, we floated happily along, letting the river do the work. Ordinarily this is where I'd tell you about sheer, majestic cliffs or forests of lodgepole pine and Douglas fir. But when you're on the Merced all you really notice is State Highway 140 running along the river's left bank. Less conspicuous is the one-lane dirt track on the right bank called Incline Road. It was along that washboard road that we'd probably see prospectors, searching the river for gold dust just as they had since 1849. But for now, we were alone, except for the occasional motor home that rumbled down 140 headed out of Yosemite for Mariposa.

After a while, we noticed that we were seeing a lot of one particular motor home. The first time we floated past it, the family inside watched us from the windows then pulled onto the highway and raced past us, only to pull off the road again alongside the next rapid. As we approached the rapid, the family poured out of the boxy Winnebago and hurried to the safety rail, cameras at the ready. We waved and shouted as we dropped into the rapid and cheered, fists pumping the air as we made it out the other side. The family climbed back into their motor home and hurried down to the next large turnout and the rapid that lay below it.

They'd raise their cameras and tense up as we dropped into Can Opener, Ned's Gulch. or Son of Ned's. When we got to the bottom the entire family would shake their heads and slump their shoulders. Dad would comfort the kids as they climbed back into the motor home. They would drive away without a wave or a honk of the horn. They seemed enormously disappointed by our performance. But when we reached the next rapid, the motor home would be pulled into the turnout, the family waiting breathlessly at the safety rail. We finally understood. They didn't want to watch us run rapids. They just wanted to see us flip boats. To see us swept downriver and swimming for our lives—now that would be a picture.

Passing under the bridge at Briceburg meant saying goodbye to Highway 140 and our family of death-obsessed vacationers. At the same time, mining claims began to pop up along the river's north side. But there were no twinkly-eyed, sourdough miners with white beards and red suspenders. In eddy after eddy, scowling men with beer guts and tattoos stood chest deep in the water, wrestling with noisy vacuum hoses as they sucked gravel off the river's sandy bottom. Their claims were a tangle of rusting metal, dented, dirty trucks and the litter left by a life of snack cakes and bargain beer—an unholy marriage of Little Debbie and Meister Brau.

Each makeshift camp was a tableau of debauchery. Some miners were drinking and arguing around campfires that spewed inky, foul-smelling smoke. Others lay sprawled on dredges, dozing or smoking pot as they monitored the compressors that pumped air to their partners working underwater. Each miner we passed looked at us with an uncomfortable mixture of boredom, booze, and resentment. Miners are secretive by nature. And we were 20-plus cheerful vacationers, enjoying some time in the wilderness. Happily, they were all on the right side of the river and we would be camping on the left. But where? It was well after 4:00 p.m. and we hadn't seen anything that looked like camp.

Around 4:30, I pulled the group into a tiny eddy on river right. I walked the guides back upstream so we could discuss our options in private. Had we missed our camp? Was it time to grab the next beach we could find on river left and call it a night? Or should we press on, fingers crossed, hoping that our perfect sandbar was still somewhere downstream? I stared across the river as I weighed our options. That's when I saw our camp.

The river had been turning to the south so slowly that I hadn't noticed the large eddy. But across the river, at the lower end of a sweeping crescent bend, I could see the beach everyone had told us about. It was big and beautiful. But it was also 50 yards upstream. The African Queen portion of our trip was about to begin.

Mike was the biggest of the guides and I was leading the trip, so I elected us to wade into the water and push the boats upstream. As Mike and I struggled in waist-deep water, Del and Myles stood on the bank, keeping the boats from catching on anything that might slow our progress. But our passengers were doing the real work. Positioned on the rocky bank upstream they pulled on the bowline of the boat we were working on at that moment. As we pushed the boat, they would walk backwards along the rocks, keeping the rope taut. When we reached the top of each small eddy, Mike and I would push the boat into moving current. Then, it was up to the passengers to pull against the current, muscling the boat into the next small patch of quiet water. There the process would begin again. To get the four boats up to where we could row across to camp took us the better part of two hours. By the time we were all across the river, the sun was disappearing behind the rim of the canyon.

Even after all that, our passengers were still upbeat. I'd need to tap that enthusiasm if we were going to get our camp set up and dinner served. Bouncing around like a cheerleader, I rallied small groups to help us unload the boats, gather firewood, and set up the kitchen. Once we had got the fire going and our kitchen table in place, we unloaded the passengers' personal gear and sent them off to change into dry clothes and relax. As Mike, Del and Myles began to pull the food for dinner, I shuttled around the group, making sure everyone had a cocktail and a flat place to sleep. Satisfied that everyone was okay, I joined the other guides in the kitchen. We worked as quickly as we could, but still didn't serve dinner until after dark. By 9:30, as I squatted at the line of buckets to wash the dinner dishes, most of our passengers had climbed into their sleeping bags. And within an hour, we were fast asleep as well.

Del and I were the first ones up the next morning. In spite of the work of the previous day, everything felt brand new. It was quiet. A light haze rose from the river. I felt good about where we were and what we were doing. Even if it only lasted as long as that morning, we'd found a peaceful, perfect world that wasn't filled with bloodthirsty tourists or drunken miners.

And then I heard the shouting.

"Help meee!" It was a man's voice, coming from upstream. "Help meee!" It wasn't the terrified outburst of someone hanging from a ledge, but a strange, monotone plea of someone who'd been in trouble for a while. "Help meee!" It came again. By now passengers were scrambling out of their sleeping bags, horrified by what they heard. They gathered near the kitchen, unsure how to react. Del joined me by the river.

A guy in his mid-20s came floating around the corner on a homemade raft. He was dressed in a windbreaker, flannel shirt, jeans and boots—and was soaking wet. Calling his watercraft a "raft" is a little misleading. It was a pair of inner tubes lashed together with a couple of 2x4s that he straddled. It was rigid enough to support him, but so poorly designed that it was almost useless when it came to getting anywhere.

His paddle was also a 2x4 and equally useless. Its narrow face cut through the water with almost no effect. Since he was only paddling on his right side, what little power he did generate spun him in a slow circle as the current carried him down river.

Del jumped onto my boat and unclipped a throw bag—a safety line coiled up inside a canvas sack. If you knew how to use it, you could hit a swimmer with pinpoint accuracy. Then, whoever was in the water could grab hold of the rope and pendulum to shore downstream. "I'm going to throw you a line," Del shouted. The guy shouted back, "Help meee!" Del let the bag go at just the right moment. The paddler watched as it traced a sweeping arc through the air, rope unspooling from its ass-end like some kind of magic trick and leaving a length of rescue line within arm's reach. The guy stared blankly at the rope then paddled another small circle. He yelled the only words he seemed to know. "Help meee!"

"Paddle on the other side!" yelled Del, and the prospector complied. The little raft stopped spinning. The guy looked amazed. Another magic trick. Paralyzed by wonder, the guy drifted past Del. Downstream, I took over the lesson, shouting commands that finally steered our miner to a hard collision with the rocky bank a few hundred yards downstream. Splashing clumsily into the waist deep water, he scrambled onto shore and disappeared up the hill without looking back. Del was coiling the rope back into the throw bag when I got back to where he was standing. There wasn't much to say. We still had to make breakfast. When we got back to the kitchen area, the passengers stood in a knot near the fire, staring at us in disbelief.

Ten minutes later, after I'd pulled our blackened coffee pot from the fire and set it aside to let the grounds settle, one of our passengers got my attention and pointed discreetly up the hillside. Our misguided paddler was passing our camp as he picked his way back upstream. I headed up the beach to see how he was doing.

At first I gave the guy the benefit of the doubt. Was he trying to reach a mining claim on the south side of the river? He shook his head. Something he lost that needed retrieving? "No." Finally, he admitted that he just wanted to see if he could get across the river. Fully clothed. At 6 a.m.

"You know there's a waterfall downstream," I said, as neutrally as possible. He nodded sheepishly. Then he brightened a little.

"You smoke pot?" asked the guy, hoping to repay me for our morning rescue.

Bouts of crippling depression have always been ample motivation to keep me away from high balconies and drugs that play with my mood. But even if I had smoked pot, after seeing this guy in action I would have stopped. Still, the offer made me curious.

"Is your pot dry?"

He smiled confidently and nodded as he reached into the pocket of his soggy windbreaker and pulled out a cellophane bag that was full of water. I half-expected to see a gold fish in the bag, as if he'd won it at the fair. His expression changed as he stared at the bag. Almost losing his life had been an abstract concept. But losing his pot? You could feel his heart breaking as he carefully slipped the bag back into his pocket and shuffled sadly upstream.

Running the same stretch of river a second time meant closing up camp, loading the boats, rowing to takeout, breaking everything down and loading it into a truck. Then we'd drive back upstream, unload the boats, tie everything down again, squeeze back into our wetsuits and do it all again. It was a lot to do, so we moved as quickly as we could, breaking down camp as our passengers finished eating. When breakfast was over, we threw their bags onto the boats and headed for takeout.

Twenty minutes later, we pulled up to our destination.. It was here the road ended, spilling into a large campground called Railroad Flat. Clearly, it was where the miners lived when they weren't working their claims. Even at 10 a.m. people were shouting, swearing, and laughing around campfires of cardboard and newspaper. Women with bad teeth flashed their breasts and spanked their children. The ping of ricocheting bullets echoed down the canyon from upstream, where a group of miners fired guns at the rusting sides of a 100-year-old stamp mill. Desperate to spend as little time as possible on what we'd later refer to as "Freak Beach," I bounced around enthusiastically, trying to get everyone focused on the fun we were having carrying boxes to the truck. I tried to make a game of it. A game I quietly called, "let's not die here."

But slowly, guides and passengers began to tire. We were all exhausted from the day before. No amount of joking and clapping and running up and down the beach could make anyone move any faster or work any harder. I needed to say something profound to light a fire under the group. Something inspirational. I couldn't think of anything. Luckily, the Merced drove the point home more clearly and eloquently than I could have on my best day.

A girl of about 10 years old scrambled through the middle of our group like a wild animal, her eyes glassy. Her high pitched, manic laugh made it seem like she'd lost her mind. She was either horrified or happier than she'd ever been. She paused long enough to shake her head of stringy hair and graze each of us with her vacant stare before scampering away. We instinctively turned to see what she was running from. Time seemed to stop the way it does before a car wreck, when you see something so terrible that every detail comes into clear, unbearable focus. In this case we weren't looking at an oncoming semi. It was a 12-year-old boy.

He wore cut-off jeans, no shirt, and oversized hand-me-down sneakers of some generic type, unlaced and loose around his ankles. His body widened like a cone, from his bare, narrow shoulders to an ample ring of meat around his waist that bounced as he ran. His head rose out of his neck, a soft cylinder of flesh, topped with a red crew cut, like the end of a new pencil stuck into a pear. He grinned with stubby teeth, his freckled cheeks rising to press his eyes into slits. He stopped, wheezing as he tried to catch his breath. Then he took long slug from a 16-ounce can of Budweiser. He wiped his mouth with the back of one dirty forearm and stumbled drunkenly after the little girl.

Myles is a pretty resilient guy. But at this moment he looked at me with abject fear. "We have got to get out of here," he said, without a trace of humor. Ten minutes later the truck was loaded, the passengers were in the bus and we were bouncing up the road toward our second day on the Merced.

Except no one wanted to do it again. As the bus rolled toward Cedar Lodge, where the folks had left their cars, a pair of passengers asked if they could stop and use the bathroom. When we piled out of the bus they admitted that they didn't need to pee. They wanted to go home.

It turned out that whether or not the passengers would get a partial refund for this ill-conceived tour of California's biker-backwoods depended on how unhappy they were with their experience. They gathered around the pay phone as I called the office. "Are they upset?" asked one of the company's owners. I repeated the question so the passengers could hear it. They all shook their heads emphatically. They weren't upset at all. They would have loved to do another day on the river. Just not on this river. So I did what any good guide would do. I lied.

I told the office I had a full-blown mutiny on my hands. After a worried moment, the owner asked me to extend his apologies to everyone, assure them that we'd do better next time and send them on their way knowing they'd get refunds for the unused day. I've never seen a happier bunch of passengers as they gathered in the parking lot and waved good-bye.

Back in Briceburg, it turned out that all our disabled truck needed was a jump. We promised to replace the generator as soon as we got back to Groveland. And that was it. As we piled into the truck, I yelled thanks and good-bye to Jack Bass, but he wasn't listening. He was lost in the joy of lording over that beer and gas-oline-soaked stretch of river, his arms around a pair of teenage runaways from Modesto. Downriver, the miners were still shooting guns, smoking, pot, and scraping the bottom of the river for tiny flakes of gold. That crazy little girl was keeping just ahead of the drunk 12-year-old chasing her, both of them laughing. And our passengers were headed home. As nearly as I could tell, everyone was happy to be exactly where they were at that moment. And as I steered the truck onto Highway 140 and watched the Merced disappear behind me, so was I.

WHALE

JERRY HUGHES

YEARS BEFORE CURT HANSEN BECAME "WHALE," we grew up together in tiny Hazelton, Idaho. Curt's big brother Larry and big sis Connie were high school upper classmen we all admired, as was my sis, Roberta aka "Bertie" who was a classmate with Connie. Small town Idaho for sure.

Curt and I were pals, and eventually at a young age got into our first misadventure together. We decided to raid Mr. Thompson's gooseberry patch. We made the raid but did not escape cleanly. Curt (age five) had a relatively high-speed bike with training wheels and did get away. At age four, I tried to elude pissed-off Mr. Thompson on a tricycle. I was dead meat. Curt's parents and mine were bummed that it seemed like the two of us were started into a life of crime. They didn't know about river running yet.

The next adventure of note was playing Little League Baseball for the Hazelton Lions, sponsored, of course, by the Hazelton Lions Club. What fun. Practices, games, fans, uniforms, road trips, no groupies…Bob English was coach. Whale and I shared playing catcher and outfield, depending on the game.

From 1963-65, we played football for Valley High School—the Vikings. Whale was a tackle and I was tailback. I carried the ball many times behind Curt's blocks. I remember all those practices, games, chilly fall days in pads.

In 1965 when Curt graduated, I was A junior. He had already signed up for the US Army. On graduation night, Whale and some pals did the expected. They drank some beer and got in trouble. Not serious trouble, but trouble nonetheless. No charges against Curt because he was off to the University of Viet Nam.

My high school senior year 1966, Curt showed up at school, and he was in uniform and lean and mean after boot camp. Curt was never actually very mean. But he was slim and fit. I worried about him going to Southeast Asia. He seemed okay with it. The girls flocked to hug him in his uniform.

After my first year at University of Idaho, I hired on with Hatch River Expeditions in May of 1967. I Worked that first year in Dinosaur National Monument and Idaho. I started guiding in Grand Canyon in June of 1968.

I would hear bits and pieces about Curt in Viet Nam throughout the time he was there. Nothing directly from him. Then, during the college spring break of 1969, I was boating a geology field trip (Doc Barrs, Four Corners Geologic Society—wow what fun trips) for Hatch during March. Whale was there training on the Hatch crew. He took me aside, and told me that he had heard about Hatch from our mutual high school friends Mike Weatherwax and Brick Wells who were already on the Hatch crew. He told me he used me for a reference with Ted. Hoped that was okay. Of course it was. Curt and I were back together, this time working for Hatch River Expeditions. We boated together in The Grand Canyon, on the Yampa/Green, and the Middle Fork of the Salmon during the next few summers.

Curt became "Whale" on the Hatch Crew. Story has it that, after a night of revelry, Curt was "sleeping" very soundly (perhaps passed out) on the beach. Early in the morning the Colorado was lapping up against him while guests were waking up. A woman exclaimed, "My God, he looks like a beached whale." It stuck. Curt was "Whale," "Whaler," or "The Whale."

In those Hatch years, Whale didn't like to talk about Viet Nam. But one night he did. We were camped illegally in the bay at Havasu with the moonlight reflecting off the white cliffs. He was haunted by the war. I'm sure he would be considered a PTSD victim today. Door gunner firefights with a 50 caliber machine gun in his hands were over the top for sweet, mild mannered Whale. His first crew on a gunship were all wounded or died, and Whale was still there. Then, many of the replacements to the wounded/dead crew members were also wounded or killed. Whale lived on. Sitting on top of his bullet proof vest to save the family jewels rather than protecting his body cavity. He made it through. Survivor's remorse. Curt came home and went to Grand Canyon.

From then on, we all know the story. Over the years, Whale was the best guide, or the maybe much less than best, depending on the trip. Mark Smith, Grand Canyon Expeditions, sent me a large color image of Whale's wrecked Hatch 33 footer at Hance rapid. Mark knew Whale visited us in Idaho, and wanted me to have that image with the NPS helicopter hovering over the wrapped pontoon. I put it up on the Hughes River Expeditions office wall for the next time Whale would come by. He never made it back to see Mark's picture. The picture is still hanging in the same place, right over the copy machine. I think of Curt every day when I see it.

After one of Whale's firings from Hatch, he worked for Fred Burke. Fred wanted to have a father/son talk with Whale to help him get some positive direction. Whaler was in such a "give a shit" mood that the "father/son" conversation ended with Fred firing Whale on the spot. Whale bounced around all the Grand Canyon outfits a bit. Worked for most or all of them, and was fired by some more than once. But everyone loved the Whale, even the outfitters who fired him. And, in balance, Whale was a damned fine, knowledgeable Grand Canyon river guide. He carried a heavy burden the rest of us didn't, and my guess is he did the best he could.

What a blow to hear of his death.

I've shared some images of Whale. River photos from around 1969-71. High school images of Curt. I Wish it were still the fall of 1964 and we were getting ready to play the dreaded Wendell Trojans in football, or 1971 scouting Lava Falls before rowing some Hatch 33-footers down the left side, or taking out 10 man rafts and loading the trucks at the Confluence of the Middle Fork and Main Salmon.

In Idaho, we have the beginning of an organization similar to the Whale Foundation: The Redside Foundation (www.redside-foundation.org). This offspring is a tribute to beloved Idaho guide Telly Evans—also a suicide victim, and indirectly to Whale. From afar, all of us Idaho guides have admired the Whale Foundation. I'm confident that The Redside Foundation will be a big success too.

I hope this message brings a smile to some old boatmen. I loved the Whale.

OLD DAN

DICK LINFORD

WHITEWATER RAFTING BEGAN IN CALIFORNIA in the 1960s, on the Stanislaus River. The section we ran was in the central California foothills between the towns of Sonora and Angels Camp. The river was amazingly remote, having carved a beautiful and inaccessible canyon through limestone. It gave us a nine-mile stretch of river that had Class III rapids, spectacular canyon walls, beautiful tributaries and great campsites.

Joe Daly and I started our company in 1972. We were the eighth company in the state and we apologized to the other seven companies because we felt that we were going to overcrowd the river.

Everyone ran two-day trips on this nine-mile stretch. We would meet our guests at our takeout, Parrott's Ferry, the morning of the trip, and drive them to the put-in spot, called Camp Nine. It was a two-hour ride on a bumpy, windy road. In the early days none of us had buses. We packed people in the backs of trucks. Some were stake-side vehicles. One outfitter built benches in a trailer to carry his people. I have to admit that, in our first year, we would rent a U-Haul box-bed truck, pack our guests in the box, and shut the door on them. They would arrive, two hours later, half-asphyxiated by carbon monoxide and car sick, but happy to be there. Rafters were tougher in those early days. They were also expected to bring their own sleeping bags, tents, and eating utensils; to do their own dishes and cook their steaks. As for chairs, are you kidding me? We sat on logs and rocks.

Once we got people to Camp Nine, we would float maybe three miles to Rose Creek, a lovely tributary, where we would spend several hours hiking, swimming, and diving into deep pools. Sometimes we would have lunch there. Sometimes we would float a bit downstream to help thin out the crowds.

We were floating through public land, managed by the Bureau of Land Management, or BLM. The agency issued us special use permits, and then pretty much stayed out of our way. They had no interest in and no knowledge of how to manage rafting companies. They charged us a whopping twenty-five cents per user-day, and let us report our own numbers. (A user-day is a paying passenger per day. Ten passengers on a two-day trip constituted twenty user-days.)

The biggest issue was campsites. We had several shouting matches over who got what site, and once two outfitters squared off, one with an axe, the other with a pistol. Fortunately, after a bit of chest pounding, they worked things out.

But the near-brawl informed us that we needed a forum where issues could be discussed rationally, so we founded The Pacific River Outfitters Association, or PROA. One of the most responsible things we did was agree to limit our trip size to 25 guests and five rafts. We also agreed to store nothing but porta potties in camp. The 25-guest limit helped us spread river use away from Saturday-Sunday trips. Friday-Saturday trips were next most popular and, by the late 1970s, outfitters were often running trips every day of the week. Spreading the river use out not only preserved a semblance of a wilderness experience; it also made economic sense. Using a few rafts several days a week was much better than using a lot of rafts just on Saturday and Sunday. Plus it gave our guides several days of work per week.

We all put in at Camp Nine and took out at Parrott's Ferry. There was no river access between these two spots. You could float an additional four miles to the Highway 49 Bridge, but the river was neither exciting nor pretty.

Old Dan lived in a cabin at Parrott's Ferry. We never got a last name. He was simply Old Dan. He must have been well into his seventies. He had white hair and a white beard; he wore Levis, cowboy boots and a black Stetson, and he had a pistol holstered on his side. He was never hostile or threatening, but the sidearm demanded respect. And he did mean business. He told us that we were welcome to take out on his land as long as we kept the place clean AND paid him a dollar per raft. Cash only. He would appear as soon as boats landed, expecting payment.

Old Dan wasn't getting rich. Maybe a hundred rafts would take out there each week, for maybe four months. But keep in mind that this was the early 1970s, and a hundred bucks went a lot farther then that is does today. In 1972 we charged $45 per person for a two-day trip, and we paid our guides $20 a day. Still, we were more than willing to pay Dan. It was his land after all, and it came to about what we were paying BLM.

Rafting evolved from a cutting-edge sport to mainstream recreation in the late 1970s. The number of people taking trips increased exponentially, our prices soared, and we made trips more comfortable for the general public. We started to supply eating utensils, tents, sleeping bags, expensive sleeping pads and chairs. Some people brought tables and cots. The price of a two-day trip is now around $280—a six-fold increase. Our costs soared as well. Guide wages pretty much kept up with trip prices, and our fees to the government rose to 3% of our gross income, which is a thirtyfold increase. If Old Dan's fees had risen in pace with our income and expenses, he could have done very well for himself. He could have been sitting on a gold mine. But that was not to be.

When we arrived early one spring, sometime in the late 1970s, Old Dan was gone. So was his cabin. We thought this was a bit strange, and called BLM to find out what had happened. BLM told us that Dan had been squatting on the land for years. He had never owned it. They had evicted him and razed his cabin. They had no idea he had been charging us.

Nobody likes to be scammed. But somehow I have no hard feelings toward Old Dan. The guy either had brass balls, or he really thought we owed him. Maybe both. Here we were, urban hippie types playing in his backyard, even if he didn't own the yard. Whatever it was, he saw a good thing and took it. And wasn't that the spirit of the Old West?

Dick and Suzie Linford, with daughters, Eliza,
Coral and Rachel. Rogue River, 2013.

Peter Fox

All The Difference

PETER FOX

WE WERE BOTH NAKED. SHE WAS NAPPING and I was propped against a sleeping bag next to her in the shade. Life appeared to be going perfectly. We were just behind the beach, good current in the South Fork of the American River passing close to our screen of branches. It was May 24, 1981. I was watching a commercial raft trip passing on the water. My gray Avon Pro was pulled up on the beach, bowline well secured to a tree, river bags, boxes, and a red 60-quart Gott cooler piled in the shade.

A boatman rowed an oar boat past, and then the paddle boats drifted by, each steered by a guide and filled with guests. For every guide there were eight passengers taking in the sights. They were looking at the river, each other, at the canyon. Meanwhile, the guides looked over and read our beach.

I watched each of them start by looking over the pulled up raft, then the overnight gear unloaded, and the bowline tied off with care. I was close enough to see the understanding in their eyes that this raft was squared away for the night, because they quickly switched to looking for us. Anyone on that beach would be keeping out of the blazing sun, so they began scanning the shady spots.

We were well hidden, not easily picked out from the water. One by one, their gazes traveled along the tree line, probing into the coolest pockets till they alighted on my face and the suggestion of bare skin through the thicket. I grinned at them and they grinned at me.

Every one of the guides saw us. I watched them each follow the same path of discovery to where we lay, while not a single passenger had the slightest idea we even existed.

That summer I was starting my second season guiding in the foothills of California. I had started as a total neophyte the year before. I hadn't so much found river guiding as river guiding had found me; rescued me more like. I was six years out of college with no prospects and no long term plans. Linda was a very good friend, a smart directed classmate on her way to medical school. For a couple days on the river, our hearts beat to the same tune. The heat and titillation of a new beginning mirrored by the California sun caressing a beautiful beach.

It was a day that almost never happened. Our friendship almost never had this brief bloom of romance. Because four days earlier, I had been locked in a very different kind of embrace. Cut off in an Idaho canyon by a wild flooding river, my heart had pounded to a very different beat, the beat of adrenaline as I rowed the biggest rapids I had ever seen. My new life as a river guide was all over the map.

The Idaho trip came up out of the blue a couple weeks earlier, when Bob Melville and I had faced each other, shading our eyes from the afternoon glare, outside the South Fork guide house. Bob, my rafting manager, was as experienced as I was new at river rafting. His craggy face mapped a thousand river days and testified to the limitless stories he had to tell. He had just made me a proposition and it hung in the air between us as we studied each other's faces. His friends, from years guiding in the Grand Canyon, were doing a private trip on the Selway River in Idaho and they needed another hand. My rendezvous with Linda was still a couple of weeks away. Bob and I would be well back in California by the time she and I planned to be together. The Selway trip was only going to be five days on the water. No problem.

Bob's brown eyes sized me up like a man about to buy a horse. I was big and strong enough to help with the heavy work. More to the point, I had a truck and he needed reliable transportation for the thirty hours driving back and forth to Idaho. My '78 orange Datsun was standing demurely by. I tried to judge if it was me, or the truck he really wanted. But it really didn't matter "Yeah," I said, " I'd love to go."

Topping the pass from Sun Valley into the Salmon River drainage, we were twelve hours into our all night drive to the Selway when Bob opened gritty eyes to the first light over the Sawtooth's. He turned to me, voice hoarse from a night of storytelling, and told me he had decided not to go on the Selway. "Don't worry, he said "you can row the boat. I just have a bad feeling."

At the Selway putin, we stood looking at the flow gauge reading 4.5 feet, a moderately high level for the river. Big water, but considered in a safe range. But Bob could not be convinced to change his mind. Everyone else was feeling good about the trip. His friends looked like the cast of a cowboy movie, drooping mustaches and tanned faces, all seasoned guides, with years at the oars: Bob Center, Randy Breckinridge, Steve Dupuis, Steve Cutright They slouched in a semi-circle listening to what Bob had to say as if it were the most natural thing in the world that a man might have a bad foreboding, and it made perfect sense for him to act on it, no matter that he had just driven 15 hours from California to go on the trip. They respected Bob's decision, even if it meant missing their friend and putting a rookie at the oars of one of their boats. The faces around me looked focused and prepared. I looked inside myself and I just felt excited. Deep in the mountains of Idaho, as the newest conscript of the Butch Cassidy and the Sundance Kid gang, I watched Bob drive my orange truck back up the road.

We had a clean first three days on the river, challenging rapids but good runs. Our head boatman, Steve Dupuis looked like the Sundance Kid, blond and dashing. He had chosen our camp at the top of Moose Creek Gorge for the third night, and had planned for a two-night stay there. We all rousted out on morning number four onto a trail heading back upstream a half mile to a suspension bridge across the main branch of the Selway. Hiking up and over the hump of a narrow peninsula we passed the sign for a ranger station on our way to a second suspension bridge, this one over Moose Creek, a medium sized river almost as big as the main Selway. On the far bank, we turned down a trail traversing the canyon wall a couple hundred feet above the river, and spent all day scouting the succession of big rapids, which we were preparing to run the next day.

This was the only way to see them all: Double Drop, Ladle, Little Niagra, Big Drop, Puzzle Creek. This was the stretch of rapids that earned the Selway its reputation as a famous whitewater river, too serious to run sight unseen. There was no place to stop on the river once you got into the gorge. At the end of our hike, we were eight miles by trail from where we started, six miles as the river flows from our camp.

Foot weary and almost back to our tents, we stumbled into the camp of another party just upstream of ours. There is only one private permit issued each day for the 47 miles of the Selway's Wild and Scenic stretch. This reasonably experienced and nice group of folks had launched the day after us and were planning to do what we had just done, go look at the rapids on a layover day. We trudged the final feet back into camp, made dinner and were driven to our tents by a sky opening up and dumping rain. In the morning everything had changed.

Where the night before our boats had been cinched up tight and our tents a safe 30 feet from the river's edge. That morning we woke with the river inches away from our sleeping bags and boats milling in waist-deep water like spooked horses, wide-eyed and straining at the ropes.

The Sundance Kid stood on a rock in the gray morning, his raincoat open, sucking his mustache and studying the river. After a while he stepped down and in a matter-of—fact tone, made it clear that we weren't going anywhere except to hike someone up to the ranger station's airstrip and fly out for a couple of extra day's food. A river that had been 4.5 feet at putin, had just risen vertical feet. The Selway at levels over 6 feet was a very serious proposition. What we were looking at was a lot higher than that and not something to mess with.

The neighbors in the upstream camp put in their hours on the scouting hike that day, and came to the same conclusion Steve had made in about a minute. Stay put till the water level backed down.

By late afternoon, when the rain had mostly stopped, a third rafting party careened around the corner and bundled themselves into a makeshift camp above the other two. This group, obviously the least experienced and least well equipped of the three rafting parties woke up the next morning, hiked far enough to get a quick look at the first rapids and said they were going to run the gorge. "Piece of cake," their leader proclaimed. Steve tried to talk them out of it. Others tried too, but they had their minds made up. There was nothing left to do but grab our cameras and head downstream.

Clouds pressed onto the tips of cedar trees on the ridge. We were glad for our sweaters and rain gear. Most of our group agreed that the main action would take place at Ladle, the longest and most renowned rapid in the gorge. But I had a feeling that Double Drop, the very first rapid, was going to cause some trouble. So I watched my companions disappear around a curve in the trail, and scrambled and slid down the canyon wall to a flat boulder at eye level with the first whipsaw turn of the rapid. I levered a fresh roll of Kodachrome 64 into my Canon FTB and waited.

When they finally came, it was over in a minute. The red stripes on the rafts and the drawn faces above orange life jackets materialized suddenly out of the gloom and plunged into the rapid. I was close enough to see the terror grow in their eyes. Straight down the bore of my 200 mm lens I watched three out of four rafts slammed upside down, driving their occupants deep into the maelstrom a few feet from where I sat. Panning my view downstream, I cranked off several more frames of wetsuited figures scrambling onto an overturned raft and the one upright boat swamped and floundered against the cliff wall, before they both disappeared around the corner and I was again alone at the bottom of the canyon.

The first thing my companions saw waiting downstream at Ladle was the black bottom of a solitary overturned raft with a broken oar bobbing next to it as it ran through the rapid alone and disappeared downstream.

I scrambled up to the trail above Double Drop as fast as I could and jogged toward Ladle. About halfway there, something ghostly white moving through the trees ahead on the trail brought me to a stop. The apparition resolved into man with wild hair shuffling fast toward me in a pair of ripped up wetsuit booties. In his mid-thirties, wearing a turned down farmer john's wetsuit over a soaked white t-shirt, he had obviously found a place to clamber up the steep canyon walls from the river. He had no jacket or rain gear to brace against the chilly afternoon, just the wet clothes on his back. He grabbed me by the arm and I could feel the heat of his breath as he shouted into my face.

"Where the hell is that airstrip? My son of a bitch brother-in-law flipped me twice already and today he just about killed me. I am getting a plane and I am never setting foot in a raft again as long as I live and that son of a bitch brother-in—law of mine can go to hell!"

Stepping out of his grip, I pointed up the trail and watched his T-shirt melt into the forest in the direction of the suspension bridges at the confluence. Our guys flying in the extra food found him by the dirt runway when their single engine plane taxied up to the ranger station. He jumped right on board with the motor still running and the ranger reported that they bee-lined straight to the Boise Airport where he bought a one way ticket and boarded the first flight back to Milwaukee, still in his wetsuit and booties.

The next day, with the water down a couple of notches, we got through Double Drop with almost all of our boats right side up.

From the vantage point of being the last boat in line, I watched the cowboys rope the one upside down stray and turn it back right side up with a guy in the rowing seat before the river swept us all around the next turn. It was damned impressive. These guys knew what they were doing. By the time we made it through the Gorge—we learned later the river was still running over 7 feet—I had learned some lessons I would never forget, and I made it back to California only two days late for my date with Linda.

It was an eventful summer. I flew to La Jolla to see her again in July. In bed together, she broke down. Since she last saw me, she realized she still loved her old boyfriend, one of our best friends. I got dressed and spent the night in a park under a tree. As my flight was about to board, she rushed into the departure gate in tears, to say goodbye. They went on to get married. He became a lawyer and she became a doctor. We are all still good friends. It turned out to be for the best.

However, it didn't feel that way when I was flying alone back to my less than straight and narrow path; to water that was getting lower and lower in the foothills of northern California. But even a broken heart healed up fast that summer. Fantastic things were happening. A boatman named Ian Madin brought this cutting edge new piece of technology down the river. It was the highest tech thing we had ever seen and it threatened the electronics free purity of life on the river. Change is hard. We eyed the device like it was a rattlesnake in our camp. That is until we tried it. It was called a Sony Walkman.

The water kept going down. Each week saw a lower water level on the Tuolumne and new challenges to be met. We were a new generation of boatmen. For some reason all the seasoned guides had moved on and some very athletic but inexperienced rookies were left to figure things out, either for ourselves or from a couple of smart, slender, experienced women who didn't have the strength to muscle their way down a river. That summer, as we all walked the water level of the T down the ladder, these women taught us that to get a heavy boat down a hard river, you had better let the water do the work.

Now Dewi Butler was one of that cadre of athletic new boatmen and there are some important things to know about him. First, he is a Welshman and a rugby player. Never get in a wrestling match with him. Second, by his standards, grabbing your balls at the bottom of the scrum is funny as hell. Though as he would tell it, "Peter, I am a Welshman and a gentleman. We never grab balls, we grab testicles."

Dewi and I both started guiding in '80, and cut our chops together among an outstanding cohort of boatmen, rowing Avon Pros on the Tuolumne. Dewi and I couldn't have been any more different in the way we approached the craft of rowing a river. My way was about feeling it, becoming locked in to the movement and flow of the moment. Dewi's way was to calculate the precise number of strokes to take, especially at the crux points in rapids, and then to execute the plan flawlessly. As different as they were, our two approaches yielded about the same amount of success.

That is, until this one time, late that summer, on a three day Tuolumne trip, where I was having the worst run of my life. I just couldn't get the feel, couldn't get into any kind of a rhythm. As frustrated as I was, I was also blind to good judgment and tried for a little sympathy from my Welch friend at takeout. He found this hilarious and a good opportunity for good old fashioned Welsh therapy to help me get over myself. He and the other guides tackled me and wrestled me to the sand. This was where I learned my lesson about wrestling with a Welch rugby player. But that was just a side show.

The last morning of the trip, we had all woken at the North Fork camp. Geologist, philosopher, and man ahead of his time, Ian Madin with his Walkman, John Storrer (called JC—short for Jesus Christ—because of his long hair and saintly appearance), Dewi, and me.

It was after breakfast that I got my turn to try Ian's Walkman, and I remember exactly where I was standing: on a gravel ledge overlooking the peaceful canyon, with the Talking Heads blowing the top of my head off. Nothing remotely that size or sound quality had ever existed. If I hadn't tried it myself, I wouldn't have believed it.

It took me a while to recover. The morning was a Sunday and as usual on Sundays we were waiting for the water to come up. Rocks choked the river in front of our camp. The hydroelectric draw on the dams upstream were not as great on a Sunday. We were dawdling around, packing boats in a leisurely fashion and keeping an eye out for water.

At some point, after lunch we began to wonder if the water might be coming up a little later than usual. A late summer trip still afforded plenty of daylight, but we had an appointed meeting time with the passenger bus at Ward's Ferry Bridge. Somewhere as the afternoon started to wear on toward 2 o'clock, we realized that we no longer had the luxury of waiting in camp. We pushed our four boats about ten yards off the beach, which was the first place they got stuck. Then on into a puddle of water leading to a trickle of current into the place where the main channel should have been.

It was an afternoon of seeking enough water between rocks to place our oars. We scrabbled our boats from one little pond to the next. At the end of each, we would jump into knee-deep water to heave the rafts one by one over the rocks and drag them to the next bit of water where they could actually float. Each of our Avon Pro's carried four passengers and all the camping gear, cooking gear and stuff needed for 20 people to camp out and eat for three days. They were heavy and I can't ever remember "rowing" that long afternoon for more than a hundred feet before we again had to heave the boats by brute force over the rocks. The entire remainder of that August day was spent with heads down, muscles straining, and eyes glancing upstream for signs of the river coming up. The sun fell below the rim of the canyon. Dusk found us still manhandling boats from pool to landlocked pool. Dark caught up to us as we reached a little beach above Pinball rapid miles of heavy labor since we left the camp at the North Fork.

Standing above Pinball, we could just peek around a bend in the canyon to see the headlights of the bus sweep the hillside as the driver gave up on us, turned around and headed back up the road, leaving us stranded several hundred yards away. In the gathering dark, it was now too dangerous to have any of the passengers on the water, so we unloaded all their black rubberized canvas river bags onto a small beach, and sent them carefully picking their way down the shore toward the bridge at takeout.

We tied two boats off above the rapid, and cursing and grunting, hauled the other two boats with kitchen gear and remaining food over a wall of rocks and through the boulder field that was Pinball rapid minus the water. It was a low snow pack year, and the reservoir was very low so that when we reached the bridge, we were able to park the boats right along the bottom concrete footing of the bridge tower. There we built a fire and made a camp kitchen with the bridge 100 feet over our heads against the starry sky; until the heat of the fire exploded an air pocket in the concrete and we had to move it to shore.

JC had jogged up to the road and hitch-hiked a ride from a lone truck, to go get us some transportation. Down around us in the dark, the passengers were rummaging through their bags, changing clothes, and doing their best to settle in when one gentleman came up to us and said he and another fellow couldn't find their bags. Leaving dinner preparation where it lay, we spread out to search the makeshift camp with the light from our headlamps, looking for the bags we were sure would be there. No luck. We searched again all around the area. It was about this time that we heard a low rushing sound. Be damned if it wasn't the river finally coming up, its pulse getting louder and the level of the inky water rising up the bridge abutment.

We were all standing at the edge of this concrete dock, shuffling our feet and wondering what to do next, when Dewi started to reason out loud.

"We unloaded all the black bags onto that beach above Pinball before it became too dark to see."

"Everyone grabbed bags and walked downstream."

"The bags aren't here. Could they somehow have been left on the beach? That's not too likely, but it was pretty dark and if they're not here…"

"If they're not here, and the water just came up, it would have washed right over that little beach up there and the bags, being waterproof would float… would have floated away and been carried downstream by the current…and since we are on the same side of the river as that beach, they would probably have to float past us right about here where we are standing."

As Dewi turned toward the river, his headlamp swept out across the dark river now flowing past us at a good rate, We all followed his reasoning and his gaze exactly as he turned. At that exact moment, his light swept across two black bags bobbing by in the current at the foot of the slab. Dewi just took a step, reached down and neatly plucked them out of the water saying, "I believe these are the bags you are looking for."

A month later, with fall coming to the foothills, I was back driving my orange Datsun truck up a winding road out of a winding river canyon, this time all by myself. It was the end of the season and I was moving back to the Bay Area for the winter. Another winter without a girlfriend, but this time I would *not* be lacking a plan. I had a good feeling. Come spring, my truck would be loaded again and I'd be driving back down this very road. Not the straight and narrow road of making something out of my life. Just a winding road leading down into a canyon where rivers and river guides rarely followed a straight line, but always knew exactly where they were going in a way that now, to me, made perfect sense.

Dan Steiner, circa 1982

THE BIRD

DAN STEINER

BACK IN '81, AS I WAS FINISHING UP MY FIRST YEAR of law school at UC Berkeley, I hit the summer job trifecta. I lined up a salaried weekday position with the county prosecutor's office in Bakersfield, a weekend gig as a Kern guide, and free full-time lodging at a guide house in Lake Isabella. Three months of crime-busting, whitewater and beer! What wasn't there to like?

No one warned me about the bird.

Tom Moore was our Kern River bossman that summer. When I rolled into town in mid-June, the bird was already shacking up at the guide house. It only took me a New York minute to see what was going on. Tom had fallen hard for the bird. Under normal circumstances, of course, neither I, nor any of my fellow guides, would have given a damn. After all, as the poet says, the heart wants what it wants. And river guides, to their credit, tend to be a live-and-let-live bunch. So yes, none of us would have given a rat's ass about Tom's thing for the bird. Had it not been for the one complication.

Before we get to the complication, there's something you need to understand. This bird of Tom's wasn't just another pigeon, fresh from the park. The bird was an *Ara chloropterus*—a green-winged macaw—and what a magnificent macaw it was! Glossy emerald wings. A dazzling scarlet breast. Taut trim talons. And that beak! Too big, to be sure, but somehow that big old beak only added to the bird's overall allure. To describe Tom's macaw in, ahem, a nutshell? A practically perfect parrot package.

The guides all knew this, of course. The bird knew it, too, and what's more, the bird didn't hesitate to flaunt it. Truth be told, I've never been much into macaws. I've always been more of a lorikeet man, myself. But when that bird of Tom's got to strutting, and preening, and flashing those tail feathers? Well, let's just put it this way. It didn't matter what kind of parrot you were into. A guide couldn't help but notice.

And therein lay the one complication. *A guide couldn't help but notice.* Chief among the noticers were a pair of first year guides whose names I've long since forgotten, but whom I can still picture in my mind's eye: a bantamweight blonde and her big, bearded lug of a boyfriend. Blondie coupled boundless energy with the attention span of a fruit fly. Lug was strong as an ox and, on a good day, perhaps half as bright. Between the two of them, they possessed about as much common sense as your average house fern. Even so, they were pleasant enough, and as first year guides go, you could certainly do worse. But you could tell, right off, that both of those tinhorns had serious things for the bird.

The tinhorns weren't alone. Practically all of the guides struggled with bird things of their own. Even I had a twinge of a thing for the bird. The sole exception was Mike O'Malley, who had no bird thing himself and was critical of those who did. As a veteran guide, Mike believed in time-tested protocols. And as everybody knows, you don't mess with your bossman's bird. It's a cardinal rule of the river. Violating the rule breeds tension and disharmony in a guide house and can only lead to tragedy.

Those first few weeks, as June gave way to July, all of us guides tried very hard to adhere to the cardinal rule. I'll tell you this, though. It wasn't easy. Tom would no sooner turn his back than that bird of his would start waggling its tush at whatever guide was nearby, bobbing its beak and squawking "Ooh, baby!" or "You're a peach!" or some other pet phrase it had picked up from Tom in a private moment. I'm no prude. But the bird was utterly shameless. I felt bad for Tom. And I worried about what might happen downstream.

Meanwhile, I was doing my best to settle in at the Kern County prosecutor's office. At first, the career prosecutors didn't know what to make of me. Gauged by river guide standards, duded up in a tie and jacket with my hair brushed and my beard trimmed, I looked downright corporate. Gauged by prosecutor standards, however, I looked more like Charlie Manson's kid brother. My Berkeley connection didn't help. It took a good month for the career guys to stop thinking of me as an anarchist, and to accept me as their dedicated, crime-busting brother-in-arms.

Over this same period, mid-June to mid-July, weeknights at Lake Isabella rapidly became a living hell. Following ten hours at the office and an hour-long commute back from Bakersfield, I'd return to the guide house to find the bird strutting and screeching, the tinhorns looking and leering, O'Malley tsk-tsking and tut-tutting, and Tom, still smitten, simply sitting and smiling, oblivious to everything but the bird. It got to the point where I was hanging out at the Duck Blind Inn practically every evening—shooting pool and drinking and spending money I didn't have—just to get away.

The nights he was off river, O'Malley would sometimes wing-man me at the Duck Blind. We'd feed the jukebox and drink beer-and-shots right up to last call. O'Malley and I have been friends for a long time. In all the years I've known him, Mike has always been reasonable and fun to be around. Except for that summer of '81, when he was neither. Mike was positively puritanical when it came to the bird, and unrelentingly rigid when it came to the cardinal rule. Evenings at the Duck Blind, he could talk of nothing else. Meanwhile, Blondie and Lug were exhibiting increasingly erratic behavior. One weekend on the river, they started arguing over which one of them the bird liked best. Those two tinhorns nearly came to fisticuffs, right in front of the guests.

If my work at the prosecutor's office taught me anything, it's just how wacko people can be. Every day, I dealt with cases where seemingly normal folks had gone right off the deep end and done some truly crazy shit. It's not as though I was convinced that Lug or Blondie—or, for that matter, O'Malley or Tom—would get violent and do something stupid. Still, I couldn't rule out the possibility. The situation was clearly getting out of hand. Something needed to be done. The time was ripe for bold and decisive action.

Even so, as July marched towards August, I took no bold or decisive action. Instead, I dithered and dallied and did nothing at all. You remember Act III of Hamlet? Those endless scenes where Hamlet roams around Elsinore, spouting iambic pentameter, basically admitting that he has no frigging clue what to do next? That was me. Kern County was my Elsinore. But with less fog. And more bikers.

Even Hamlet eventually got off his ass. In early August, I finally got off mine. I developed an action plan. My plan was to seize the floor at our upcoming all-guide meeting and propose that we banish the bird. I marshaled a host of arguments in favor of my proposal. Given my extensive legal training and the sheer intellectual force of my arguments, I was confident that I could persuade my fellow guides to go along. The evening of our scheduled all-guide meeting, I left the prosecutor's office just before sundown. I hopped in my battered VW bug, cranked down the windows, and headed for the guide house.

Outside of Bakersfield, where Route 178 enters the Kern River Canyon on its ascent to Lake Isabella, the narrow, two-lane road zigs and zags for eight or ten miles, flanked by a sheer canyon wall on one side and a vertiginous drop down to the river on the other. As I drove uphill in the twilight, rehearsing aloud my forthcoming pitch to my colleagues, a great winged creature materialized from out of the canyon. The creature swept low over my VW, nearly brushing the windshield, before gliding away into the dusk. I'll admit I was startled. No shame in that. You'd be startled too, if a hellhound-sized harpy came at you from out of the abyss.

It might have been an owl, I suppose. I don't know. But I definitely know a portent when I see one. That creature was a sure sign that something really bad was at hand. Sure enough, when I arrived at the guide house, most of the guides were lounging moodily on the front porch, drinking beer. Lug, looking pale and out of sorts, was guzzling bourbon straight from the bottle. "The meeting is cancelled," he said. "The bird is dead."

The words no sooner left Lug's lips than my prosecutorial instincts kicked into overdrive. I knew, in an instant, that the violence I'd feared had come to pass. An Aracide—a murder both foul and fowl! Committed right in our very own guide house! As to the particulars of the bloody business, there wasn't a scintilla of uncertainty in my mind. The bird was obviously the victim of a crime of parrot passion, a crime that had doubtless been perpetrated by one of my fellow guides.

Needless to say, I felt terrible. To be sure, I hadn't done the deadly and dastardly deed. Yet hadn't I been the one who had dithered and dallied? And but for my dithering and dallying—but for my abject failure to take bold and decisive action—wouldn't the bird be alive and fluttering with us still? Didn't ultimate responsibility for this senseless tragedy thereby fall on me?

My orgy of self-recrimination was soon interrupted. Lug explained that the bird, after perching in the sun all afternoon, had collapsed and died. The cause of death was heatstroke. On hearing Lug's post-mortem, I felt a little sad. Mostly, though, I just felt sheepish and relieved. I grabbed a couple of six-packs from an open cooler on the porch and walked around to the rear of the guide house. There, on the back patio, I found O'Malley and Blondie and Tom, sitting in lawn chairs, side-by-side in the dark. I pulled up an empty lawn chair and cracked open beers for the four of us. We then sat in silence. We sat for a long time, sipping our brews and staring out into the night.*

*AUTHOR'S NOTE

In order to ensure the accuracy and authenticity of this story, I commissioned a pre-publication fact check by Mike O'Malley and his wife, Lauren. Mike agrees that he and I both guided on the Kern River back in '81, that I worked weekdays at the county prosecutor's office, and that Tom Moore had a pet bird that died sometime in the early 1980s. As for the other events I have reported, Mike claims that they didn't happen, or at least not the way I remember them. Lauren, for her part, claims my story "is pretty much wrong on all salient points." Their claims are not surprising. As any prosecutor will tell you, conflicting testimony between and among eyewitnesses is not uncommon, particularly when testimony is not solicited until long after the events at issue have transpired. For the record, I would simply note that this is not the O'Malleys' story. It's mine. And I'm sticking to it.

John Cassidy

Batman

JOHN CASSIDY

THE ROAD TO LUMSDEN BRIDGE ACROSS THE TUOLUMNE RIVER in Northern California is a steep 6 miles of dirt and big views that was originally carved for horse and foot traffic before the turn of the last century. During the Depression it was widened to take the occasional truck or flivver but has not, in the intervening 80 years, received a great deal more of road engineering attention.

The geology is typical of the Sierra Nevada foothills, a fractured and upended mix of bedrock, chert and various sedimentaries. Lumsden road cuts across the layers at a steep angle and the result is a ragged and bumpy ride.

In July of 1981 I was on the Lumsden road, driving with two friends and filled with the intent of kayaking the 11 miles of river that started at the bottom of the road and that all of us had done many times before. This day, however, was a little more fraught than usual. The stretch just upstream of ours—Cherry Creek—was our real goal. The plan was to paddle our kayaks on the familiar 11 miles, and then, properly emboldened, take on Cherry Creek tomorrow morning. Today's trip, in other words, was no more than a warm-up, the undercard for tomorrow's big matchup.

But all of that was still 3 bumpy miles away as we crept down Lumsden road, hairpin by hairpin.

"I heard a boatman got bitten on the lip by a bat a few weeks ago," I said, over my shoulder. "During the day. He was napping at lunch."

Barry and Rimbeaux were in the back. The three of us had known each other for years and been on countless trips on various rivers together, either as professional river guides or on our own in kayaks, as we were today.

"Where?" Asked somebody from the back of the van.

"On the lip. On his mouth."

"No. I mean what river?"

"This one. The Tuolumne."

"I don't believe it. A bat lands on his mouth in the middle of the day and bites him? No. Wrong."

"That's what I heard. A couple of weeks ago. At the Clavey."

"Who?"

"I don't know. Some guy."

"Ridiculous."

"No really. It happened."

"No it didn't."

We passed another mile or two of sparkling repartee like this.

Neither of them had the slightest faith (or interest, for that matter) in my amazing and fascinating fact.

Until Jerry Jacques paddled up.

The three of us had just finished launching our boats and were making final preparations in the little piece of still water called Lumsden's Pool (now known as Meral's Pool) when we were joined by a single boater who'd put in, apparently unseen by us, just upstream. He paddled up to Barry who was drifting a bit behind. The two of them fell into conversation.

"Hey!" We heard Barry holler after us, "This is the guy that got bit by the bat!"

"Really?" I said, after a pause but happy to take the low road. "But I thought that was impossible. Remember? Back in the van? You guys knew."

Jerry Jacques, it turned out, was very much the guy who'd been bitten by the bat. On the mouth. But as we gathered around him and drifted downstream, listening to him talk, we learned that the bat bite was no more than the opener. What follows is his story, the way I tell it.

"I've been down in LA for the last little while, at a clinic, getting rabies shots. The serum is from horses and they give it to you in your abdomen. It's supposed to work, and I'm not totally sure it took. But I came up here because figured if I was going to die of rabies, I'd rather do it on the river than down in LA."

It was a good start and as a river story obviously had serious potential. Jerry's delivery, deadpan and almost weary sounding, removed any doubt about its veracity.

"A month ago I was working a trip here and we'd just finished lunch at Clavey Falls. I was snoozing on my rowing seat when this bat landed on my face and bit me in the lip…drew blood even. A guy on the trip was a doctor and he said I'd better get it checked out. What kind of bat bites people in the middle of the day?"

The three of us looked at each other and had no answer to that one. The story went on.

"So I drove down to my where my folks live in LA and set up this doctor's appointment. And I did a lot of reading. If you start showing any signs of rabies, it turns out, you're a goner. So the shots are supposed to prevent rabies. Not cure it. If you get really sensitvie to the light, or really irritable and crazy, or some other things like that, you've got it and it's too late.

You get the shots once a day at an outpatient clinic. So I was living at home. No one's ever survived rabies except one kid from France. Plus, in the last stages, you get super-contagious and they quarantine you. Lock you up.

Anyway, I finished up all the shots —there are 12 —and I called the nurse to see how my test had come out. They test you at the end to make sure you're clear. But when I called, the nurse made up some bogus story and said I should come in to see the doctor to talk about the test. That's when I figured the shots hadn't worked. I figured if I went in, they'd drop a net over me and lock me up. There was no way I was doing that.

We were bouncing through rapids at this stage, but paying far more attention to the story than anything on the river.

My mother knew this woman who did holistic cures in Santa Barbara and I started off to see her. But then this kid got in my way on his bike. It wasn't that close but for some reason it really pissed me off and I knew something was wrong. On top of that, the sun felt super-bright and hot and it just kept getting worse and I finally stopped the car and turned around. After another day or so of feeling weird I just got all my stuff together and drove up here.

At this point he stopped and there ensued one of those pregnant pauses.

"When?" somebody finally asked. "When did you come up?"

"Last night," he said. "I drove most of the night. I just got here a couple of hours ago."

We let that sink in.

"So you don't know if you have rabies or not? Still?"

He shook his head.

At that point the river intervened and we were forced to pay some attention to where we were actually going. We caught a necessary eddy and began the process of reading and running the rapids, Jerry's last line resonating in our heads: "If I'm going to die, though, I'd rather do it here."

The rest of the trip was uneventful. The day was nice, the water was familiar. Jerry, we discovered, was just learning how to boat and on a few occasions fell over and had to swim. But no harm done. We pulled over for a simple lunch on a beach to ourselves and finished the day without any real mishap. As we were taking out though, we received a surprise.

"Mind if I join you guys tomorrow?" Jerry asked.

We paused for an awkward moment. Jerry was a bare beginner; the three of us had years of experience and were just now ready to take on Cherry Creek ("*Maybe*," I thought.) Today, we'd been able to rescue Jerry and his boat from all his swims with little trouble. Tomorrow would be a whole different story.

Cherry Creek was 6 miles of straught-up serious water with a number of Class V rapids. It was a do-not-swim stretch.

"Like I said," he added, looking at us carefully, "this is where I need to be."

Eventually, we shrugged and nodded. "Sure." What else was there to say?

Over the course of my kayaking career I ran Cherry Creek maybe half a dozen times, but I never was able to sleep well at the put-in. But that night, the first night, was probably the worst. I got a couple of hours of restless tossing.

I had seen the stretch once before, a few years earlier when I'd done it in a paddle boat, but all I could remember was steep, fast and rocky. I couldn't single out any rapids except the last one, something we had named "Flat Rock Falls." It was a huge drop onto a boulder but I remembered it mostly for where it was: just above the Big One, Lumsden Falls. You had to run Flat Rock clean and you had to get out then. If you didn't, you were going over the falls and that was something you definitely didn't want to do.

Lumsden Falls was the only rapid you could see from the take-out and the road. Over the years, especially if there was time on the evening before a commercial trip, we boatmen would sit on the bridge, drink a beer and check it out, trying to find a runnable line. Eventually, we'd all just shake our heads and head back down the road. It was a monster rapid, starting with a series of steep boulder drops before funneling into an undercut wall. The boulder drops looked at the edge of possible, but nobody wanted to find out what was in the undercut. There were only a few kayakers in the state who'd run Cherry Creek at the time, but none of them, we knew, had ever run the falls. It was the knock-out punch at the bottom of Cherry Creek. A no-question walk-around.

But all that was far from our minds when we put in that morning. Between us and there we had a ton of Class V and our focus was very much in the here and now. We went through the put-in rituals without the usual banter. There were a couple hundred yards of easy warm-up water before the river turned a corner and it all started.

We paddled away, agreeing to meet in an eddy just above the corner —the starting line. We had game faces on and none of us was thinking about anything but what was coming.

Until we got to the eddy.

"Where's Jerry?" somebody said. We looked upstream. We could see all the way to the putin. No Jerry.

"He's got to be here. I know he put in."

Then we saw him. Swimming, hanging onto his boat.

Somehow, in the bouncy little Class II stretch we'd just come through, he'd fallen over and failed to roll it back. A bad sign.

We managed to catch him before the real stuff started. His boat was bent in half, "a taco." We could still see the truck at the put-in and we all heaved the same sigh of relief: Jerry would have to take out. There'd be no beginners on Cherry Creek today.

Wrong. Up on the bank, Jerry proceeded to stand inside his boat and jump up and down enough to bend it back to semi-straight. A rough-and-ready fix. A few minutes later, he was back in his boat and pulling on his spray skirt.

"Are you sure you're up for this?" somebody asked—*reasonably*, I thought.

"Let's go," he said.

Confidence? I thought. *Arrogance? Indifference?*

We set up our order and joined the current, one by one. Since it was all new, we ran it eddy to eddy, rapid by rapid, boatscouting over our shoulders where we could and where we couldn't, we pulled over and scouted from the bank. It was slow going.

At least it was for us. Jerry had a less laborious approach. He didn't bother scouting, preferring to wait in the eddy while we did the legwork. I don't think he was cocky so much as fatalistic. And logical. Why over-plan a route when your steering wheel is a little sketchy?

But the river gods were in a good mood that day. At this distance in time, the rapids blur together, but we must have made the cuts where we had to and squeaked through the must-do chutes.

I remember Jerry went for a swim or two, but not in the places where you couldn't. We had a Spartan lunch on a beach mid-way and geared up for the final leg.

It must have been getting late when we finally came to Flat Rock. I remembered the route we'd taken in the rubber raft: directly onto the namesake boulder. I didn't want to try it in a kayak.

We scouted from the right bank and examined another drop. Steeper, and skinnier, but the pool below looked clean. If there were rocks in it, they were out of sight. We decided to try it with as much speed as possible. Hit the pool flat. *Don't probe the bottom.*

Rimbeaux went over first and when he appeared below, intact and upright, we all followed in relieved succession, nothing but water at the bottom.

Almost immediately we found the take-out eddy on the right. There was the bridge, startlingly close. The river dropped out of view and we could hear the ominous roar of Lumsden Falls. We were done. The sense of relief and profound exultation is hard to describe.

As we pushed out of our seats and began to shoulder our boats for the climb up the bank, Jerry made an announcement.

"I'm going to run it."

We looked at him blankly. "Lumsden? You're going to run Lumsden?"

It was a shocking moment and for the first time since put-in I looked at him as I had the day before: a guy who might have a disease, a fatal disease.

We mounted a little resistance, putting up the obvious objections, but under the circumstances, we ended up just wishing him luck and offering a last bit of advice:

"Stay off the wall," we said, "on the right. About halfway down."

The bridge offered ringside seats and as we stood in the middle of it, watching Jerry get ready to pull out of the eddy, I would be lying if I didn't confess to some morbid curiosity. *"Are we watching this? Or rubber-necking?"*

Jerry got out into the main current and from the beginning, it didn't go well. The only possible line was directly over the boulder drops, hoping for clean exits. Getting pushed to the right meant the wall.

We watched him go over the first drop and disappear into the foam. When he reappeared, he was upside down. We saw one effort to roll—unsuccessful—before the current took him hard to the right. He slammed into the wall and vanished. We started to run for our boats when someone shouted: "He's out!"

Sure enough. His helmet appeared in one place, his boat another, and his paddle a third, but Jerry made it through. We scrambled down to the river in time. Someone went after his boat while the rest of us helped him out. He was holding half a paddle. Jerry hadn't run Lumsden so much as swum it, but he was here, alive, and we were finally ready to go home.

We separated that evening. Jerry said he wanted to go find another paddle and as he drove off, we bid our adieus, wondering when, if ever, we'd see him again.

We met up with Gail, Rimbeaux's our shuttle driver, and as we drove back home, celebratory beers in hand, related the whole tale. When we finished with our thrilling adventure, she asked what seemed like the most irrelevant question.

"What did you have for lunch?"

"Lunch? What'd we have for lunch? *Who cares?* A sandwich. A couple of apples. Why?"

"Did you share?" Gail was a nurse.

Silence.

"Do you know how rabies is spread?" She looked at us. "Saliva. Did you share the apples?"

We felt like kids who'd been caught underage. "Maybe. I don't remember..."

"You shared an apple with a guy who's got rabies." She declared flatly. The beer suddenly tasted weird.

The next day I was working the phones, calling various clinics.

"Is it possible to get rabies from somebody by sharing food with them?" I finally got a doctor to talk to me.

"People who have rabies aren't on the street." He responded bluntly.

"Just for argument's sake, let's say somebody was."

It was no use. No one believed me. Rabid people are in horror movies, not kayaking on the Tuolumne River. It got to the point where I started to doubt myself. *Maybe the whole story's a crock*, I thought, hopefully. *Maybe Barry and Rimbeaux were right!*

Jerry had mentioned the outfitter he'd worked for. I called him up.

"Does Jerry Jacques row for you guys?" I asked.

"He used to," the man said, "but then he had to go get some shots. A bat bit him." *Great.* I thought, *when I need a guy to be lying through his teeth, he's not..* "Do you know where he is?" the guy asked me. "He ran away before they could finish with him. Some doctor down in LA really wants to talk to him."

I put down the phone a vindicated but unhappy guy. A couple more phone calls and I finally got a nurse friend of mine to look it up.

"They have to be showing symptoms," she read to me, "before they're considered dangerously cantagious. Sensitivity to light, irritability. And foaming."

Foaming? I didn't remember any of that. And he didn't seem that irritable. A little crazy, sure. But he's a boatman.

I was rationalizing, but the days went by and I failed to do any foaming of my own. Barry and Rimbeaux, for their part, thought I was being completely paranoid. "You don't have rabies," they said dismissively, "Don't be ridiculous."

It would have been easier to take some consolation from their opinions if they weren't the same geniuses who were so certain nobody'd never been bitten on the lip by a bat in the first place.

But eventually, my paranoia faded away and more trips intervened. As the seasons wore on, the story fell into the pile of all the river stories we'd tell around the campfire.

The years passed. I retired my kayak, got married, with a family ("the full catastrophe," in Zorba's famous phrasing). When my kids got to the wide-eyed stage, I used to tell them some of the river lies, including the rabies story, embellishing it without any shame.

"Whatever happened to that guy," they'd ask. "Whatever happened to Batman?" I had to shake my head. I didn't know. No one knew.

Until one day the phone rang.

"Hello?" I said.

"Do you remember that time on Cherry Creek when I went down with you guys in kayaks?" the voice said. "Like about twenty years ago?"

"Jerry?"

"I ran Lumsden Falls. Do you remember?"

"Is this Jerry Jacques?" I said.

"Yeah. I need to know if you remember that run."

"Where are you?"

"Alaska. I moved to Alaska years ago."

"You don't have rabies?"

"No. It turned out to be OK. Nothing ever happened." He said. "But I need a favor…"

Jerry, I learned, had moved shortly after the whole incident, running rivers, scuffling a boatman's living, running his own out-fit. With hundreds of new adventures, he'd pretty much forgotten that July day with the three of us on Cherry Creek.

Until just recently. He'd been in a bar in Anchorage and struck up a conversation with the guy in the stool next to him, a lawyer from California who'd been a big kayaker back in his day. The subject of big bad rapids came up and eventually, as often happens in these circumstances, the name Lumsden Falls surfaced. Jerry must have put his beer down to inform the lawyer that he was talking to the very man who'd run it first.

"The jerk didn't believe me," Jerry explained curtly. I felt a faint wave of sympathy and understanding for the lawyer.

And the favor?

"We bet $100. I'm going to give him your number. When he calls you, you know what to say, right? You saw me, right?"

What could I say? I was there.

RAFTING WITH CHARON

DAN STEINER

MY FIRST RIVER GIG? We're talking a long time ago. Eons ago, actually. Though plenty of people still ask me about it. They want to know what it was like, working for such a legendary boatman. And of course, they want to hear about the goddamned dog. As a rule, I deflect these inquiries. I murmur "it was hell," and I smile, and I change the subject. Folks are understandably curious about my time down under. But there's no point in getting into it. They'll all be finding out for themselves, sooner or later.

It's a good rule. I'm making this exception for only one reason. I need to get Linford and Volpert off my case. For months, they've been pestering me. "We'll share your story with the world," promises Dick. "We've got legions of loyal readers," swears Bob. I don't believe these claims. The last book those two jokers published was when, back in 2012? Legions of loyal readers, my ass.

Even so, the duffers have finally worn me down. I've agreed to sit with them for a Q&A session. In return, they've agreed to spring for drinks at a bar of my choice and thereafter to leave me alone. That's our deal. The Q&A session follows, which means that I'm honoring my end of the bargain. The rest is up to them.

. . .

Dick: Thanks, Dan, for joining us to chat about your first river gig. Let's begin with some background. Tell us about your youth.

Dan: Not exotic, Dick. Pretty conventional, really. I grew up as your average middle-class kid from Thebes. My parents owned a vase and urn shop. I wrestled varsity for Thebes High School, but I wasn't very good, and our team sucked. In fact, we used to joke that the "T" on our letter sweaters stood for "terrible."

Dick: That bad, eh?

Dan: I'm afraid so. We weren't like those guys at Sparta High. They were animals. I swear to Apollo, you'd get pinned by a Spartan in, like, a nanosecond. I remember my junior year, they had this one wrestler, totally ferocious, a freshman. He bit the ear off one of my teammates and swallowed it. Without chewing! I shit you not. But that's a Spartan for you.

Dick: What about college?

Dan: As I say, I wasn't much of an athlete in high school. But I did test well. I always just assumed I'd end up at the University of Athens. And sure enough, that's exactly what happened. Of course, it wasn't as though kids could pick and choose their colleges back then. Not like young people today. Back then, you went where the Fates decreed. Those three Fate gals were seriously bad ass. You didn't dare piss them off, I assure you.

Bob: Thanks for sharing your early memories, Dan. Our legions of loyal readers will be fascinated. What did you do after college?

Dan: After graduating from U of A, I fell into a funk. I had no clue where I was going with my life. I mean, I knew the Fates would be calling the shots. I just had no idea what the shots would be. I hopscotched around, supporting myself with a series of temporary jobs. Stomping grapes here, pressing olives there. I drove an oxcart for a while. Didn't stay anywhere very long. I wandered the Peloponnese. I must have climbed every mountain on that entire peninsula.

Bob: Wow. Was that a Rodgers and Hammerstein allusion, Dan? I don't imagine you fellows are aware of this, but I'm a total R&H fanboy. *The Sound of Music* is my all-time fave. The live television version blew me away.

Dick: It was terrific, Bob, no question. Yet in my mind, the 1965 film remains the gold standard.

Bob: True that, Dick. But let's get back to Dan. Before we got sidetracked, he was still in a post-college funk.

Dan: Yup. After a year or so in the Peloponnese, I remained as directionless as ever. So I thumbed a ride to Delphi. Figured I'd consult the Oracle, ask her what to do. Have you ever been to Delphi? If you want my advice, don't waste your drachmas. The whole deal is a total scam. You stand in line, you take a ritual bath, you sacrifice a goat. And then some withered old crone speaks in riddles and instructs you to follow your bliss. That's basically it. Disappointing, to say the least.

Dick: And thus, you found yourself right back at square one.

Dan: Well, yes and no. The funny thing is, as the weeks went by, I kept thinking about what the Oracle had said. About following my bliss. Finally, I thought to myself, why not? Why *not* follow my bliss? At U of A, I had double-majored in outdoor recreation and mortuary science. I decided to find something that would permit me to combine those interests. Then I stumbled across the A.A. ad.

Dick: The A.A. ad?

Dan: "Trainee boatman wanted," it read. "B.A. in Outdoor Recreation and/or Mortuary Science preferred. Absolutely no river experience required. 'People persons' need not apply. Contact C.H. Aron, Pres., A.A. River Trips, Inc."

Bob: What was your reaction?

Dan: My reaction? I was pumped! I had the perfect academic background. I had absolutely no river experience. Plus, I've never been much of a people person. It almost felt like the Fates had arranged this particular gig, just for me. And of course, they had. That's what they do. But it also almost *felt* that way, you know? Like higher powers were at work. Anyway, to make a long story short, C.H. hired me at A.A. That was my first river gig. Are we ready for those drinks now?

Bob: Whoa there, Danno. We're not done yet. I'm confused. What's with all the initials?

Dan: Must everything be spelled out for you, Bob? This isn't complicated. Afterlife Adventures River Trips, Inc., a/k/a A.A. River Trips, a/k/a A.A., was founded by my old boss, Charles Hitchcock Aron, a/k/a C.H. Aron, a/k/a C.H.

Bob: I mostly hear him called Charon.

Dan: That's because you mostly listen to folks who ignore punctuation.

Dick: Enough about the name. Tell us about the man.

Dan: C.H. Aron was a visionary, plain and simple. No one else was running commercial river trips in the Underworld, not back then. Frankly, no one else even dreamed it could be done. C.H. made it happen. He built a financially successful operation and paved the way for the countless generations of Underworld outfitters who've followed. He's a legend in the industry. Deservedly so, if you ask me.

Dick: I can't quite picture Charon. Can you describe him?

Dan: Physically, he was nothing special. Virgil described him thusly: "a sordid god: down from his hairy chin/A length of beard descends, uncombed, unclean/His eyes, like hollow furnaces on fire/A girdle, foul with grease, binds his obscene attire." In my opinion, Virgil pretty much nailed it. Basically, C.H. looked like your typical old-school river guide.

Dick: I've heard that Charon could be extremely nasty, and a real demon to work with.

Dan: Untrue. Myths and lies, fostered by small-minded bards who never met him. On the outside, C.H. Aron was tough as Iron Age nails. But underneath that thick skin? A total pussycat. Meow.

Bob: I, too, never met Charon. I would have liked to. He certainly enjoys quite the reputation. Folks at URGA—the Underworld River Guides Association—still worship him as a god.

Dan: No duh! That because he *was* a god, Bob. For all intents and purposes, anyway. His parents were both primordial deities. The two of them were quite elderly by the time I worked for A.A., although they still managed to totter over occasionally for guide dinners. Erebus and Nyx. Cute old couple.

Dick: Whatever else may be said, Charon has long been acknowledged as a shrewd and savvy businessman. Our readers would doubtless like to hear more on that score.

Bob: Did I mention that Dick and I have legions of them? Readers, I mean. And they're loyal, too.

Dan: As a businessman, C.H. Aron subscribed to one simple maxim. "Start small, dream big, and always look to make money on your way downstream." C.H. began humbly, with a single skiff, working solo, ferrying half-day float trips on the Styx River. And yet, in the blink of a millennium, he built A.A. into the biggest, most profitable outfitting company in the entire ancient world. In my book, that's about as shrewd and savvy as it gets.

Dick: Impressive.

Dan: Beyond impressive. Think of the challenges inherent in the original business model. For starters, there was no profit margin in those early Styx trips.

Bob: I don't understand.

Dan: Of course you don't, Bob. Let me illustrate. In Thebes, my mom's dad lived with us when I was little. One day a minotaur gored him and he died. There we were, with the hole all dug, about to get the geezer in the ground, when my mom screams, "Wait! We need an obolus for the boatman!" She's adamant. Nothing will do but my father has to fish around in his own pockets, pulling out wads of cash, until he finally finds an obolus to stick in the old man's mouth.

Meanwhile, us kids, we're waving madly at the corpse and yelling, "Goodbye, Grandpa! Don't forget to wear your life jacket!" True story.

Bob: A drachma wouldn't do?

Dan: No. That's the whole point. From time immemorial, the tradition's been to use an obolus, which you must place under the tongue of your dearly departed. Don't ask me why. An obolus is worth what, a lousy sixth of a drachma? Small wonder a boatman couldn't earn a buck.

Dick: Sounds like the Styx trips may have been underpriced.

Dan: The margin was certainly razor thin, Dick. Far too thin to make it up on volume. Plus, there was no repeat business to speak of. And to make matters worse, those early Styx trips were one-way. We'd debark on the other side of the river, at the Pylai Haidou Gate. We'd hand out box lunches and wish our guests good luck in the Underworld. Then, if you'll pardon the expression, we'd deadhead back.

Dick: Were all the trips really one-way? And no repeat business? There must have been exceptions.

Dan: Not many. Odysseus took a round trip once. So did Hercules and Dante, as I recall. But it was rare. Our only regular repeat guest on the Styx was Persephone. She liked the Underworld fine until she came down with a wicked case of seasonal affective disorder. That's when the doctors recommended she get some sun, take annual R&Rs at her childhood home in Attica. We hosted her on a couple of trips every year, going and returning. Things were always pretty gloomy in the Underworld while she was away, although Hades never seemed to mind. Whatever made Persephone happy was okay by Hades. "Happy wife, happy life," he used to say.

Bob: How did Charon turn the business around?

Dan: Skillful application of three BBPs, Bob. Basic business principles. BBP No. 1: "Expand your product line." The Styx has always been a great marquee river. Talk about your original "River of No Return"! But Styx trips are short, and they can be awfully crowded. C.H. recognized that there was a huge, untapped market out there, comprising folks who were literally dying to have a true Underworld wilderness experience. C.H. catered to this market. He pioneered multi-day rafting adventures on a number of the region's lesser-known rivers. Fewer souls in the seats on those pure wilderness trips, of course. But much higher margins. And certainly more enjoyable for us guides.

Bob: How could multi-day wilderness trips be profitable, at an obolus a head?

Dan: Excellent question, Bob, which leads us directly to BBP No. 2: "Develop new revenue streams." It didn't take C.H. more than a couple of centuries to see that the old money-in-the-mouth way of doing things would have to, heh-heh, change. His introduction of the online death-dough account revolutionized the Underworld's entire adventure industry. With death-dough, you can prepay and preselect afterlife trips for yourself and your loved ones. Alternatively, you can sock away a designated sum and wait to select your afterlife trips until after you reach your, well, afterlife. As C.H. liked to say, "with death-dough, you CAN take it with you!" And of course, death-dough has given Underworld outfitters much more flexibility in pricing.

Dick: Charon was a clever dude.

Dan: To be sure. But C.H.'s real genius lay in his implementation of BBP No. 3: "Market your product." I'm sure you remember that late night television spot with the cute young couple opening their "pay now, play later" death-dough account. The spot where the wife is a gazillion months pregnant and the guy looks straight into the camera and says, "I'm planning ahead, for myself *and* my family." C.H. crafted that spot. There was also his famous two-page print ad. Both pages were all gray and misty and indistinct, except that you could just barely see the ghostly outlines of a couple of rafts on a river. Printed across the bottom of the right-hand page, in bold black type, were the words, "Float the FUNderworld." A true classic, that one.

Dick: We're about out of time here, so we'll need to start wrapping this up. Bob, do you have a last question for Dan?

Bob: Yes. What's the deal with the hellhound? The one who guarded the Underworld at Pylai Haidou?

Dan: Why does everyone always ask about that goddamned dog? Cerberus was a total neurotic. A complete pain in the ass. Nowhere near as ferocious as his legend. Contrary to what you hear, his bites weren't a big deal. The barks were the problem. Yap, yap, yap. Constantly. Yap, yap, yap. I'm telling you, the mutt definitely had issues. The whole three heads thing. His relationship with Hades. The stray poodle genes.

Dick: I have a final question of my own, Dan. You've run all the major rivers in the Underworld. What's your personal favorite?

Dan: Wow. That's tough question, Dick. There are so many good ones. I like the Pyriphlegethon. Fast, lots of whitewater. Several its rapids—Heel of Achilles, Cassandra's Corner—are underworld-class. Be sure to go in the spring, though, because come July, the Phleg is actually *hotter* than hell. The Lethe is also a great river. Fantastic scenery, with a nice layover at the Cave of Hypnos on Day Four. The only problem with the Lethe is the water. It's not potable, and you need to be very careful. A single sip will pretty much nuke your memory. They don't call it the River of Oblivion for nothing.

Dick: Your top choice?

Dan: I'd have to say the Acheron. The River of Woe. Fantastic trip. 8 days, 7 nights. Thanks to the perpetual twilight, the trip seems even longer. Imagine northern Finland in February, but way warmer, practically tropical. There's an incredible segment where the Acheron winds for miles through a host of rolling hills. The landscape is so barren, so austere, that it feels almost lunar. And as you float downstream amidst all this desolation, you hear the strangest sound emanating from those hills.

Dick: The sound of what, exactly?

Dan: Hard to say. It's an eerie sound, weirdly enchanting. The cries of a vast chorus of lost souls, perhaps? The keening of a myriad of doomed spirits, adrift in the Underworld? To me, though, and this might seem crazy, but it's almost the sound of…

Dick: Yes?

Dan: The sound of ... music.

Dick: Double wow. Unfortunately, I see that we're completely out of time. Many thanks to you, Dan, for sharing the story of your first river gig.

Bob: That's right. We really appreciate it. As do our loyal readers, of whom there are legions!

Vladimir Kovalik with son Kyle & grandson VK

Vladimir Kovalik, circa 1970s

Basket Boat, 1971. Photo by Larry Orman

VLADIMIR KOVALIK

DICK LINFORD

WE CALLED HIM VK OR VLAD BECAUSE HIS FULL NAME, Vladimir Kovalik was such a mouthful. Sometimes, when his behavior warranted it—which was often—we called him Crazy Vlad, or sometimes The Cancelled Czech. The amazing thing is that he rarely talked about his past, and his past is a story that would make a fine book, and then a movie. Starring Daniel Craig maybe. It would be an action movie, involving being shot at by Germans, escaping from a train headed for Siberia; sneaking across the Iron Curtain; coming to America; going to Stanford; working in intelligence in Viet Nam, circumnavigating the earth by motorcycle, bus, ship and train; and becoming a river outfitter. Had we known about his many escapes along the way we might have called him Houdini.

VK was born in 1928 in Poprad, a small town in what was then eastern Czechoslovakia. In 1993, in an amicable split called "The Velvet Divorce," the western part of the country became The Czech Republic and the eastern part became Slovakia. Poprad is now in Slovakia. His father was an engineer, and an important man in the community.

VK was ten years old when the Germans invaded Czechoslovakia. although his village was far from the front, the Czech partisans were waging guerilla warfare against their invaders even in his rural area. One of his vivid memories of those years was when he was wandering the woods near town and smelled something terrible. Upon investigation he found a body of a German soldier who had been killed by partisans. A large black German Shepard was standing guard over the soldier. When VK approached, the dog growled menacingly. He wouldn't let VK near his dead master. VK went home and got a bowl of milk, returned to the scene, and slowly approached the dog, offering him the milk. Close to starvation, the dog alternated between growling and whining as VK slowly pushed the bowl toward him. Finally the dog gave in and licked the bowl clean. Then he reluctantly let VK pet him. VK petted the dog for a while, picked up the bowl, and headed home. The dog followed him. He told his father about the soldier and they gathered some friends, who went out and buried him, marking the grave with a cross made of sticks.

The dog meanwhile had found a new master. He followed VK everywhere, and would stand just to his right and a bit behind. If anyone reached into a pocket for something the dog would growl a warning: "Don't go for a weapon." When VK went to school the dog followed, and sat outside until school was over. He named the dog Greif, the Czech word for griffin, the mythical beast with wings, the head of an eagle, and the body of a lion—whose job was to guard treasure.

In 1944, when VK was sixteen, the Germans were losing the war and were desperate for both soldiers and factory workers. They started drafting young Czechs. VK's father feared that VK would be conscripted. He also knew that a west-bound train was coming through town, said to be carrying military scrap metal back to Germany to be re-used. He decided that the best thing for VK to do was to hitch a ride on the train to a small town a 150 or so miles west of Poprad, where he would be taken in by his uncle, who was a farmer and active with the partisans.

When the train arrived, his father found that no one was riding in the caboose, so he bundled VK up, sneaked him into the caboose, and gave him a cigar, telling him that, when he got really cold he should take a couple puffs on it and that would warm him up.

The train was very slow and it was very cold. In a few hours VK had smoked the cigar and was freezing. He decided that he had to get to the engine to get warm, regardless of the consequences. This was, of course, a steam engine, driven by heat from burning coal, so the engine room would be warm if not hot.

He left the caboose, climbed the ladder to the top of the next car, and slowly made his way to the engine. Suddenly someone yelled in German for him to stop. He turned and saw that a soldier had opened a door on the roof of the car, and that he had a rifle. Not thinking clearly. VK continued toward the engine. The soldier shot at him. VK could either surrender or jump. He jumped, hitting the ground and rolling several times before stopping. He was quickly captured by Slovak police working for the Germans, imprisoned and interrogated for a week, and then conscripted into a small army unit composed equally of German and Czech conscripts. He was given a gun and trained in the use of anti-tank weapons. On their first patrol the unit attacked by partisans. One German was wounded and the rest scattered. VK hid in the woods. There he made contact with the partisans, who helped him find his uncle. He found out later that the train he was on was not carrying scrap metal. It was secretly carrying German soldiers to the western front. Shortly after Vladimir jumped, the train entered a tunnel where the partisans had set explosives. The engine was blown up and everyone on the train was killed.

So VK had three escapes on this one adventure. He escaped town on the train, escaped the Germans by jumping from the train, and escaped the Germans in the shootout.

VK spent the rest of 1944 and early 1945 with his uncle. As the Russians poured in from the east, the German army retreated, but destroyed as many roads and telephone and telegraph lines as they could, making travel and communication virtually impossible. The country was in chaos, and VK wanted to go home. He knew that his parents didn't even know if he was alive, and he was homesick. His uncle had taught him how to live off the land by seeking food stored in barns and cached in remote huts for shepherds. It took several weeks to reach home, and when he arrived he was so thin and haggard that his mother didn't recognize him at first. She thought he was just another of the many stray children seeking food and shelter. It took him some time to recover.

With considerable help from the Czech partisans, the Russians forced the Germans out of Czechoslovakia by early 1945. The war in Europe officially ended on May 18, 1945. The Czechs evicted over two million ethnic Germans between May and August of that year. Most of them went to The Federal Republic of Germany, better known as West Germany. About 600,000 ended up in The German Democratic Republic, or East Germany. The name is a perfect example of Orwellian doublespeak. The country was neither democratic nor republican.

And of course the Russian "liberators" didn't exactly leave. Along with many other eastern European countries, Czechoslovakia became a satellite state of the Union of Soviet

Socialist Republics, or USSR. The Iron Curtain dropped across Europe, and Czechoslovakia became part of the Eastern Bloc. The Russians were an occupying force no better than the Germans, but they didn't need young men for the military or factory work, so VK was safe.

He lived a fairly normal, somewhat privileged life for a few years, going to school and doing what young men of his social class did. He hunted, hiked, climbed mountains and even floated the Vah River on a German inflatable assault raft he and some friends found. Thus began his love of rivers.

At first his life was not terribly affected by Russian domination but, like most Czechs and Slovaks, he resented Communist repression, and yearned for national independence. He and his friends watched a lot of American movies, especially westerns, which gave them a very bad idea. They decided to make up some WANTED: DEAD OR ALIVE posters like they saw in the movies, and place a photograph of Stalin on them with a list of his crimes. The reward offered was insultingly small. Many people thought the posters were funny, but Communists have never been known for their keen sense of humor. It didn't take them long to figure out who did it, and Vladimir and his two friends were sent to a prison in Bratislava, a large city on the Danube.

The prison was a converted school and most prisoners were there for minor offences. Security was relatively lax. So were health conditions. The place was cold and damp; it was winter, and prisoners were often beaten with rubber hoses, the weapons of choice because they inflicted terrible pain but left no marks, so the beating could be denied if and when prisoners were released.

One of VK's friends contracted pneumonia and died, and one of Vladimir's lungs filled with liquid. He could easily have died. There was no hospital and no doctor. Fortunately one of the guards was an ex-nun and nurse. She recognized the problem and knew what to do. She had several people hold VK down, and jammed a large syringe between two ribs, and into the lower lung. She then drained the liquid into a bowl. VK remembers that the liquid looked like beer: yellowish and with a frothy head.

Vladimir spent about six months in this prison, much of the time sick. Then an older prisoner proposed that the two of them escape. The prison was right next to the Danube, which was at least a quarter mile wide at this point. They figured that if they could just get to the river, they could submerge themselves and swim downstream to safety, surfacing only to breathe. Remember that security was lax. They waited for a moonless night, made their escape, and plunged into the river. What they hadn't anticipated was that the Danube was a foot or so deep near the banks. Submersion was impossible. As they ran for deeper water, they created a lot of noise and splash. Guards turned a spotlight on them and yelled at them to stop. VK stopped. His friend said that he was a dead man either way, and kept running. The guards riddled his body with bullets. VK froze with his hands up, and watched the body of his friend float slowly away.

Another escape, though it failed.

This attempt elevated VK from subversive pest to enemy of the state, and he was sentenced to ten years of hard labor in Siberia. Sentences like these were seldom completed. The prisoners froze, starved, or died of exhaustion before their time was up. VK had, in reality, been sentenced to death.

He was herded into a boxcar with sixty or so other prisoners. His boxcar was one of many with the same payload. The train made its way east, transporting several hundred people to the gulags. Hundreds of thousands of people experienced this fate during Stalin's reign. Many starved or froze to death en route.

There are documented cases of trains stopping to dump bodies that were frozen solid, as stiff as fence posts. Luckily, Vladimir was not traveling in the winter. Nevertheless, traveling in a boxcar with sixty people, with little food and nowhere to go to the bathroom, was an ordeal. When VK's train reached the border between Czechoslovakia and Ukraine, everything and everybody had to be transferred to new trains. The Czech railroad tracks were the standard European width—1,435 millimeters apart—while the Ukraine and Russian tracks were—and still are—1,529 millimeters apart. This difference, of about three and a third inches, saved VK's life.

In those days it took time to unload and re-load a full train. As Vladimir's train sat in the rail yard in Ukraine, he and another prisoner scouted the situation by peering through cracks and holes in the boxcar's walls. They noticed that there were several "turntables" or "wheelhouses" in the vast rail yard. Unlike the diesel locomotives of today, the steam engines couldn't run backward nearly as fast as they could go forward, so sections of track were built on a platform that could rotate 180 degrees. The engines were placed on these turntables, which slowly turned them so they were facing back the way they came.

What caught Vladimir's eye was that one of the turntables seemed to be out of service. In fact, a fence, separating Ukraine and Czechoslovakia, bisected it. On the Czech side was freedom, or at least a reasonable chance for escape. He and his new friend quietly clawed a hole in the bottom of the boxcar, bloodying their fingertips in the process. Then, in the dead of night, they slipped out and darted to a trapdoor that led under the turntable. Once inside they waited for daylight so they could figure out the mechanism that pivoted it. That mechanism was a simple set of gears, but they were somewhat rusted and extremely hard to get moving.

Desperation breeds innovation. They lubricated the gears with their own urine and feces. They then spent the next forty-eight hours rotating the turntable so slowly that no one would notice it was turning. The process was excruciatingly slow and strenuous. They were close to death from dehydration and exhaustion by the time the door was on the other side of the fence. And then they had to wait until dark to make their move.

Another escape.

But they were a long way from safety. Their goal was to reach West Germany, which meant navigating the length of Czechoslovakia (east to west), a distance of about 650 miles. Today you can do the trip in about eleven hours in a car. But they were walking and hiding. They traveled mainly at night and hid in the woods, barns, and shepherd huts during the day. They foraged for food. VK used what he learned on his last cross-country trip, finding cheese and sausages in shepherd huts, and taking eggs, potatoes, and meat, etc. from farmhouses when they could. Sometimes they threw themselves on the mercy of peasants who hated the Russians as much as they had hated the Germans, and risked their own lives to help. Many of them told the fugitives that but for the grace of God, they or their sons could be in the same situation.

It took them close to six months to reach the border, near the German town of Regen. By this time many people were seeking freedom in the West, and the Communists were determined to stop them. They had built fences the length of the border, and evenly spaced guard towers along the fences. The guards had orders to shoot those who tried to cross. VK and his friend watched the towers for several days, working on a plan. What they realized was that not all of the towers were manned all the time. The Communists seemed to be short on manpower, and had to rotate guards, leaving some towers empty. After a few more days of observation, they figured out the rotation system. Then they hid near a tower that was scheduled to be empty one night, and slipped across without incident.

Another escape.

Once safely in West Germany they let their identities be known, and were interned in a displaced persons camp near Munich. His fellow escapee was delirious at this point and taken to a hospital and they lost touch with each other. VK was once again exhausted and half starved.

Conditions were primitive in the camp. Inmates slept on cots in over-crowded tents and the food was barely edible by most standards. But VK felt like he had died and gone to heaven. He quickly regained the thirty or so pounds that he had lost on his journey. He was soon exploring his surroundings, making trips into Munich when possible. He had only the clothes on his back when he arrived, but there were piles of used clothes to choose from.

He soon noticed a pretty young American woman who was working at the camp. Nada Skidmore, a recent Stanford graduate, was recovering from a romance gone sour by burying herself in refugee work. Nada spoke English and French, while VK spoke Czech, Polish, Russian and German, but no English. The relationship began with long walks, and to overcome the language barrier they spent hours going through old magazines, naming objects in their respective languages. It wasn't long before they fell in love.

They got married in 1950. Vladimir borrowed a suit for the wedding. They soon moved to Portland, Oregon.

Another escape.

They lived with Nada's parents while VK attended Portland State University, where he excelled. He majored in economics. He applied to several top graduate schools and was accepted everywhere. He chose Stanford because Nada had gone there.

Vladimir loved his time at Stanford. He was a good student and still had time to play. He hiked and climbed in the Sierra and started running whitewater rivers in a rather unique way. On his first trip down the Rogue River, he swam some 70 miles of it, wearing a wetsuit and fins. And he picked up capitalism quickly, making good money buying and selling cars. He loved school so much, and was such an apt student that, after getting a master's degree in economics, he stuck around and got one in physics as well.

Upon graduation, he went to work for The Stanford Research Institute, where he put his knowledge of physics to work advising the Army in weaponry at Fort Ord, near the Monterey Bay in California. While there he helped develop the rocket propelled grenade, or RPG. He and Nada settled in, had kids, and bought a house in nearby Pacific Grove. He held the job well into the Viet Nam War years. During this time—the mid 1960s—his college friend Ron Hayes, who went on to a successful acting career, introduced him to Martin Litton, who at the time was running private trips in the Grand Canyon. Vladimir joined him on a of couple trips, and those trips fed his love of rivers and whitewater. Martin would go on to become a legendary Grand Canyon outfitter and eloquent spokesman for wilderness. He was the relentless driving force that galvanized the environmentalists and saved the Grand Canyon from dams planned by the U.S. Bureau of Reclamation

One day at Fort Ord VK came across a big, black German shepherd that was a dead ringer for his childhood dog Greif. The dog was caged. Upon inquiry VK found that the dog had been trained to sniff out drugs on soldiers, but had started eating the drugs he found. Soldiers using drugs was bad enough, but a dog on dope? Intolerable. He had been sentenced to death. VK begged the sergeant to give him the dog, but the sergeant told him that orders were orders. The dog had to die. VK came back that night with bolt cutters, rescued the dog, took him home and named him Greif.

Another escape, Not VK's exactly, but he made it happen.

The dog remained a loyal pet for years. Only Kyle, VK and Nada's oldest son, had mixed emotions about Greif. As a teenager Kyle was experimenting with drugs, and when he would try to smuggle then into the house Greif would rip his clothes apart to get to them.

In the late 1960s VK switched gears and went to work for the U.S. State Department as an economic advisor to General Westmoreland in Viet Nam. At the time, Westmoreland was sure that we were going to win the war, and VK was part of a team to develop an economic recovery plan for the country we had devastated. After a few years there VK became disillusioned with the war. He resigned his position and, with a couple friends, bought Honda 250 motorcycles and headed west.

Another escape.

Their goal was to reach Europe and then return home to the US. They traveled unharmed through Viet Nam, Cambodia, Thailand, and Burma (now Myanmar), but were stopped at the border of India. They were told that they could proceed but their motorcycles were not allowed in the country. They crated the motorcycles, had them shipped to the United States, and continued west, alternately riding buses and hitch—hiking. Once in Europe, and with his American passport, VK was able to visit his family in Poprad. In West Germany he bought a Porsche, drove it around for a while and had it shipped to Canada. He crossed the

Atlantic by boat, picked up the car, and drove across Canada and down to Pacific Grove. The whole trip took six months, during which he had a lot of time to think about his future.

Once home Vladimir told Nada he didn't want to work for anyone ever again. He wanted to be a river outfitter like his friend Martin Litton.

Another escape, this one from the normal world of work.

That was the birth of Wilderness World, which was to become one of the premier rafting companies in the West. His timing was perfect. The year was 1971. Rafting was just being discovered, rivers were just starting to experience crowding, and Federal agencies were planning to limit use by not issuing any more permits to run commercial trips. For a nominal application fee the United States Park Service granted Wilderness World a "concession" to run commercial trips in The Grand Canyon, and the Forest Service and Bureau of Land Management granted "permits" to run trips on the Middle Fork of the Salmon, the Main Salmon, the Rogue, the Stanislaus, and the Tuolumne Rivers. He was set up.

A big challenge for river runners in those days was rafts. Nobody was making rafts strong enough for whitewater use. Everyone relied on military surplus rafts, and they were hard to find. Outfitters combed surplus stores and warehouses. Grand Canyon outfitters bought inflatable bridge pontoons for their large motorized rigs. Outfitters on smaller rivers looked for assault rafts like the one Vladimir had found in Czechoslovakia. These were incredibly heavy and often not very puncture proof, but they came with rubber cones. In war these cones could be crammed into bullet holes when the rafts got shot up.

Never one to sit around and complain, VK took it upon himself not only to design boats, but to find people to manufacture them. His designs included the original Havasu, Miwok, and the Shoshone. The Havasu became the model for many rafts to follow, including the Avon Adventurer, Pro, and SuperPro. I would venture that every raft built since then has been some variation of these rafts.

The first manufacturer VK found got the design right but used a fabric that was far from airtight, and the boats became the joke of the industry. But Vladimir stuck with it and found manufacturers in China who used hypalon and neoprene, fabrics that were durable and air-tight. They became a huge success.

Another challenge in the early days was life jackets. The only jackets that met the safety standards of the government agencies were the Coast Guard-approved Type III jacket informally called the Mae West because people wearing them looked like they had large breasts. The jackets were made for one-time use for passengers on ships, and not designed to be used day after day like river outfitters used them. They had a canvas shell inside of which were plastic bags filled with a cotton fiber called kapok. While they would float unconscious people with their heads out of the water, they were incredibly bulky. Worse yet, the plastic bags were fragile, and when they broke water seeped in. The kapok absorbed the water and the jackets soon served better as anchors. Outfitters went through lifejackets almost as fast as they did toilet paper. We all had mounds of dead jackets, and the cost of replacing them was huge.

So Vladimir went to work on that problem too. Working with the man who built the faulty rafts, and then wending his way through the mountain of governmental red tape, Vladimir designed a life jacket that was durable and met Coast Guard standards for carrying passengers for hire on whitewater. Instead of plastic bags filled with kapok the new jackets featured ethafoam, an aerated, close-celled plastic that could never become water-logged and would float forever. Instead of canvas, the cloth was a tough synthetic. Instead of having tons of floatation in front, the new jackets had a collar to keep the head up. Getting the approval, first of the Coast Guard and then the other Federal agencies regulating commercial rafting, was close to a miracle.

So in many ways, VK was a godsend to outfitters. That said, he wasn't easy to get along with. He could be charming one minute and a pain in the ass the next. He was incredibly smart, very aggressive, devastatingly blunt, and extremely volatile. He could also play fast and loose with the truth. These traits helped him survive Nazis and Communists, get to America, and succeed. They also engendered the sobriquet "Crazy Vlad." His guides loved him, but were wary of his moods. They referred to them as VK1 and VK2. VK1 was jolly, friendly, funny. and incredibly generous. VK2 was furious with everyone and everything. These many years later, those who remember him talk mainly about his idiosyncrasies.

Take his first rafts. The ones that didn't hold air. I remember VK saying to me, "I tell you Deek, I tie thees raft behind my truck and drag it five miles. Not even scratch mark!" No reference to the fact that it didn't hold air.

Some of his guides remember a spring meeting at his beautiful house on the beach in Pacific Grove now worth several million dollars, where VK, with tears in his eyes, told the guides that his kids were going hungry because business was so bad, so there would be no pay raise.

My first encounter with him was in the early 1970s, during an outfitter discussion about campsites on the Stanislaus River.

Earlier outfitters had staked out campsites and there seemed to be nothing left for his company. No one was willing to concede his camp. I don't remember how things worked out, but I do remember being blown away by VK, an adult male, yelling and threatening others with bodily harm. There is no question that he had a hair trigger, but I think he also used his anger to get what he wanted.

My favorite VK story is about a meeting we outfitters had at The Miwok Inn, a bar and café he had bought in Angels Camp, California, near our favorite river, the Stanislaus. We held an outfitter meeting there one night, with probably seven or eight outfitters in attendance. I have no recollection what we were talking about, but things got heated. Suddenly VK stood up, shouted that we were all against him, stormed out, got in his pickup and drove off, spewing gravel behind him. We were surprised. Not by the outburst —we were used to those-—but by the fact that he had left his own place. Twenty minutes later he quietly drove up, came in, sat down and joined the conversation like nothing had happened.

An escape that backfired.

Nor was VK all that sensitive to the feelings of others. Winning was what was important. That and letting the world know he had won. In the early 1980s Bryce Whitmore, a venerable Rogue River outfitter, offered my partner Joe, Daly, and me a property on the Rogue River. Two riverfront houses on two acres, for $60,000. We opted out. Too rich for us. Three months later VK called to brag that he had bought the property for that amount and sold it two months later for $100,000.

Bob Rafalovich, who bought Vladimir's operation on Oregon's Rogue River, and certainly over-paid for it, tells about being in his office on a cold spring day. Bookings were slow and Bob was depressed, wondering how in the world he was going to survive.

In walked VK, happy as a pig in shit. He waved a check in Bob's face. It was made out to Wilderness World and in the high six figures. Enough to set Bob up for life. It was the second installment on Vladimir's sale of his Grand Canyon business. He said to Bob, "You see Bob, this why (sic) I love America. In 1971 I pay thirty-five dollars for Grand Canyon permit. This is second payment on sale of that permit. What a country!" Bob was torn between congratulating him and killing him.

In an argument with his guides about pay, VK once said, "A rock could row a raft! If I could teach rocks how to cook I could fire all of you!" On another occasion he told his guides "Is privilege to raft in Grand Canyon. You should be paying me!!" And guides knew they were in trouble when he addressed them as "Mr. Smarty Pants."

VK's son Kyle recalls being with VK when he was meeting a group who had arrived in the middle of nowhere for a trip on the Usumacinta, a river in the jungles of Guatemala. The people had come a long way, and were nervous and excited about their trip. VK began his talk by saying "I know you will bitch like everyone else." Pre-emptive strike? Setting the tone for the trip? I suspect that he just said what he was thinking.

There have been a lot of unique river outfitters. The business, especially in the early days, attracted offbeat, adventurous, interesting people, people not firmly tethered to reality. But none could claim a background as colorful as VK's, and none were as fascinating to watch in action. He was eccentric, brilliant and volatile. He saw things differently, and he held nothing back.

While he could be intimidating and difficult, people who got to know him came to love him. He could flip his switch from Dr. Jekyll to Mr. Hyde in a nanosecond. But Mr. Hyde never lasted long and Dr. Jekyll would give you the shirt off his back.

I use the past tense when writing about VK. He isn't dead. But he is no longer the man I knew. At 90 years of age he's in the memory care unit in a rest home in Salinas, California. But he doesn't like it there, and I won't be at all surprised if he escapes. It's in his DNA.

John Hunt

Lodge Trip

JOHN HUNT

I'D BEEN WARNED ABOUT BOB SMITH. His house overlooked the road between the Galice store where we picked up our passengers and Almeda Bar where we launched our five-day Rogue River trips. "Whatever you do, don't drive fast past Bob's house." There was no need to mention consequences; Bob was clearly not a man to be trifled with. A few people in our California-based company had dealings with Bob about passenger shuttles and other river business, but I'd seen him only from a distance and I figured it was best to keep it that way. At a time when the newly-elected Reagan administration was signaling an upsurge in every-man-for-himself individualism and a disdain for resource management, Bob had never needed encouragement to assert his praise for self-reliance and his contempt for the Bureau of Land Management, which had recently assumed authority over the Rogue Wild and Scenic River area. Wild and Scenic status was often sought to protect out-standing river canyons from inundation caused by building dams downstream, but Bob adamantly declared to anyone listening that he'd rather see the river dammed than have it managed by federal bureaucrats, even if the resulting reservoir would have taken away his livelihood and flooded his own home.

Bob Smith was a stocky, powerfully built man in his early fifties, with a round bald head and level gaze. I never saw him in anything other than a plain white T-shirt, blue jeans, and work boots, even on the river. He was well known in the southern Oregon river community and was an imposing presence in the Galice area where we worked. I, on the other hand, was an obvious interloper from California: a post-hippie, long-haired surf kid in my mid-twenties, wearing baggy trunks, sandals and Grateful Dead T-shirts. I had walked precincts in the San Francisco Bay Area to collect signatures for a ballot proposition to save the Stanislaus River from flooding behind the New Melones Dam, and was likewise politically involved with any number of big government attempts to regulate everything from offshore oil drilling to firearms. I suspected that any conversations I might have with Bob would get awkward quickly, with untold repercussions for my employment and physical well being.

I'd driven past Bob's house (slowly) many times in the two or three years I worked on the Rogue and Upper Klamath. In those days the distinction was pretty clear between the local river guides and the guides brought in by out-of-state river companies, particularly those from California. Most of the guides in my company were recent university graduates, many with resource management or biology degrees from Stanford or UC Berkeley. We tended to come from financially successful families, and most of us had plenty of experience in the fine arts of partying and substance exploration. I only got to know a couple of the local Rogue guides, but generally their on-river temperament was no-nonsense, and their relationships with passengers and others on the river seemed much more formally constrained. The dress codes were different, too, but the most obvious distinction was that the California guides usually ran rapids and worked their boats downstream by pulling on the oars, whereas the locals always rowed by pushing forward. Our habit of pulling was engrained from rowing rivers like the Tuolumne, where every ounce of leverage was needed to dance the rafts through difficult boulder-strewn rapids. The Oregon guides, on the other hand, came from the drift-boat fishing-guide tradition, where guides always pushed on the oars because their aluminum-hulled drift boats had high prows and flat sterns, and because rowing forward gave their fishing clients the best angle for casting into eddies where the biggest steelhead and salmon lurked. There was a general tolerance among guides from the different companies, but these distinctions clearly marked our crew as outsiders in the Rogue Valley.

The Wild and Scenic section of the Rogue River is a gorgeous palette of every shade of green you can imagine. The abundant rainfall keeps even the shrubs verdant all summer and the river itself is a translucent jade green tinted by phytoplankton and the reflections of forested canyon walls crowded with Douglas and white firs, sugar and ponderosa pines, incense and Port-Orford cedars, understory rhododendron and riverbank alders. The wildlife is spectacular; osprey and bald eagles whisk away fish in their talons, and bears amble along the river bank or through our campsites at night. This section of the river is home to a small number of secluded rustic lodges tucked up in the trees above the highwater ledges. One of these lodges is Paradise. A typical river trip would reach Paradise Lodge after three days of rafting the most remote reaches of the canyon, capped by runs through Mule Creek Canyon and Blossom Bar rapids. It was something of a tradition to tie off the rafts and climb the rock steps to the lodge for ice cream and cold drinks, then take in the quiet history of this isolated settlement that had barely survived the greatest floods of the past century. We knew that some of the local river companies, especially those using drift boats for the fishing season, would bring their passengers to spend the night at Paradise and some of the other lodges. This seemed a luxury well beyond the means of regular rafters, who hauled food and kitchen equipment, bags and tents and all the other weights of civilization up the sand banks each afternoon to set up our camps. Even though we didn't rate as overnight guests, we enjoyed knowing that the lodges were there, adding a stately air of endurance to the rugged coast range landscape.

One late summer day the word came down from World Headquarters that I was to run our company's first lodge trip. A wonderful idea! I was delighted. It was to be a two-boat trip with some long-time clients, and the thought of getting dinners from the lodge cooks with no dishwashing involved was blessed relief. The other guide on the trip would be Bob Smith.

It had been years sine I had eaten sausage. I wasn't a vegetarian and hadn't yet heard the term "vegan;" but I'd had a vague notion of eating light on the land and avoided red meat. I ate a lot of vegetables, especially potatoes. Bob had invited me to his house for breakfast before put-in and I was happy to accept. It would have been rude to turn down such an offer, of course, but I also had set my mind to being all in on this trip and learning as much as I could about Bob's way of doing things. While I had a pretty well established framework for viewing world affairs, I didn't have much aptitude for confrontation, and I was eager to take on the challenge of getting out of my cultural comfort zone. The first step was to chow down the two huge sausage patties that Bob's engaging wife, Jean, had piled on the plate next to three sunny-side-up eggs and a stack of toast. I was hungry, and damned if them sausage patties don't fill you right up. It was a bright sunny morning and the conversation, mostly with Jean, was cheerful. I was surprised to see that the dog Bob doted upon was a bouncy little cockapoo rather than the Rottweiler/Doberman mix I would have expected. The kitchen table was on the second floor of their two-story house, and looking out the window I was reminded again of Bob's vantage point for observing speeding vehicles.

I was genuinely glad to make Jean's (and Bob's) acquaintance, and thanked Jean for such a hefty breakfast. As Jean cleared the table, Bob and I drove down to Grave Creek to set up the rafts. I had a gray, 16-foot Avon Pro and Bob had his own raft of similar size, the same dark red color as the rafts used by local companies. After we inflated the rafts, Bob went back to Galice to meet the passengers and I busied myself organizing gear in my boat. I tied down everything the same way I tied down every load: ready to survive any manner of wrap, rip or flip. When the passengers arrived, I introduced myself and started meticulously tying in their waterproof bags and personal gear. I was getting ready to give the usual sixteen-part safety talk when I realized that Bob had tossed all of his passengers' bags in the stern of his boat, and without tying a single thing down or putting on his own life jacket, he'd shoved off and was pushing on the oars toward Grave Creek Falls. While frantically strapping in the rest of my passengers' bags, I offered a distracted few words about making sure their life jackets fit then hustled everyone into the boat and started pulling downstream. I glanced nervously about the boat for loose ends and bags that might pop free, while taking frequent looks over my shoulder to keep Bob in sight. Bob went out of sight immediately, of course, because Grave Creek Falls starts with a section of fast current through haystack waves and then drops over a four-foot ledge around the corner. I didn't catch up to Bob until we were another mile downstream.

One reason Bob was moving quickly, and the reason we'd started at Grave Creek instead of further upstream at Almeda Bar, was that we planned to row all the way to Paradise on the first day, a section usually covered in three days. Our regular trips made few miles on the first day because we had to negotiate Rainey Falls, which always required a scout and an orderly sequence of positioning boats while walking the passengers down the left bank around the falls. It's an impressive rapid. The main Rainey Falls section sucks most of the river's flow thundering over a twelve-foot drop into a wide reversal wave that flips about three boats out of every four ill-advised attempts. Luckily, there are two alternate routes. One is the middle chute, which splits the drop into two five-foot falls slicing down a narrow bedrock slot. It has a tricky fast-moving entry that has to be done just right or you risk either drifting sideways into the main falls or getting wedged suspended above the double falls of the tight chute. We always scouted this rapid because the chute can't be seen from upstream and there's always the possibility of another boat stuck in the narrow falls, a nasty surprise you wouldn't want to encounter as your own raft dropped in. The other alternate run is the line channel, sometimes called the fish ladder, which eases the gradient by spreading the drop over a shallow 100-yard-long section along the right bank. That channel is too narrow to allow any oar work, so boats are usually lined through with ropes. I always took the middle chute because it was a challenge to row, had a fun drop and allowed me to skip all the fish ladder hassles of getting out of the raft and dealing with ropes while scrambling over rocks and through brush to cajole the raft down the long channel. I had never seen anyone do anything but stumble while lining boats down the fish ladder.

Bob and I floated toward Rainey Falls without discussion. He was still well ahead and was pushing his raft far right toward the fish ladder. As I approached the falls Bob already had his passengers out of the boat and marching down the trail. He had a long stern line in hand and was working nimbly along the bank, guiding his raft down the channel ahead of him like a carriage driver reining a well-trained horse. By that point I had committed to running the middle chute, and seeing Bob's pace I realized there was no time to scout and no time to drop off the passengers to walk around the falls. I had run the middle chute many times, including the last trip just a week before, but I'd never run it blind with a boat full of passengers. They were all experienced and able-bodied, so I took a deep breath, took a good look at the wisp of current through the boulders lining the entry, and let the oar blades find their spots in the shallow swirls and eddies approaching the falls. I took one last tug on the left oar to turn the corner and swung my hands wide to ship the oars and keep the blades off the narrow rock walls. The raft lunged straight over the ledge and we went bucking down the falls. As we slid out into the main river below I was feeling more relief than usual; if I'd blown this one I'd have been out on an island with four passengers hanging in the bow above that grinder of a double drop.

The boiling water from the main falls swept us along and I headed for an eddy downstream of the fish ladder to wait for Bob. Before I got there I was amazed to see that he had already lined his raft through, had all his passengers back in the boat and was just then tossing the coiled rope back into the stern to head down-river. I wish I'd gotten a better look at how he'd single-handedly worked a 16-foot raft down 100 yards of tricky footing as fast as I'd rowed straight down the middle chute. I was getting a sense that there were things Bob had learned about this river that I would never know.

After a long stretch of rowing we stopped for lunch. Like everything else Bob had done, lunch was short and to the point. No fancy spread of cold cuts and sliced vegetables. Just peanut butter, jelly and sliced bread propped up quickly on the lunch box. We sat in the shade on a small beach, and the passengers clearly enjoyed their BP&Js after the long hours since breakfast. A ragged little squirrel was making a nuisance of himself, and I told the passengers to avoid it since you never knew when the little vermin might be rabid. Bob wasn't one to do any avoiding, however, so he nonchalantly put out a piece of bread with peanut butter on it, and as soon as he turned his back, the squirrel darted over and gobbled it up. The little beast spent the rest of the lunch break off to the side and out of our way, clucking over and over to pop the roof of its mouth off the peanut butter. No more worries about rabies.

Toward the end of the day we ran the two largest rapids on the river. I followed Bob and watched as he executed a classic move in the Coffee Pot section of Mule Creek Canyon: he just parked his stern on the boil and kept it there while the raft bounced for nearly a minute until the surge turned him in the right direction and he let the raft slide cleanly downstream, never coming close to the common thrashing many boaters get in that narrow rock-wall chamber. As we approached Blossom Bar, a long boulder-filled rapid with some serious consequences, Bob casually pulled straight into the entry chute without a thought of scouting and with not a bag tied down. He did, I noticed, put his life jacket on for this one rapid. I followed close behind and had a good run down the middle while watching Bob slide cleanly through the right side maze with barely a push on the oars.

As the sun dipped low over the canyon wall we pulled over and tied off the rafts at Paradise Lodge. On a regular trip we never had quite enough time to fully enjoy this place; if we stayed too long, we'd end up cooking dinner in the dark at our camp downstream. This was a lodge trip, however, and now I would experience the difference. It's a fifty-foot climb up the rock steps to the lodge, and I was checking the weight of my passengers' bags in anticipation of the haul when two dutiful teenagers walked up to the raft and asked for all the bags. They even hauled mine up while I untied everything in my boat that Bob never needed to tie down in his.

Once up at the lodge I found Bob talking to the proprietor, Allen Boice. Allen was about the same age as Bob, with the same short-and-to-the-point style of conversation, and they seemed to be old friends who hadn't seen each other in a while. I figured he had similar political leanings as Bob, based on the prominence given to a large framed photograph of J. Edgar Hoover in the main room. I later learned that Allen was a WWII Marine and former Curry County Sheriff notorious for his hard line and his animosity toward hippies, a few of whom were said to have been taken down to the jailhouse for a head shaving. He was fired as sheriff after some of his deputies, apparently with his approval, shot and killed several suspected drug dealers at a remote cabin. From a respectful distance, I listened in to a bit of their conversation, expecting to hear some irate remarks about the Bureau of Land Management or the general degradation of a society increasingly populated by the likes of me. Instead, the first thing I heard was Bob asking how the tomatoes were doing that summer. They exchanged a few words about gardening, the weather and family, then decided they'd done enough socializing and got back to the tasks at hand.

The guests were put up in a series of small cabins while Bob and I were shown the bunkhouse. Our bags had already been delivered, and with not an ounce of work to do before dinner, we sat out on the porch overlooking a lazy stretch of river as the late afternoon sun sent slanting rays through the forest. Bob pulled out a bottle of whiskey and passed it over. After we'd both had a taste I went inside the bunkhouse and pulled a bottle of rye from my ammo box. We passed them back and forth judiciously for an hour or so and had a good long conversation. I can't remember specific topics, but I do remember feeling comfortable offering my honest opinions, listening more than talking, and learning a whole lot about the river, the mountains that surround it, and the people who've had the fortitude and perseverance to make a living here through every season, year after year.

The last two days of the three-day trip were uneventful. I continued to wear my life jacket but passed on tying down the gear. The passengers were pleasant and enjoyed the trip, and it was relaxing rowing short stretches each day after covering so many miles on the first. We stayed the second night at the Illahe Lodge, just upstream from our usual take-out. The lodge owners were genuine and friendly, and the food was good; I think there was a fresh berry pie. On the last day we floated past the Foster Bar take-out and went another five miles downstream to Agness to fill out the river day. I hadn't rafted that section of the river before; it had some fun waves along the river bends and a wide steady current that made for pleasant late-summer drifting. As the sun's rays took on the colors of afternoon, they were joined by that subtle melancholy that creeps in towards the end of a good Rogue trip.

It's that moment when you realize that time and rivers flow only one way, and that anticipation has turned to memory.

We drifted another mile, rounded a bend and landed the rafts on the bleached gravel bar at Cougar Lane. Take-out was easy with no kitchen gear and little to untie, so we said our goodbyes to the passengers and packed up the boats. I rode back over the mountain in the gear truck with Bob. I remember enjoying the ride, hearing stories about snow, keeping my ears open for river lore and my eyes fixed on the horizon as he pointed out distant mountain landmarks. There were long stretches between comments on that four-hour drive, but the connection stayed open and easy in a way that I wouldn't have thought possible just three days before, before the river once again bridged differences that perhaps we only imagine.

Skip Volpert, circa 1994

Skip Volpert

Dolphins In Stanley

BOB VOLPERT

THE WALL STREETERS THAT SHOWED UP IN STANLEY, Idaho for our June 3, 1995, Middle Fork of the Salmon launch had been promised a trip they would long remember. Promises commonly mirror demands and this group had a bunch. Two appetizers and three entrees at every dinner, fresh New York bagels to accompany every breakfast, individual tents, special beverages, a specific brand of pillows and other gear and food requests. And this wasn't going to be the usual trip down the Middle Fork. We were going to "turn the corner" when the Middle Fork joined the Main Salmon and head down that river as well. 185 miles in six days.

Our friend and fellow outfitter, Mark Evans, had organized this group. Mark lived and worked in Houston and was one of the owners of Texas River Expeditions. He would be a guide on this trip and was in Stanley to help get the group ready. I had come to Stanley to do the same, although I was not going down the river with them. Accompanying me, just for the fun of it, was my four-year old son, Skip.

Friday, June 2 brought some kinks. It was raining and the forecast called for much of the same for the next week. The river was rising and many groups were opting to start their trips at Indian Creek rather than from Boundary Creek, the upstream launch site accessible by road. Indian is reached by plane so the air charter services were busy. The weather wasn't fully cooperating and flights were starting to back-up, delaying people and gear. It was becoming clear that flights the next day would be impacted by today's delays and with the addition of up to eight groups flying tomorrow, Indian Creek was going to be a very busy place. When I asked one of the pilots about plans for morning, he told me it would likely be a chaotic, very long day and to get our guests and their bags to the airport as early as possible.

Our pre-trip meeting was at 7:30 that evening and it was there that I presented an idea to our group that would have placed me in the outfitter hall-of-fame if things had gone according to plan. I went through the usual litany, like how to pack our waterproof bags, and then told them about the turmoil we were likely to encounter on arrival at Indian Creek the next morning. But, I assured them, "There is a way of outsmarting the other groups and getting on the river quickly. We will be ahead of everyone else."

My directions for implementing this terrific plan were simple:

"Get up early, grab some breakfast, and when you get back to your room, put on your wetsuit, pack your waterproof bags and be out front by 7:30. When you get to Indian Creek, you'll be ready to go since you'll already have your wetsuits on and your gear packed."

The next morning was overcast but it wasn't raining. Our guests started assembling early in front of the Mountain Village Lodge, and by 7:30 we had all their bags loaded in our truck. Mark Evans, and a couple of the guests got in the truck and we headed to the nearby airport. The pilots quickly loaded their planes and Mark and the two guests took off for Indian Creek. The planes were still in sight when the fog started rolling back in. Within minutes the nearby mountains were obliterated.

Until the fog lifted there would be no flight departures from Stanley. I would have to find something to do with the 14 guests in wetsuits outside the Mountain Village. They had checked out of their rooms and their personal belongings, including wallets, were on the way to Indian Creek. I met with them, and tried to sound confident that the delay was temporary. They told me not to worry about it and that they would just hang out, walk around town and be ready to go when flights resumed.

An hour went by and then two. It was raining. Our group had broken into pods of four to six men wandering around Stanley. Knowing they didn't have their wallets and probably no cash, I decided to visit every bar and restaurant in town and arrange for these guys to buy food and drinks if they stopped in. At each stop, I told the person at the cash register "if anyone comes in here wearing a wetsuit, give them anything they want. I'll pay for it." Some places took my credit card info; others told me they would just run a tab in my name. I would take care of it later.

As we walked through town, Skip asked me, "Daddy, why are all those men dressed up like dolphins?"

Volpert Family, circa 1992

Trails and Transitions

BOB VOLPERT

A Continuation of Dolphins in Stanley

BY LATE MORNING THE RAIN HAD ABATED but fog still socked in the valley. No flights were arriving or leaving Stanley and from my perspective I couldn't imagine the sky ever clearing. My four-year-old companion had grown restless and irritable and was tired of marching from place to place. We both needed to escape our wetsuit clad guests and I figured a short hike and a Snickers rush would do us both good. We grabbed some candy bars and a bag of chips at the Mercantile, and escaped in a company truck to a trail-head adjacent to the Salmon River a few miles northwest of town.

The trail was initially flat but soon narrowed and steepened. I would walk about 20 yards and wait for my son Skip. His pace was neither joyful nor quick. At every stop I could look up and see switchbacks snaking through boulders and trees. In places, a visual distance of 50 yards might entail a route four times that length. We'd been on the initial uphill section for about 20 minutes and really hadn't gone far when he sat down and called it quits. His arms crossed his chest and he glared at the trail that descended to our truck. "I'm done," he announced.

I didn't try to talk him out of his decision but offered some guidance. "You can stay where you are until I come back or you can sit here for awhile and then follow me up the trail. The one thing you can't do is walk down the trail towards our truck. The choice is yours. Either come after me or stay where you are."

I delayed leaving him by needlessly adjusting my daypack and rummaging around for a Snickers bar. He sat staring dead ahead with little movement and no words. After a few minutes I reminded him of the rules, gave him half the candy bar and a water bottle and headed up the trail. Even with the switchbacks it was steep, so the vertical distance I covered in the next 15 minutes wasn't much. I paused, and glanced down the slope to where he was sitting. Nothing had changed. The arms were crossed and he maintained the down-trail stare. I continued for another 15 minutes or so and then ducked behind a large trailside boulder where I couldn't be seen to check on him. No movement had occurred, and the arms remained defiantly crossed, and the stare persisted. This maneuver of climbing, hiding and checking on him repeated itself a few times with no noticeable alteration of posture from him.

I had been hiking alone for about 45 minutes when I heard what I thought was a truck. Aside from the rumble of the Salmon River it had been quiet and the truck engine reminded me that leaving a four-year old a hundred yards or so from the highway probably wasn't the best idea I had ever had. It took me awhile to realize that the engine noise was from a plane and not a truck. That sound meant that flights would soon be departing from Stanley and we could get out of there. The nightmare would soon be over. We high-tailed down the trail to the truck and returned to Stanley.

TWENTY YEARS LATER

By the time 2015 rolled around, we had been outfitting in Idaho for 37 years. Mary and I had raised our family of three sons primarily in Point Reyes Station, California, but we spent non-school months in Salmon, Idaho. When they were youngsters, the boys always looked forward to returning to the big city of Salmon because it had a movie theatre, gas stations, and food venues that the small village of Pt. Reyes, population 600, lacked. They grew up in the chaos and fun of living with river guides, knowing other outfitter families, and doing outdoor things that today would seem appallingly dangerous. The seeds must have taken root since all three have now embarked on outfitting careers: Will on the Rogue River, Matt on the Kern in Southern California, and Skip on Idaho's Middle Fork.

That year, Mary and I had taken a few weeks off in September for a hiking vacation and returned to Salmon in October to close things up for the winter and help Skip map out the chores that he would need to tackle in the off-season. We were planning to stay in Salmon long enough to celebrate his 25th birthday later that month and then head back to Point Reyes.

"What would you like to do for your birthday?" was the question I posed to him a few days before the event. Most of Skip's river guide friends had left Salmon when the rafting season ended, but we could celebrate with dinner in town or a trip to Missoula, or a small party at our house, or maybe even a round of golf. Mary would bake a cake and although it wasn't destined to be a huge bash, we would do something fun that hopefully would be suitable and memorable for a milestone birthday. "I'll let you know," he replied. A few days later, he did.

"On my birthday, you and I will get up really early and drive to the Stoddard Trail and hike to the top of the ridge to see the sun come up over the Middle Fork and Salmon rivers."

The Stoddard Trail is about a two-hour drive from our house. It is located just beyond the confluence of the Middle Fork and Main Salmon on the opposite side of the river from the road. The trail is reached by crossing the Stoddard Bridge. If you have ever done a Main Salmon put-in at Corn Creek or a Middle Fork take-out at Cache Bar, you have driven past the bridge and trail. If you look up from the road, you can see the switchbacks that go back and forth across the face of the hillside that rises several hundred feet from the river to the overlook above. In the nearly four decades that we ran those rivers, I never saw anyone hiking the Stoddard Trail.

It was dark and cold when we arrived at the Bridge. I told Skip that I wasn't going to head toward the trail until I could at least see or sense an outline of the bridge so we remained in the warm truck waiting for the first tinge of light. We ate the cookies he had grabbed as we left our house and finished off a thermos of coffee. A few minutes later the bridge appeared, ghostlike, shrouded in fog and we headed out.

At the second or third switchback, Skip let me know that my pace was too slow and that he was going to head up the trail without me. I continued up the barely visible trail alone. In the semi-darkness, I imagined that each of my steps was along a ledge that plummeted hundreds of feet to the river, so my pace was more a cautious shuffle than a stride. As the morning lightened the switchbacks became visible and the imagined dangerous drop-offs proved to be only a steep, sloping hillside. I trudged up the trail and took a break at the next switch to catch my breath and take in the scenery. The view was spectacular. Below I could see miles of river and above the steep, serpentine trail. I noticed that Skip had paused maybe 100 yards above me and was glancing in my direction.

At each successive change in direction, I'd pause and look up. I no longer could see Skip but occasionally the top of a metal pole, periscope-like, poked up from behind a rock. The pole was the top of the tripod he was carrying and it gave away the hiding locations he had chosen to spy on me. Nearing the top, the Stoddard Trail became easier and crossed an open field away from the earlier precipitous route. When I got to the top plateau I found Skip fiddling with his camera. He handed me some water and half a candy bar and headed to an outcropping that afforded a view of both rivers. "You probably shouldn't go out there," he cautioned. So while he climbed to the top of a nearby boulder to get a sunrise photo, I walked the trail high above the Middle Fork pausing to take in the majestic views that went on for miles.

We took our time and didn't start back down for a couple of hours. A morning mist had partially obscured the sunrise we had hoped to see, but just being on that plateau was its own reward. The sun soon burned off the fog and we hung around enjoying its warmth. The climb had been tiring, and I took an opportunity to prop against a tree for a short sun-drenched nap before descending to our truck.

It was just after noon by the time we got back to our place in Salmon. I grabbed a piece of cold chicken from the fridge and plopped into a comfortable chair in our living room. Six hours later I awoke for the celebratory dinner Mary had made.

The following day we packed for our departure. Skip would be staying in Salmon for a few more days before heading to Bozeman for the winter. Mary and I would drive to Ashland to meet our new grandson and then head to Point Reyes from there. Early the next morning we finished loading and began the trip with a slow drive down our dirt driveway as if sightseeing.

When I got to the edge of our property, I turned onto Wagon Wheel Road, stopped, and stumbled out of the car for a moment to look around. My back and legs were still feeling the stiffness and pain from the hike. I looked at the three buildings, the frost covered grounds, the few boats that remained partially inflated waiting to be put away, a fence still needing repair, and I turned around towards the sun that was just starting to poke through the clouds partially obstructing the view of the Beaverheads. I gave the place a season-ending wave goodbye, then gingerly got back behind the steering wheel and set off down the road. Mary broke the silence.

"Do you ever have any qualms or concerns about Skip taking over our Idaho business?"

"Not anymore," I said.

---

* The Stoddard Bridge collapsed when struck by a rockslide in March 2017. The Forest Service has plans to reconstruct it.

ACKNOWLEDGEMENTS

WE HAD A LOT OF HELP COMPILING THIS BOOK. First, Callan Wink's story "What did I do Wrong?" was first published in *Big Sky Journal*'s 2015 Fly Fishing issue. Moira Magneson's poem "Apparition" first appeared in the anthology *What's Nature Got to do With It?—Staying Sane in a Mad World* and her poem "Green Room, Havasu" was published in *The Boatman's Quarterly*, Winter 2003.

Moira Magneson and Emerald LaFortune laboriously helped edit the whole book. Their input was invaluable. Thanks to Tara Mayberry of Teaberry Creative for designing the book and to Mark Unger of Sky Lakes Media for use of the cover photo.

The following people read one or more stories, and found an embarrassing number of typos, misspellings, and punctuation errors: Nancy Boever, Terry Correia, Cort Conley, Joe Daly, Toni Dudley, Carin Eddy, Carolyn Hammond, Carolyn Kramer, Larry Linford, Suzie Linford, Kathleen Meyer, Barbara Nixon, and Gail Sabbadini.

Dick's writing critique group, Writer's Bloc, offered encouragement and gentle suggestions on all of his stories.

Our wives Mary and Suzie watched the process with amazement and amusement and offered advice and occasional encouragement when asked, and when not asked. They seem exuberant that the book is finally completed.

CPSIA information can be obtained
at www.ICGtesting.com
Printed in the USA
LVHW051502141218
600488LV00017B/511/P

9 780692 136256